An Introduction to Colonial African-American Evangelical Theology

An Introduction to Colonial African-American Evangelical Theology

Colonial Identities, Sense of Belonging, and Shared Space

CORY J. MAY

☙PICKWICK *Publications* • Eugene, Oregon

AN INTRODUCTION TO COLONIAL AFRICAN-AMERICAN EVANGELICAL THEOLOGY
Colonial Identities, Sense of Belonging, and Shared Space

Copyright © 2025 Cory J. May. All rights reserved. Except for brief quotations in critical publications or reviews, no part of this book may be reproduced in any manner without prior written permission from the publisher. Write: Permissions, Wipf and Stock Publishers, 199 W. 8th Ave., Suite 3, Eugene, OR 97401.

Pickwick Publications
An Imprint of Wipf and Stock Publishers
199 W. 8th Ave., Suite 3
Eugene, OR 97401

www.wipfandstock.com

PAPERBACK ISBN: 978-1-7252-7973-5
HARDCOVER ISBN: 978-1-7252-7972-8
EBOOK ISBN: 978-1-7252-7974-2

Cataloguing-in-Publication data:

Names: May, Cory J., author.

Title: An introduction to colonial African-American evangelical theology : colonial identities, sense of belonging, and shared space / Cory J. May.

Description: Eugene, OR : Pickwick Publications, 2025 | Includes bibliographical references.

Identifiers: ISBN 978-1-7252-7973-5 (paperback) | ISBN 978-1-7252-7972-8 (hardcover) | ISBN 978-1-7252-7974-2 (ebook)

Subjects: LCSH: African Americans—Religion. | United States—History—Colonial period, ca. 1600–1775.

Classification: BR563.N4 .M39 2025 (paperback) | BR563.N4 .M39 (ebook)

01/30/25

My inspiration derives from those colonial voices that have been silenced, minimized, and ignored. I write hoping to shed light upon their genuine faith in Christ.

Contents

Introduction: The Nature of Christian Influence and the Character of God: Concerning Our Identities, Sense of Belonging, and Shared-Space with the Human Other   1

1. Constructing Our Identities, Sense of Belonging, and Shared-Spaces Through Essentialist/Racialized-Binary Reasoning and the Cycle of Dehumanization   17

2. The Melodrama of Fragmented Blackness: King and Essentialist/Racialized Binary-Reasoning   42

3. Colonial African-American Self-Awareness, Obliviousness, and Fragmented Whiteness   73

4. Jarena Lee (1783–1864) and "Old Elizabeth" (1766–ca. 1863): A Dialogue Between the Preacher Who Wrestled with Satan and the Humble Servant of Christ   98

5. Maria W. Stewart (1803–1879): The African-American Evangelical Prophetess   140

6. Julia A. J. Foote (1803–?): "The Sanctified Preacher"   171

7. Homage to Harriet E. Wilson: An Evangelical Reading of "Our Nig"   197

8. Homage to Harriet Wilson: The Concluding Evangelical Reading of "Our Nig"   219

Conclusion: The Authenticity of Our Christian Faith   245

Bibliography   249

Introduction
The Nature of Christian Influence and the Character of God: Concerning Our Identities, Sense of Belonging, and Shared-Space with the Human Other

EVANGELICAL CONCERNS

As an African-American Christian, I have noticed issues within our contemporary context that have confused, frustrated, and angered me. Naturally, these issues reside within the religious and political world. I am continuously dismayed by the increasing superficiality of racialized politics in America and the relative obsession with race by some African Americans who, claiming to be psychologically free from White Supremacy, ultimately do the bidding of its adherents by contributing to the prevalent distortions of racialized reasoning. Yet, my views regarding certain African Americans do not negate or dismiss my disdain for the repulsive notions of Eurocentric imperialism and White Supremacist discourses throughout the world. Nevertheless, connected to my previous views is the shock of witnessing how counterproductive and counterintuitive Black discourses and other agendas deteriorate common knowledge about Christianity, and how they have shaped African-American existence. Examples of this are seen within the Black academia in America, whereby certain scholars have routinely secularized Christianity, aided by African-American Christians, who elevate Black solidarity above their call to articulate their Christian faith. Yet, this is likely exhibited by African-American Christians who prioritize their racial identity on par or above their Christian identity. Ironically, their Blackness becomes the central hermeneutic, much like Whiteness, to interpret Christianity, God, and reality in its entirety. From my vantage point, theology, for them, is reinterpreted as an anthropology, the spirit of Western Democracy replaces the Holy Spirit of Judean Christianity, and the worship of the human-Self replaces worship of the real God.

My concern, in part, is that aspects of African-American culture, politics, and the academy appear to be gradually losing their sense of reality concerning the view of God as the "really real." For some, God is continually reinterpreted as an individualized philosophical concept with limited emotional, psychological, and moral value as determined by Western Democracy and racialized politics. Subsequently, segments of African-American culture, politics, and the academy are losing their connection to the *essence* of Christianity, and the divine revelation of God-Self as the ultimate reality from which everything else derives. Interestingly enough, I fear some of us are also losing a grounded understanding of freedom and equality as defined within Western Democracy.

True equality inside and outside the Church is genuinely transformative within the Evangelical tradition and does not occur before sincere repentance, forgiveness, and reconciliation. These principles are also applicable in the secular political world. Historically, African-American Christians have embodied these principles within their *religiopolitical* world. We have a rich history of Christians who upheld the integrity of Christianity, and their love for Christ as they engaged the political world, to create lasting change and transformation. A deceptive illusion exists and permeates America that states religious faith is politically inept and should be imprisoned within our internal worlds. Yet, when we believe this illusion to be a reality, aspects of our culture, politics, and academy experience an identity crisis, embracing a fragmented existence. Connected to this is losing a healthy understanding of colonial African-American Christianity, particularly within American Evangelicalism, and those who self-identified as such, who emancipated themselves from the very things in which we choose to enclose ourselves: namely the distorted self-contradictory racial ideologies and the concealed influence of White Supremacy.

The general purpose of my book is to establish a new theological starting point for a larger project discussing the literature and theologies of colonial Evangelical African-American Christians. This process involves excavating some of the African-American slave narratives that have been buried under theological and sociopolitical obscurity because of their genuine Christian faith and adherence to the Gospel narrative, which greatly influenced their engagement in the secular sociopolitical world.[1] For me, their theologies, Christian faith, and overall lives have become the relative antithesis of our contemporary hyper-racialized identity-politics and adherence to ambiguous religiosity within the quasi-religion of Western Democracy. Connected to this is what I also refer to as the complementary religious disposition of *African-American Civil Religion*.

However, more specifically regarding this current book, I aim to establish an introduction to my views by bringing increasing awareness to the presence, activity, and voices of pioneering colonial Evangelical African-American women. These are Christian women who, by some, have been ignored, dismissed, and rejected because they represent a distinct reality, types of Christianity, and forms of Blackness that constructed its *identity, sense of belonging*, and *existence in shared-spaces* with the human-Other, that is antithetical to aspects of our contemporary culture, politics, academy, and understanding of religion. I will discuss the theologies, ministries, and lives of Jarena Lee (1783–1864), Old Elizabeth (1766–1866), Mrs. Zilpha Elaw (1790–1873), Maria W. Stewart (1803–1879), and Julia A. J. Foote (1883–?). Each person articulated distinct messages through their narratives, and their lives shaped African-American culture, Christianity, the Black Church, and their theologies. Yet, I will also take an orthodox and possibly controversial approach in providing an evangelical interpretation of an ambiguous autobiography/novel by an African-American spiritualist named Harriet E. Wilson (1825–1900). Wilson wrote a work called, *Our Nig; or Sketches from the Life of a Free Black*. Wilson provides an intriguing and captivating story that I feel is

1. I initially came to the awareness of the African-American slave narratives as a source of Black theology, and conceptions of colonial Black slave theology through the scholarship of Dwight N. Hopkins. I have always found Hopkins's scholarship interesting and frustrating, as he demonstrates the legitimacy of articulating a Black slave theology, but employs his interpretation through what I refer to as the "Conian" school of thought. Hopkins is the protégé of James Cone (1938–2018), the founder of contemporary Black Liberation Theology. I am not a follower of Cone and the hermeneutics/methodologies he employs for his theology. Nevertheless, despite my reservations with Hopkins, his work must be engaged as a valuable interpretation of colonial Black theology. See Hopkins, *Down, Up, and Over*; *Introducing Black Theology of Liberation*; *Shoes That Fit Our Feet*; Hopkins and Cummings, *Cut Loose Your Stammering Tongue*. For a critique of Hopkins's scholarship, see Anderson, *Beyond Ontological Black*, 97–98; Carter, "Contemporary Black Theology." For my critique of Cone, Hopkins, and an aspect of African-American studies that utilizes similar hermeneutics and methodologies, see May, "Racialized-Politics."

greatly influenced by Christianity. For me, it is a great story of a young Black girl who had a similar identity, sense of belonging, and conception of shared-space with the human-Other, like other colonial African-American women had, inside and outside of the Church. My aim is not to deceive anyone into thinking it is a Christian text, but a beautiful text influenced by Christianity with a relatively concealed Christian message.

My book is divided into three sections. The first section, *Contemporary Dilemmas*, establishes my interpretation of our contemporary religious and sociopolitical Western American context. I will focus on the problems I perceive in the exaggeration, obsession, and distortion of how we construct, embody, and weaponize our identities, sense of belonging, and shared spaces with the human-Other. Chapter 1, "Constructing Our Identities, Sense of Belonging, and Shared-Spaces through Essentialist/Racialized-binary Reasoning, and the Cycle of Dehumanization," discusses my general view and specific examples of what I refer to as the cycle of dehumanization that produces a pendulum effect of self-inflicted trauma, that extends outward as oppression when imposed upon the human-Other. Connected to this is the destructive usage of essentialist and racialized-binary reasoning. In part, I assess the aspects of the present influence of secularism and ambiguous religiosity that produces spiritual ignorance and biblical illiteracy, which contributes to sociopolitical oppression. I discuss my perception of the lack of religious authenticity and genuineness within African-American religiosity. I argue that some of its proponents have made a quasi-religion of Western Democracy and hyper-Black racialized politics.

My second chapter, "The Melodrama of Fragmented Blackness," employs the sociopolitical philosophy and theology of Martin Luther King Jr, as representative of the conservative tradition of African-American Evangelicalism. I situate King within the same or similar school of thought that Lee, Elizabeth, Stewart, and Foote helped establish. Naturally, in discussing King's views, I examine aspects of the Civil Rights Movement relating to conservative and liberal Black religiosity and sociopolitical philosophy. I interpret King as one of the earliest African-Americans during the Civil Rights Movement to observe and fight against essentialist/racialized-binary reasoning. For me, King understood its usage as antithetical to genuine human equity and equality. I will also encourage my readers to critically reflect upon the present and past context of the Civil Rights Movement, relating to authentic religiosity and its hyper-politicizations that create manufactured civil religions. My aim is also to demonstrate the positive contributions of African-American Christianity and forms of its sociopolitical theologies that take seriously the orthodox Christian faith, devoid of an obsession with race and identity politics. In this, we witness a unique form of how King imagined a series of healthy identities, senses of belonging, and conceptions of shared-space representing genuine freedom and reconciliation.

Chapter 3, "Colonial African-American Self-Awareness, Obliviousness, and Fragmented Whiteness," completes my transition from progressing from the present to the colonial context. In this chapter, I examine certain African-American slave narratives to demonstrate their awareness of essentialist/racialized-binary reasoning. I will demonstrate their knowledge of how this destructive reasoning perpetuated a cycle of dehumanization, starting within Anglo-American society through their allegiance to slavery. My aim is also, in part, to express the different ways African-Americans were affected by this reasoning inside and outside of the church. I will demonstrate how there is an almost completely different understanding of race, Black solidarity, and sociopolitical views that are in relative opposition to those embodied by some African-Americans during the Civil Rights Movement and our contemporary period. This chapter serves as a transition to the core chapters of my book.

Section Two, *Commentary on the Theology of Classic Evangelical African-American Women*, is the core of my book as it discusses together the narratives of Jarena Lee and Old Elizabeth (chapter 4), then I will progress to Maria W. Stewart (chapter 5), and Julia A. J. Foote (chapter 6). I interpret these women as evangelical African-American theologians. Their theology and sociopolitical views were devoid of the destructive essentialist/racialized-binary reasoning that has imprisoned America today. I will provide a commentary-like examination of their work to demonstrate the uniqueness of their lives, ministry, and relationship with God that shaped their identities, sense of belonging, and conceptions of share-space with the human-Other. In this, we will also see a different form of evangelical African-American Christianity, and "Black theology" compared to what is popularized today. I do not advocate replicating these women or their theologies. Rather, in part, my aim is to place further attention on the foundations of *genuine* African-American Christianity and its various contextualized theologies. In doing so, I hope to contribute to nurturing our history and allowing this aspect of our Christian tradition to be a conduit for authentic Christian faith.

The last section of the book, *An Evangelical Interpretation of Literature Influenced by Christianity*, examines the writing of Harriet E. Wilson. "Our Nig," is a beautiful story that I was surprised to have stumbled upon. Again, I do not interpret Harriet's work as a Christian text, but I do interpret it as *influenced* by the principles of Christianity. I understand my opinion may be absurd to some people, but I sense Christian overtones within the discourse that I aim to demonstrate to the reader, not as an evangelizing tool but as a means of encouraging more African-American Christians to appreciate *secular* literature that may be influenced by Christianity, although they are likely not authored by Christians. I express my views as such because there is a shroud of ambiguity upon Wilson's life and her work that intrigues me.

An underlining and central point I want my readers to reflect on is the *nature of Christian influence* by genuine Christians and the essence of Christianity when they embody the righteousness of Christ Jesus. Before turning to the substance of my work, it is important for me to introduce a brief theory on the nature of Christian influence, that I hope you employ when reading my interpretations.

A BLACK EVANGELICAL INTERPRETATION

The Nature of Christian Influence

As an Evangelical African-American, I interpret my culture and the foundation of our sociopolitical views as deeply influenced by the Bible, but specifically through the Gospel of Jesus as the Christ. During colonialism, Christ was at the center of how many African-Americans defined their individual existence, participation in loving communities, and contribution to American culture. Theologically, African-American existence is deeply Christological. I also suggest there is an interesting relationship between divine *concealment* and divine revelation that has shaped our existence. In the Old Testament, verses like Jeremiah 29:12–14 come to mind:

> "Then you will call upon Me and come pray to Me, and I will listen to you. And you will seek Me and find *Me* when you search for Me with all your heart. I will let Myself be found by you," declares the Lord, "and I will restore your fortunes and gather you from all nations and all the places where I have driven you,"

declares the Lord, "and I will bring you back to the place from where I sent you into exile."[2]

Again, I am emphasizing the intentional hiddenness of Yahweh and the command, not suggestion, to search for Him. For me, this is a central principle within African-American Christianity, especially within colonial slavery, as many people sought not only emancipation, but knowledge, spiritual enlightenment, peace, and eventually the fulfillment of their eschatological hope in complete union with God.

As Christians, we worship a *hidden* God. God is not self-evident or as visible as some Christians portray Him. Divine concealment is intentional as it serves to elicit the internal desire in humanity to sincerely seek God as God is, presented through divine revelation. We are not alone in the process of seeking God. The voice, presence, and activity of God vis-à-vis the Holy Spirit initially and continuously engage humanity. The New Testament provides similar principles as the continuation of Jeremiah 29:12–14, and one is viewed in Matthew 7:6–8,

> Do not give what is holy to dogs, and do not throw your pearls before pigs, or they will trample them under their feet, and turn and tear you to pieces. Ask, and it will be given to you; seek, and you will find; knock, and it will be opened to you. For everyone who asks receives, and the one who seeks finds, and to the one who knocks it will be opened.

Within this context, I am emphasizing the divine confirmation of human success when we are obedient to God's will and voice. There is only success, but we cannot determine how this success manifests, and it may not be to our liking. I want us to reflect on this regarding the hearts of genuine African-American slaves and emancipated people who sincerely sought God, and God revealed Himself in ways that nobody outside of their relationship can fully understand. This is another central principle within authentic African-American Christianity.

Humanity cannot override the universal principles that God has established within our reality, especially concerning religious faith, and ultimately the journey towards accepting Christ as Lord and Savior. Numerous African-Americans, enslaved and emancipated, sought to understand God as God is and discovered Him through Jesus Christ. It is impossible for a White supremacist or secular historiography to erase this reality. I will also include various contemporary secular Black

2. I am employing the New American Standard Bible throughout my work.

sociopolitical historiographies and their complementary quasi-Christian discourses.

I must stress this crucial point: an orthodox or traditional understanding of the Bible, Gospels, and Jesus Christ has shaped how genuine African-American Christians have constructed and embodied their *identities*, sense of *belonging*, and conceptions of *shared-space* with the human-Other. This is not in a way that places an irrational focus on race, White Supremacy, and the social construction of Whiteness in any idolatrous way. Rather, in a grounded, practical, and transformative way that take seriously the integrity of the essence of Christianity, the humanity/salvation of the human-Other, and potential reconciliation of everyone. However, this does not mitigate, ignore, or dismiss the natural and divine rights of the human-Self within the sociopolitical articulations of freedom, equity, and equality. These are natural elements of our conceptions of Western Democracy and its distinct relationship to broader conceptions of Western Christianity. Both have central importance to African-American existence. We did not originate within a vacuum, detached from other cultures and ethnicities. Additionally, African-Americans, like countless examples within humanity, have responded to God's presence and voice in varied ways. Yet, my dogmatism encourages me to emphasize the point that God, for colonial African-American Christians, as articulated in their narratives and oral accounts, was truly real to them. God, as God-Self revealed through Christianity, the Gospels, and Jesus Christ, was more real than any pain and suffering endured through enslavement.

The influence of Western Christianity upon African-American Christians was not in the abstract, emotionally deceived, psychologically detached, or superficial epistemological sense. Rather, it was through the synthesis of a *genuine* religious faith in the concrete reality of a solitary deity, responsible for creating reality as they comprehended it, which included His central desire to be in union with humanity. I am emphasizing religious and Christian transformative belief in knowing God truly exists, as the "really real," that *intrudes* upon the human experience. Connected to this is the central desire to respond to God's intrusion, seeking to know God-Self as God truly is, and at some point, determining to submit to Him as Lord and Savior, or choosing external factors as quasi-justification to reject Him. The very essence of Christianity has been, currently is, and my dogmatism advocates that it will continue to influence people in positive way, regardless of their knowledge of it, as it stems from the real God.

In the Western world, I present the case that the very nature of how we understand Evangelicalism has a distinct relationship to colonial African-American Christianity. However, historically, this relationship has been severely neglected, and often unjustifiably dismissed on the grounds of *unimportance*, or that it simply is non-existent, posited primarily by those within Anglo-American culture. In part, this is observed through forms of Eurocentric revisionist historiographies. The overt paternalistic racism, and covert paternalistic ignorance of colonial Anglo-American society, had often seamlessly overlapped. This also continues to distort aspects of contemporary Anglo-American society. Thus, we are perpetually bombarded with the assumptions that Anglo-American Christians never, if seldom at all, learned about their Christian faith, and the distinctive existential reality of Yahweh, through the spirit, intellect, and teachings of some African-American Christians.

My point is that the influence of African-American Christianity upon Anglo-American Christianity may have been relatively entirely ignored by Anglo-Americans, but through the written and oral traditions of African-American Christians, some people may see that this is a deceptive lie. The employment of colonial racism and White Supremacy deeply scarred Anglo-American and European Christianity to the point they relatively lost the ability to discern those things that were obviously before them. Thus, I join with other African-American scholars who advocate that through the essence of Christianity, Black Christian faith, and the genuine engagement of Yahweh within the world, evangelical African-American Christianity has shaped the world in ways that historical documents cannot fully demonstrate. Unfortunately, within the late twentieth and early twenty-first century, we have witnessed the continual rise of some African-Americans, within and outside of Christendom, who are mimicking the distorted, and dismissive agenda of some Eurocentric, or supremacist-minded individuals within Anglo-American culture. In part, I tend to categorize these forms of historical research as secular and religious expressions of hyper-liberal *Afrocentric*, and *Black Nationalist historiography*.

Yet, I do not relegate this theory of human and Christian influence solely to African-Americans. It is universal. For me, it is obvious that Christianity and Western Democracy have influenced individuals and communities who have embraced and rejected those systems of beliefs.

Again, I am emphasizing the deceptive reality that consciously or subconsciously *rejecting* a person, event, or belief system does not eliminate their influence upon us. The sphere of influence can and does extend beyond our self-awareness, and I argue, often subsequently strengthens our self-awareness, by challenging the human-Self to delve deeper into reality, and their search to genuinely learn more about God, broadly construed. Now, I am compelled to gesture towards and begin to present my interpretation of influential African-American women within colonialism, who represented Christ to the world around them, and their distinct expressions of Christian influence that led others to establish a relationship with Christ Jesus. Connected to this is to consider the literature that does not have an obvious Christian identity, but nonetheless, have, or may have been influenced by the essence of Christianity in its articulation.

I arrive at the presence and *influence* of what I define as classical African-American Evangelical Feminism. African-American colonial women, particularly those within the Christian faith, have historically represented many positive and influential things. Theologically, I am advocating their distinct representation and embodiment of the *Fruit of the Spirit*. To a certain extent, because of Christianity's influence on African-American culture, we must also acknowledge the ethical and moral fabric of those African-American women who did not identify with Christianity. These women demonstrated aspects of the Fruit of the Spirit, *outside* of the Body of Christ, in ways that testified to Yahweh's *influence* upon humanity. In saying this, I am not rejecting traditional basic Christian doctrine, claiming they had the indwelling Holy Spirit. However, I am theorizing and suggesting that the influence of the Holy Spirit influences people's characters in various ways. Nevertheless, historically, particularly through African-American colonial literature, we can see a display of diverse contextualized African-American Christian theologies, their practical application of biblical principles, and the influence of both upon various colonial Anglo-Americans. These aspects influenced and were subsequently shaped by how these individuals constructed their *identities*, *sense of belonging*, and lives within *shared-spaces* with the *racialized-Other*.

It is helpful to discuss my interpretation of the Apostle Paul's outlines within Galatians 3–5, regarding the Fruit of the Spirit. In this discussion, I want to emphasize how salvation, righteousness, and justification are related to Christian ethics and politics but have unfortunately undergone skewed reinterpretations that influence how we construct our identities, sense of belonging, and shared space. Furthermore, I will reframe the Law within notions of Western Democracy, and the authority of the colonial slave master and mistress, within the institution of slavery. This interpretation will be contrasted with Paul's demonstration of Christ as the representative of freedom. My interpretation of Paul's theology helps the reader understand, from a biblical standpoint, how I perceive certain Evangelical African-American women representing the Fruit of the Spirit, as the Character of God.

FLESH OF BONDAGE AND THE SPIRIT OF FREEDOM

In Galatians 3:19–25, the Apostle Paul outlines the importance of the individual becoming justified through *believing* faith in Jesus as the Christ. Belief is not a superficial acknowledgment of an abstract ideology or adherence to an individual who proposes an agenda. Nor is the Christian conception of believing faith a pseudo compromise stemming from idolatrous obedience to the Law, used to supplement or replace an authentic relationship with Yahweh. Faith, as believing in Yahweh, is what credited Abraham as righteous in the sight of God.[3] Faith, as transformative belief in Christ, is a confirmation of the individual and community's existence with new identities, sense of belonging, and shared-space that points to the eschatological finality as existing eternally in an incomprehensible but loving union with the Triune Godhead of Christianity.

Salvific faith and the spiritual union between humanity and Yahweh are Christian theological truths that are gradually neglected and dismissed in our contemporary period. For example, this is observed from a religious and secular perspective. Skewed interpretations of Western Democracy are used to create and employ a secular *hermeneutic of equality* within Christianity. Equality and equity are redefined in ways that minimize the legitimacy of qualitative and quantitative differences among religions, and eliminate the beliefs of God's activity throughout the world.

Hermeneutics of equality are also employed to present a compromise. It is used to inevitably reinterpret the legitimacy of salvific faith in a real God, into a subjective *moral* acknowledgment of an abstract concept,

---

3. "Then he (Abraham) believed in the Lord; and He credited it to him as righteousness" (Gen 15:6).

solely intended to help the individual and community adjust to reality. Subsequently, we also observe the minimizing and dismissing of Christian dogma, and the general core beliefs of various religions. Ironically, this is partially achieved through the desire, and to some extent, necessity for interreligious dialogue. Interreligious dialogue is a necessary good but is often employed by ignoring the core beliefs of each religion, which define its very existence, for the sake of creating an illusion of equality and harmony with other religions. The dogma of religion is relegated to a private sphere, only to be protected from justifiable criticism from those outside the community, as they are refined further by those within the community.

Nevertheless, the Apostle Paul advocated that the purpose of the Law was, to some extent, intended to create a heightened sense of self-awareness, revealing a distinctive nature of humanity and humanity's central purpose as a creation of God, being created *for* God. Israel was the sole beneficiary of this revelation according to their covenant with Yahweh. Yet, the deeper significance of this relationship, at least from an Evangelical perspective, was that Yahweh always intended for those outside of Israel to be included within the covenant between Him and Israel. Faith and obedience in Yahweh within the Old Testament covenant is fulfilled within the New Testament covenant, through salvific faith and obedience in Jesus as the Christ, through His death, burial, and resurrection. Paul discusses aspects of this in Galatians 3:19–25,

> Why the Law then? It was added on account of the violations, having been ordered through angels at the hand of a mediator, until the Seed would come to whom the promise had been made. Now a mediator is not for one party *only*; but God is *only* one. Is the Law then contrary to the promise of God? Far from it! For if a law had been given that was able to impart life, then righteousness would indeed have been based on law. But the Scripture has confined everyone under sin, so that the promise by faith in Jesus Christ might be given to those who believe. But before faith came, we were kept in custody under the law, being confined for the faith that was destined to be revealed. Therefore, the law has become our guardian to *lead us* to Christ, so that we may be justified by faith. But now that faith has come, we are no longer under a guardian.

Paul explains that the Law was not Christ but only led us to Christ. There is a deep interconnected relationship between a heightened self-awareness of an individual's ultimate purpose and the realization of that ultimate purpose through the transcendent transformative process of salvific faith within Jesus as the Christ.

In our contemporary world, aspects of secular Western society have reinterpreted Western Democracy into a superficial *representation* of the Law. Western Democracy, for some, with its ethics and morality, attempts to create a world of equity and equality void of projecting a deity as the object of worship. A deity in the traditional sense does not exist, but an illusory conception of freedom stands as the ultimate ideal, which becomes a quasi-deity of sorts. This conception of freedom, despite one's political views, is advocated as the means to *sociopolitical righteousness*. This quasi-religious sociopolitical ideology, and complementary structures, skews the individual's perception of their ultimate purpose in life. The issue of an individual's ultimate purpose is either irrelevant or is fulfilled through the obtainment of said illusory freedom, through conceptions of Western Democracy. In many ways, this is the structure of American Civil Religions. I am highlighting the conflicting ways some individuals employ politics, conceptions of freedom, and Western Democracy as they help define how some people create their identities, sense of belonging, and shared spaces with the human-Other. The processes we experience and observe today were well within colonialism. The colonial Evangelical African-American women I discuss had engaged and overcome similar issues in various ways.

The allure of illusory freedom, equity, and equality was more enticing during colonial slavery than they are today. Skewed politics, employed in certain ways, can establish itself as the ultimate purpose in our lives. It provides subjective and/or limited situational freedom, and the perception of power, but also a distorted concept of sociopolitical righteousness, and justice. Humanity has an innate desire and capacity for self-governance. They lie within the fabric of our ethics and morality. Christianity cautions humanity against making the desire and capacity of self-governance into the fulfilment of human destiny. An example of what I'm stating is witnessed in the Old Testament. The Old Testament Law was not intended to be an object of worship, creating righteousness and justification in and of itself, for its adherents. Politics, being a means to freedom and empowerment are not aspects of humanity's ultimate purpose. They are guides, like the Law, void of granting anyone who adheres to them realities independent from God's creative order. Rather, they are in part, intended to help disclose a heightened self-awareness of humanity's desire to achieve unity, alongside its inability to do so apart from God. Christian realism, like the Law, reveals the wickedness of our human nature, as expressed within the historical evidence of perpetual war between nations, societal oppression within nations, various forms of slavery, and genocide.

Reality, and everything within it, at least in part, reveals the tension between morality and immorality, righteousness, and unrighteousness, as well as the acceptance and denial of God's existence. A constellation of natural oppositional dualisms exists, and we are perpetually subjected to them. The biblical narrative, aware of this, seeks to create a heightened sense of awareness regarding their existence, attempting to guard the Christian from lapsing into the practice of wicked desires.

The procession of thought from Galatians 3:19–26 leads Paul to state in Galatians 3:28–29 that, "There is neither Jew nor Greek, there is neither slave nor free, there is neither male nor female for you are all one in Christ Jesus. If you belong to Christ, then you are Abraham's seed, and heirs according to the promise." Colonialism's hierarchy of human value is negated and destroyed within the Body of Christ. It is not that God does not acknowledge human diversity. Human difference is a part of the creative order and has a divine purpose. Human diversity reaches its apex as an existential expression of the human-Self living *for* the human-Other within its union with Yahweh. This is an aspect of glorifying God. Secularism, in various ways, has replicated this biblical truth, creating a superficial compromise, expressed at least in part, through some ambiguous expressions of humanism, and religious humanism, which are often exploited within Western Democracy. Nevertheless, Paul introduces Christian ethics into his discussion of the relationship between salvific faith, righteousness, and justification. For Paul, there is the binary oppositional relationship between the Christian and non-Christian worlds, vis-à-vis morality and immorality, as they relate to acknowledging Jesus as the Christ. Paul refers to this in Galatians 5:19–21,

> Now the deeds of the flesh are evident, which are: sexual immorality, impurity, indecent behavior, idolatry, witchcraft, hostilities, strife, jealousy, outbursts of anger, selfish ambition, dissentions, factions, envy, drunkenness, carousing, and things like these, of which I forewarn you, just as I have forewarned you, that those who practice such things will not inherit the kingdom of God.

We may also include the practice of slavery and the dehumanization of the human-Other. This is considering most of what Paul outlines were central aspects of colonial immorality within the institution of slavery. There are many accounts of slaves being beaten, raped, and tortured, as well as families torn apart. For me, the deeds of the flesh are natural expressions of our carnal and depraved humanity. They are normalized within society. Some appear more harmless than others. The deeds, and their complementary sets of reasoning and belief systems, are the instruments of dehumanization, injustice, pain, and suffering. Reflecting and practicing them are often accomplished while maintaining a superficial expression of love, peace, compassion, and justice.

The practice of such deeds, while claiming salvific faith in Jesus, insinuates a state of self-contradiction, and self-deception of the individual. This naturally applies to the community in which the individuals reside. Human actions are guides, physical expressions of the individual's character, level of integrity, and in this context, relationship with Yahweh. The biblical narrative warns against the perception of a compromise between morality and immorality, commitment to self-interest, or a sacrificial life within Christ. Jesus clearly references this in principle within Matthew 7:16–17, "By their fruit you will recognize them. Do people pick grapes from thornbushes, or figs from thistles? Likewise, every good tree bears good fruit, but a bad tree bears bad fruit." The question posed by Jesus is designed to elicit self-awareness towards the obvious answer: "No." Contradictions and inconsistencies exist. They are intentionally and unintentionally created. However, Jesus alludes to our moral obligation to sharpen our self-awareness to those human actions and rhetoric that represent said contradictions and inconsistencies. This, too, is connected to the biblical message of being *lukewarm*. Lukewarmness has a psychological element. The employment of cognitive dissonance, and confirmatory bias from the individual, creates an illusion of the individual existing in a relationship with Yahweh that does not actually exist. My belief is that Eurocentric Christianity and proslavery Christianity are fragmented religious systems of belief. I suggest they employ forms of racialized politics that are designed to mirror conceptions of the Old Testament Law. If this belief has any merit, how do we interpret Eurocentric Anglo-American Christians articulating their identity, sense of belonging, and shared space with the supposed inferior racialized-Other?

We have discussed specific issues that have brought us to this point. The spheres of influence from African-American culture, Christianity, and Western Democracy have individually, and collectively created forms of accountability and responsibility that, although largely ignored, nevertheless, impose judgments upon Anglo-American existence. Aspects of Anglo-American society and Christianity reinterpreted Western Democracy as a pseudo-Law, which endowed *Whiteness* with a conception of illusory freedom. This illusory freedom was, and still is, perceived to represent various forms of secular and non-Christian forms of salvation, justification, and righteousness. Hence, those who embraced proslavery Christianity, or White Supremacist Anglo-Evangelicalism, developed a distorted relationship with Yahweh, and an irredeemable contextualized Christianity. This resulted in forms of distorted American Civil Religions. Examples of this can be observed in the lack of self-awareness from some colonial Anglo-Americans regarding White self-degradation, initiated from their abuse of African and African-American slaves. Dehumanization, degradation, and other forms of abuse develop initially from within the human-Self. The internal fragmentation of the human-Self eventually extends to the human-Other, creating forms of distortions within them, all of which are concealed, existing beyond everyone's self-awareness.

I invite my readers to consider these beliefs and cling to them as you engage my interpretation of colonial Evangelical African-American Christianity, through the narratives of Jarena Lee, Old Elizabeth, Mrs. Zilpha Elaw, Maria W. Stewart, and Julia A. J. Foote. Regarding Christian influence, I will include the work of Harriet E. Wilson. My work is also an introduction in the sense of my desire to provide newer engagement of colonial African-American Christianity that takes seriously the different way it has articulated a genuine faith in Christ Jesus as God. My aim is to recast these narratives devoid of contemporary fascinations, obsessions, and idolatrous conceptions of distorted identity-politic vis-à-vis gender and race. I also challenge Christians to cultivate a genuine interest in literature that may not be distinctively identified as Christian but demonstrates positive aspects and critiques of the essence of Christianity.

1

Constructing Our Identities, Sense of Belonging, and Shared-Spaces Through Essentialist/Racialized-Binary Reasoning and the Cycle of Dehumanization

EVASIVE PSYCHOSIS?

Attempts to Call into Being What Logically Cannot Exist

HUMANITY HAS AN INTERNAL impulse, a compulsion to understand its existence, and the overwhelming reality that surrounds it. Human advancement, within this vein of reasoning, is unavoidable, as it is a part of who we are and how we define our humanity. There is no advancement or progress, broadly construed, without the human mind and will, along with other *essential* things. Yet, my point is not to create or debate an exhaustive list of attributes that define us. Instead, I am initiating a line of questioning concerning how and why we can unknowingly obsess over those things we deem essential, and how they bear upon our humanity. In this context, the desire and perception of those things can be dramatically skewed, but the things themselves are essentially unaffected. Those things, whatever they may be, cannot be excluded; otherwise, the subject itself becomes something entirely other than what we currently think it to be. Continuing with my belief in the innate human drive to learn and progress: there is no advancement or progress, and only a partial picture of our humanity is portrayed *if* advancement and progress are reinterpreted without those human attributes. I am emphasizing and questioning how and why we assess what is and is not plausible within our beliefs of ourselves and the reality around us. For me, another example of what I am seeking to describe can be viewed within aspects of contemporary *progressive* Christianity in America. For some, believing in the deity of Jesus is not a requirement to receive salvation. For some, the concept of spiritual salvation is completely irrational, and it is therefore reinterpreted within a broader sociopolitical ethic. Others would even argue whether it is necessary to accept that a Jewish man named Jesus truly existed. I would also include people who call themselves Christians, but completely disregard Church history before the colonial era, with its Church Fathers and Mothers, basic Christian doctrine and theology, councils, and creeds.

I often wonder who has an identity crisis, them or me, when it comes to understanding and embodying the *essence* of Christianity vis-à-vis Jesus as the Christ. Considering this, what do we call people who, whether intentionally or not, try to describe a person, place, or concept without an essential attribute? How do we describe their attempts and what they perceive to be something or someone that is plausible within reality? Furthermore, what if we witness their inability to properly discern what is essential, and the consequences of their inability produce injustice, oppression, and a cycle of dehumanization?

From an evangelical perspective, true freedom and equality cannot sincerely exist without the inner transformation of *everyone*, oppressor and oppressed. Inner transformation is initiated, matured, and completed through genuine repentance, forgiveness, redemption, and reconciliation. For me, these processes have secular and religious components, overlapping in certain ways. Naturally, God is present and active within every step, regardless of our awareness. However, what do we make of people who believe sociopolitical equality can be achieved without the assistance of religion, and the inner spiritual transformation of everyone? How do we interpret people who ignore aspects of religious history, that contribute to the advancement of sociopolitical equality, because they desire to strengthen their beliefs in satisfying their self-interest? And, to go further with my questioning, how do we interpret the spirituality of Christians who represent this vein of reasoning?

My aim in this chapter is to discuss the persistent and decaying effects of skewed essentialist and racialized-binary reasoning. My belief is that they are more prevalent than we realize. When we utilize these ways of perceiving and understanding reality, we unknowingly lose our grounding but deceive ourselves into thinking we have obtained our self-interest. I interpret self-interest as the desires we have created within our internal worlds. We lose the ability to discern what is and is not essential when it comes to constructing our identities, sense of belonging, and shared-space with the human-Other. Subsequently, we assume a level of ability and power that we cannot plausibly possess, and attempt to redefine concepts like freedom, equality, justice, and Christianity. I will examine the theories of certain scholars who have discussed elements of essentialist and racialized-binary reasoning, directly and indirectly, and demonstrate their approaches to revealing and expunging this destructive form of reasoning.

My concern is that once essentialist/racialized-binary reasoning is further normalized, we become unaware of the cognitive dissonance and confirmatory bias that lock us into endless loops of conflict. This develops against those we view as the external oppositional-Other, and the people within our homogenous communities we interpret as the internal oppositional-Other.[1] The process affects everyone regardless of gender, political views, race, and sexuality. The employment of essentialist/racialized-binary reasoning is an unintentional taint, and to a certain extent, a form of intentional escapism. Entrapment within this reasoning compels us to ignore the people, groups, historiographies, and traditions that are devoid of these debilitating attributes.

The presence of these debilitating forms of reasoning is contradictory to the *essence* of Christianity. Thus, it distorts all contextualized Christianity and its theologies because it becomes impossible to create and embody fundamental Christian principles, particularly those of repentance, forgiveness, reconciliation, redemption, and equality.

1. The us versus them mentality is a component of essentialist/racialized-binary reasoning. I am not attempting to articulate a definitive definition of these terms. I am concerned that they are more prevalent within society than we may realize and are readily employed by the human conscience to satisfy its self-interest—one example we see within Ancient Rome. Christians and Jews were heavily persecuted within the empire before Emperor Constantine's reign (306–337) and sporadically after his death. Despite one's citizenship, everyone, in various ways, was forced to pledge religious-like loyalty to Caesar and the Roman State along with its gods. Execution was the primary alternative for those who didn't comply. The Roman Catholic Church has a history of similar persecution of those deemed "heretics," even to the extent when genuine Christians were labelled as such for political reasons, to eliminate any threat to the Pope's authority. A contemporary example is witnessed in how Middle Easterners were treated in the Western world after the attacks on the World Trade Center in New York on 9/11. For example, see MacCulloch, *Christianity*; Evans, *Roots of the Reformation*; González, *Early Church*.

Furthermore, our identities, sense of belonging, and how we share space with the human-Other experience further fragmentation, having less to do with facts, truth, and reality, but everything that involves, at least from a religious viewpoint, idolatry through self-worship. The veneer of secularism only aids in the delusion.

We live in a nation that is extremely confident, if not arrogant, about our supposed superiority and elite representation of Christianity and democracy. Yet, there is a dark irony in our inability to see how, when we attempt to redefine freedom and equality detached from repentance, forgiveness, redemption, and reconciliation, we then lose our grounding within reality. We deceive ourselves into thinking we can live fruitfully apart from one another, and that entails an existence where the human-Other has no reasonable influence on our lives. We have convinced ourselves that all significant social issues can be solved by the exertion of political power, and that coincides with an inordinate amount of hope, hope as quasi-religious faith, in political power. Political despair resides when our self-interests are not fulfilled. The persistent influence and concealment of essentialist and racialized-binary reasoning are widespread throughout our nation. It is so cunning, elusive, and mesmerizing that even those conscious of it, may find themselves negatively employing it for their benefit.

In this context, I want to stress the importance of eventually expressing the level of self-awareness some colonial African-American Christians exhibited against essentialist and racialized-binary reasoning within the dehumanizing context of American slavery. In part, this provides a historical example of the dehumanizing category of reasoning. It will help us further understand how those deemed unintelligent and unspiritual were aware of its existence and sought to fight against it. In doing so, some colonial African-American Christians refined their contextualized Christianity and theologies relating to their conceptions of identities, sense of belonging, and shared-space with the human-Other. In achieving this, I must first discuss some contemporary forms of essentialist and racialized-binary reasoning. This allows the reader to compare and contrast various theologies, employment of essentialist and racialized-binary reasoning, along with how certain people opposed them.

The first example within our contemporary period is witnessed through the academic discipline of Black theology, which for me, is essentially various replications of James Cone's theology. I will briefly discuss the scholarship of Victor Anderson, who for me provided a mature and polished critique of the discipline when I was struggling to comprehend and put into words what I was perceiving.[2]

BLACK OUROBOROS

Race has always been a controversial issue. I have long been confused about how and why it can captivate people's hearts to the extent of them obsessing over it. For some people, race appears endowed with some mythological power. Race has obviously been reified by various people, but have we scrutinized the extent it has been defied within Black religiosity and socio-politics? If this is too much of an irrational leap of thought, how about we consider the possibility of race being philosophized into *something other* than what it really is?

Now this *something other* is extremely subjective, a hyper-distortion of the human conscience that the individual cannot fully articulate or explain, because they have psychologically fallen into the same colonial anathema of the creators of racial classification.[3] Let us specifically focus on conceptions of Blackness. I question what Blackness and *being* Black mean to some contemporary African-Americans. I often wonder what lies behind the strong rhetoric and aggressive imagery of Blackness. Included in this discussion are Black intelligence and Black beauty. There is always the issue of an ideal or competing ideals of aesthetics, an *Ideal Blackness*, whether it is intentionally or unintentionally erected, like that of a quasi-religious idol. Contemporary academic African-American literature, at least for me, appears inundated with exposing White Supremacy, and always assessing Blackness in relation to dehumanized-Whiteness. Does this represent who we really are as reality dictates it?

---

2. I must also acknowledge the influential critique from James Cone's brother, Cecil W. Cone. See Cone, *Identity Crisis in Black Theology*.

3. There were many colonial Europeans who contributed to the social construction of race and the dehumanization of the non-European. It is impossible to provide an exhaustive list. However, some examples of whom I am referencing are Francois Bernier (1620–1688), Carolus Linnaeus (1707–1778), Johann Friedrich Blumenbach (1752–1840), and George Louis Leclerc de Buffon (1707–1788). See Bernier, "New Division of the Earth," 247–50; ASL, *Memoirs*, 1:360–64; Linnaeus, *Systema Naturae*; Blumenbach, *De Genesis Hamani Varietate Nativa*; Buffon, *Natural History of Man*; Linne, "God-Given Order of Nature"; Fredrickson, *Racism*; Hannaford, *Race*; Harris, *Rise of Anthropological Theory*; Isaac, *Invention of Racism*; Jordan, *White Over Black*; McCarthy, *Race, Empire*; Montagu, *Man's Most Dangerous Myth*; Smedley, *Race in North America*; West, *Prophecy Deliverance*.

Or are some of us being exposed to the manifestations of certain Black people's inner world?

Cone has always been an interesting figure to me after I was exposed to his early work.[4] His scholarship tended to invoke brief moments of peaceful agreement that were sporadically interrupted by longer segments of confusion and frustration. Obviously, I do not take issue with exposing the destructive effects of White Supremacy within and outside the Black church, African-American culture, theology, and the world. However, my disagreements stemmed from his hermeneutics and methodologies that led him to certain conclusions, most of which I thought were questionable, and possibly antithetical to scripture. For me, theology should not be racialized or nationalized. It always appeared counterintuitive and counterproductive to the *essence* of Christianity.

Conian theology, especially its early articulation, placed a heavy premium on Blackness, a particular form of Blackness, one that felt alienated and detached from the more conservative Evangelical expression, represented by people like Martin Luther King Jr. and the conservative Black Church. I empathize with those Black people during the Civil Rights Movement and many who would identify with them today. Ironically, I have never felt connected to Conian theology, nor identified with the sociopolitical philosophies of Black Nationalism and Black Power. I have never felt *Black* enough for either of them. Thus, our identity, sense of belonging, and how we conceive our shared-space with the human-Other, in many ways, can manifest itself as the internal fragmentation of Blackness. There is a tragic irony that an assortment of Black Nationalist historiographies, intent on exposing and dethroning White Supremacist historiographies, requires the strengthening of additional Black historiographies to correct those of the latter. For example, I could never settle attempts to advance a Black *Christian* theology with all Black sources. Yet, realistically, I could understand the appeal of this theory and attempt by those who continually experience extreme trauma through persecution, desperately desiring to achieve self-love attached to a respected racial identity and valuing their heritage as one of the pinnacles of humanity. Honestly, I do not view Cone in this category, at least not completely, but

---

4. The aim of this chapter is not to present a complete discussion of Cone's theology and my thoughts on how most contemporary Black theologians replicate his methodologies. An adequate critique lies well beyond the scope of this chapter. I've presented my foundational beliefs of his theology in my doctoral dissertation. See May, "Racialized-Politics."

primarily the Black people who cling to Conian theology for sociopolitical not traditional Christian theological reasons.

Nevertheless, I viewed attempts to synthesize Black Nationalism and Black Power with Christianity as self-limiting when introduced into the *Christian* world. I also could not properly settle certain questions that were elicited from engaging Cone's scholarship: Did the ancient Hebrews construct their theology completely independent from the rest of the world? What about the Jews during the era of Jesus's ministry? Did the Church Fathers and Mothers construct their beliefs according to their ethnic and national loyalty? Truthfully, do we really believe European theology, broadly understood, has managed to escape the influences of the non-European? Or is it rather that the contributors to this broad system have never been forced to be honest about how and why the non-European has influenced them?

Yet, with all of my criticisms of Cone, which I will not fully disclose, I respect the fact that he was deeply Evangelical, as he unashamedly welded an uncompromising Christology. The tragic irony is only seen by how those who were influenced by him have appeared to avoid replicating *that* element of his discourse. For me, the academic discipline of Black theology is similar to Black Religion; it has become an ambiguous term and system of beliefs, some of which have nothing to do with real spirituality or embracing the real God, as defined by the traditional sense of the terms. Scholarship within those categories seems preoccupied with discussing race, how to defeat White supremacy, and achieving what I perceive to be an illusory concept of Black solidarity. Victor Anderson was one of a few scholars who presented important observations of Cone's theology and the discipline of academic Black theology. Unfortunately, at least from my perspective, he has been largely ignored.

ENGAGING ANDERSON

A Dismissed Voice

In *Beyond Ontological Blackness*, Anderson unashamedly critiques what he perceives to be the glaring problems within the discipline of Black theology in America. This I argue is possibly influenced more by the sociopolitical philosophies of Black Nationalism and Black Power than traditional Christianity as demonstrated by the Gospels, the theology of the Church Fathers and Mothers, Creeds, and global Church history. Anderson presents a compelling conception of essentialist and racialized-binary reasoning in his theory of *Ontological Blackness*.[5] For him, ontological Blackness is "a covering term that connotes categorical, essentialist, and representational languages depicting black life and experience."[6] Anderson is concerned with the cultural, philosophical, and theological ways certain African-Americans use race to construct their Black identities. For example, Black life and experience become overly simplified and placed within categories like survival and oppression. The overuse of these and other terms creates the illusion that all or most Black people have the same lives and experiences. Connected to this is Anderson's emphasis that a particular interpretation of Whiteness is garnered, and even exploited to support and justify these particular conceptions of Blackness.

Yet, I would argue that most individuals who employ this line of reasoning tend to primarily do it for sociopolitical reasons, such as to create and obtain a form of *Black solidarity*, most of which I interpret as severely conditional and illusory. Black solidarity, at least for some advocates, appears to represent a form of communalism. Moreover, for me, the overuse of this belief-turned-methodology becomes a central issue among African-Americans who have experienced extreme trauma relating to race and their understanding of who they are in the world, yet, have not obtained some form of positive healing. For various reasons, race as the very subject under attack is conceptualized as the primary agent that represents their being. Thus, there is a consequential defence of the individual's racial identity. The difficulty is that some people lose a healthy level of self-awareness in determining the boundaries and limitations of a racial identity. Nevertheless, Anderson asserts that Ontological Blackness,

> Examines the ways that racial discourse operates rhetorically in African American cultural and religious thought. The disclosure of the ways that race is reified—i.e., treated as if it objectively exists independent of historically contingent factors and subjective intentions—in the writings of historical and contemporary African-American cultural and religious thinkers is the *first* theme of the book.[7]

---

5. See Anderson, *Beyond Ontological Blackness*; *Pragmatic Theology*; *Creative Exchange*.

6. Anderson, *Beyond Ontological Blackness*, 11.

7. Anderson, *Beyond Ontological Blackness*, 11.

The key issue is the reification of race, and to add to Anderson's thought, I would attach the psychological inability to understand what this process entails. An individual and community cannot avoid something if they do not truly understand that it can be practiced consciously and subconsciously, intentionally and unintentionally, if they are socialized to do so by their community. In principle, this applies to academics and how we critically think, do research, and construct our scholarship. Nevertheless, the overidentification of race as the ultimate representation of the individual's existence can easily elicit unacknowledged conceptions of confirmative bias and cognitive dissonance that cause them to defend race as if it were a concrete reality. Anderson highlights how certain African-Americans mirror or invert the logic and behavior some colonial Europeans employed to create their European aesthetic ideal through what he defines as "The Cult of European Genius." These are the attributes of essential heroic, epochal, and culturally progressive attributes that supposedly defined Europeans, as well as established them as the apex of human evolution. Ontological Blackness is also employed as,

> a philosophy of racial consciousness. It is governed by dialectical matrices that existentially structure African Americans' self-conscious perceptions of black life. Under ontological blackness, the conscious lives of blacks are experienced as bound by unresolved binary dialectics of slavery and freedom, negro and citizen, insider and outsider, black and white, struggle and survival.[8]

Thus, we see Anderson's concern that certain African-Americans, through reifying race, have constructed their identities by mimicking the heroic, epochal, and racial genius of colonial Europeans. They reduce the overwhelming and complex structures of human life and experience to the minute and irrational categories that colonial Europeans created or reinterpreted in skewed ways. Anderson calls this, *The Cult of Black Heroic Genius*, and it represents what he defines as the Blackness that Whiteness has created.[9]

It is important to mention secondary terms in Anderson's thought. Anderson defines a *cult* as the "disposition of devotion, loyalty, and admiration for racial categories and the essentialized principles that

---

8. Anderson, *Beyond Ontological Blackness*, 11, 14.

9. Anderson, *Beyond Ontological Blackness*, 13–134, esp. 13, 14–16, 61, 81, 85, 87, 112, 134.

determines black identity."[10] As I interpret him, Anderson appears to emphasize the borderline to overt obsessiveness with one's racial identity. I view it also as a consuming hermeneutic in the possessor's mind. For him, *racial genius* is articulated as, "the exceptional, sometimes essentialized cultural qualities, that positively represent the racial group in the action of at least one of the group's members. Insofar as the one member's actions are said to represent the genius of the group that member also exhibits the heroic qualities of the race."[11] For Anderson, Black heroic genius is a replication of a White counterpart as African-American cultural philosophers of the eighteenth to early twentieth century reacted against colonial European racial ideology. He argues that African-American cultural philosophy, "defined itself historically in relation to theories of African aesthetic consciousness inherited from the European Enlightenment and Romantic cultural philosophy. The black aesthetic must be seen in dialectical relation to white racial ideology."[12] Although I agree with aspects of Anderson's thoughts, I do have some minor reservations. One of a few interesting aspects of Anderson's observation is centered on the absence of religious African-Americans who did not cling to their racial identity. For me, the primary examples would be various colonial Evangelical African-Americans who chose their Christian identity to be the primary identity that shaped their lives, and how they understood race, and not vice versa. Christ is the subject, the person who freed some African-Americans from the allure of racialized reasoning, and the cognitive dissonance and confirmatory bias that develops from permanently relying on it. We must remember, for these particular colonial African-American Christians, Yahweh was "the really-real," the Creator of reality, not a subjective sociopolitical object to deceive White society.

I have difficulty determining whether Anderson believes an authentic colonial African-American identity can exist apart from the European racial aesthetic. This is interesting to me, considering colonial Europeans were dependent upon the non-Europeans to define their racial aesthetics. Colonial Europeans needed to interpret the oppositional-Other as an inferior existence to establish themselves as superior.[13] Second, every *exceptional* African-American should not be smothered by Anderson's inclusive hermeneutic to sustain his initial claim. For Anderson, it appears

10. Anderson, *Beyond Ontological Blackness*, 13.
11. Anderson, *Beyond Ontological Blackness*, 13.
12. Anderson, *Beyond Ontological Blackness*, 61.
13. See Jennings, *Christian Imagination*.

that any and every *counter-discourse* to European categorical racism and white racial ideology are interpreted as mirroring and dependent upon Whiteness. This is problematic, considering counter-discourses are often necessary. They can confront and ultimately reverse an irrational and/or racist discourse that rejects truth, facts, and reality. For me, some examples would be the colonial European notion that Africans were either not completely human or a separate category of humanity.[14]

A person with the intent to deceive can easily influence another who is either wilfully or naturally ignorant of a specific body of information. This is true especially if the ignorant person is dependent upon or submissive to the deceptive person who has power over them. Early Christian history demonstrates varied examples of what I am expressing, particularly through Christian persecution prior to Emperor Constantine's reign (ca. AD 272–337). One of the harshest periods may have been during and slightly after the rule of Emperor Nero (AD 37–68). To clarify things further, we can imagine the conflict of identities, sense of belonging, and conceptions of shared-space between the early pagan Roman citizens and Christians within the empire. This was a period when Christians were a minority group and viewed as the lowest and most ignorant of Roman society. Historian Kenneth Scott Latourette remarks,

> Christians had to face the dislike and active opposition of the pagan population about them. Criticism were on several grounds but arose very largely on the one hand from the fact that they would not compromise with paganism, but held themselves apart from it and in so doing withdrew from much of current society, and on the other hand because they won converts from that society and so could not but be noticed. To avoid unnecessary publicity and to escape so far as possible the notice of government officials, Christians held their services either secretly or without public announcement.[15]

I am emphasizing, at least theoretically, the improvement upon and transformation of the pagan Roman identity, sense of belonging, and

---

14. An example of this is the theory of Polygenism, the belief that each race has its distinct origin from one another. Polygenism was present throughout Colonialism, and various Christians endorsed it to justify the Transatlantic slave trade. A notable proponent was Francois-Marie Arouet, also known as "Voltaire" (1694–1778), the French Enlightenment philosopher, historian, and author. In "The People of America," Voltaire states, "The Negro race is a species of men as different from ours as the breed of spaniels is from that of greyhounds." See West, *Prophecy Deliverance!*, 62.

15. Latourette, *Beginnings to 1500*, 81.

conception of shared space that developed in relation to the supposed inferior Christian and also Jew. Likewise, those Jews and Christians who were persecuted had undergone similar forms of identity examination and evolution relating to the oppressive Roman nationalists. Conceptions of belonging and how they shared the same space with the human Other are included. During the early development of the church, Christians had to endure and find ways to define their existence amongst the intense accusations of atheism, wild incest orgies, and secretly sacrificing babies during communion. Historian Diarmaid MacCulloch expounds upon the contexts of early Roman persecution of Christians. Referencing the secretary of Christian rituals, he states,

> As a result, these ceremonies were thoroughly misunderstood by intelligent and sensitive Roman observers. There arose reports of incest from their talk of love-feasts, of cannibalism from the language of eating and drinking body and blood. As they attracted converts, many unsympathetic outsiders became convinced that Christian success must be the result of erotic magic, strong enough to tear wives away from non-Christian husbands; after all, a number of Christian accounts of martyrdom did indeed describe women leaving their husbands or fiancés for Christian life or death.[16]

It is clear within Christian and secular historical accounts that any Christians during this period created and embodied counter-discourses against the dehumanizing pagan perception of them. Some of these discourses are what people may categorize as apologetics and Christian theology. I must also include the reality of early Christians learning and employing Greek philosophy to explain their Christian faith. This should not be considered a mirroring of secular paganism as there were standards or criteria that were developed to determine what was and was not appropriate to synthesize with Christianity.

1. Nevertheless, in returning to Anderson's thought, we must remember that Anglo-Saxons did not create essentialist reasoning. It predates colonialism, and its fragmented principles are observed throughout recorded human history.[17] Within this chapter, I am

---

16. MacCulloch, *Christianity*, 159.

17. The idea of race originated during colonialism, but the ideological fragments used to construct it existed well throughout the ancient world. See Isaac, *Invention of Racism*; Fredrickson, *Racism*; McCoskey, *Race*.

emphasizing the *universal* aspects of essentialist/racialized-binary reasoning. This involves exploring the principles of *cognitive dissonance* and *confirmatory bias* that, I assert, are embedded within essentialist/racialized-binary reasoning. They contribute to the creation and sustaining of the cycle of dehumanization and oppression. These elements influence how individuals and groups create their idealized or mythic inner world, which represents not only their existence, but the totality of their self-interest. I argue that the human-Self when submitted to this form of reasoning, situates itself within the ambiguity that stems from merging fantasy with reality. Aspects of self-oppression and self-dehumanization begin within the construction of this mythic world, intensified by the refusal, or reluctance of the external human-Other's participation.

2. Principles of oppositional dualism were present within the ancient world, and possibly extended beyond recorded human history. The inspirations and elements from which we conceptualize essentialist/oppositional-binary reasoning exist within the fabric of how we perceive reality and develop self-awareness in relation to the human-Other.[18] We witness a basic oppositional-binary reasoning within the Judean Christian narrative that establishes the paradigms of Jew/gentile, good/evil, light/dark, order/disorder, and angels/demons.[19] Furthermore, it was common for ancient cultures to contextualize a set of aesthetics that represented their existence, uniqueness, and supposed superiority in relation to the human-Other. This created the foundation for nationalism and tribalism within the ancient world. Another example is viewed from the principles of dualistic cosmology within Manichaeism which promoted the basic structural paradigms of the good spiritual world against the bad material world, righteousness and unrighteousness, and purity against corruption. The basic structures of Gnosticism may fit within this discussion too.

I want to reiterate that every race is subject to it because it is a universal issue. In the context of identity politics, we can replace the issue of race with gender, sexuality, and ageism, among others. The focus within this section of the discussion is to examine aspects of our contemporary world and demonstrate that some people have "attempted to

---

18. Berger and Luckmann, *Social Construction of Reality*; *Sacred Canopy*.
19. Wills, *Not God's People*.

call into being what logically cannot exist." With the current example of academic Black theology, broadly understood, some advocates have conceptualized forms of oppression and liberation that are not *entirely* grounded in reality. They are a fusion of fantasy and reality of which the practitioner has lost the ability to distinguish both. Thus, they are locked into an unacknowledged purgatory without realizing the totality of their actual situation. Connected to this is what I refer to as *vicarious oppression and trauma*, the exaggerated identification with those who were or are oppressed. To a certain extent, in the context of healing, there is not any substantial psychological, emotional, and spiritual progress, but a deceptive stagnation and regression, revealed primarily when assessed to people outside of their community—or, as I advocate, when compared to some colonial African-American Evangelicals. Yet, I want to state that the creators of these issues are not Cone and Black theology. I argue that they have simply inherited some skewed hermeneutics and methodologies from the hyper-liberal sociopolitical philosophies of Black Nationalism and Black theology that cannot synthesize properly with the *essence* of Christianity, although its proponents clearly believe they have.

In returning to Anderson, his observations of contemporary Black theology and the forms of Black reasoning are categorized within an unacknowledged dependency upon a particular perception of Whiteness. An example would be the corrupt and irredeemable nature of Whiteness. This is a central part of his theory that I am emphasizing concerning how certain African-Americans define their identities, sense of belonging, and shared-space with the White-Other. We must ask whether they have achieved enlightenment and sociopolitical emancipation based on *their* definitions of the terms. We should try to determine if those definitions harmonize with their rhetoric and actions, and if everything represents reality as reality truly is or if everything is simply a product of their collective traumatic inner worlds.

We can then properly initiate assessing this particular spectrum of contemporary hyper-liberal Blackness, with its conservative contemporary counterparts, and those within colonialism, in seeking to obtain a general panoramic view of Blackness defined by African-Americans. My claim is that we may witness different conceptions of African-American Christians conceptualizing their identities, sense of belonging, and shared-space within two influential traditions: Evangelical and Black Nationalist. Both traditions overlap in certain ways. However, for various reasons, the hyper-liberal conceptions of Blackness that, as Anderson's theory advances, mimic a form of Whiteness, but subsequently appear to be the dominant influence in our contemporary Black academic and political worlds.

Nevertheless, in the early twenty-first century, conceptions of social justice, protest, and freedom, as well as how we construct our identities, sense of belonging, and shared-space with the human-Other, have been skewed to the point of blurring fantasy from reality, making it difficult to distinguish the authentic from the inauthentic. I argue that this, in part, stems from segments of cognitive dissonance and confirmatory bias that have complemented principles of essentialism, and oppositional-binary reasoning that permeate postmodern reasoning. Briefly reflecting upon how oppositional-binary reasoning is currently employed will serve as a contrast to how it existed during the Civil Rights Movement, and within colonial America. I am moving from discussing a certain type of religious African-Americans and their theology to a broader secular American critique. Our journey continues to move backward in time.

CONCERNS OF AN AFRICAN-AMERICAN EVANGELICAL CYNIC

Initiating a Cynical Evangelical Historical Revision

Dehumanization, enslavement, and oppression are never one-dimensional. Each exists as a constellation of beliefs, dispositions, and actions that influence how we construct our identities, sense of belonging, and shared spaces. Layers of complexity are experienced and witnessed in contexts that integrate them because, in various ways, one cannot exist without the other. Surprisingly, we are often oblivious to the possibility that the dehumanization, enslavement, and oppression we experience are achieved through the mistreatment of the human-Other. Obliviousness and denial are convenient bedfellows. Typically, people who are unaware of their oppressive nature and how they mistreat the human-Other will always deny the possibility of the accusation, despite the legitimate evidence.

Reinhold Niebuhr, one of the greatest American theologians, has stated, "The belief that human brutality is a vestigial remnant of man's animal or primitive past represents one of the dearest illusions of modern culture, to which men cling tenaciously even when every contemporary experience refutes it."[20] For Niebuhr, the contemporary Western

---

20. Niebuhr, *Faith and History*, 11.

world advocates that it has not, nor will ever, replicate the barbarism of the ancient world or the dark ages. This is despite the atrocities of the Transatlantic slave trade, World War I, World War II, etc. Niebuhr argues that this is a naive illusion. This illusion sustains a form of *historical optimism*, which advances an erroneous faith in human righteousness, and a skewed belief in human progress.[21] Yet, human progress is seldom determined by sociopolitical equality, equity, and the absence of wars. Niebuhr, as I interpret him, insinuates that each generation, captivated by notions of historical optimism, inherits the illusion of human progress from its predecessors, and ironically crafts one of its own for the following generation. Thus, we experience layers of deception, administering destructive *anaesthetic* beliefs in human righteousness, which skew our perceptions of reality.

Niebuhr's words cause me to reflect upon African-American culture, politics, and the academy. I am alerted to how historical optimism is often provided an adversary, *historical despair*. In Western America, some individuals employ forms of pessimism that confront the notions of human progress with notions of human regression or neutrality. For example, many contemporary Western Americans have lost faith in the American democratic process. These Americans argue that corrupt politics have persisted since the birth of America, and a change of leadership between political parties will not end it. Moreover, the individuals who promote this have gestured toward rampant oppression throughout the world, such as ageism, child molestation, gender bias, homophobia, racism, rape, and endless wars as evidence for their position. For them, humanity not only continues to practice the gross immorality of the ancient world but is progressively consumed by its vices, as they are normalized within society. Therefore, human progress is an illusion. From a Niebuhrian perspective, historical optimism and despair establish a set of illusions that deceive their creators. Illusions cannot exist without facts, and deception cannot exist without truth claims. There is always difficulty in discerning how facts and truth claims are contextualized within agendas and messages.

I often wonder if each generation of African-Americans since colonialism has created and reinforced a false sense of sociopolitical progress and despair regarding equality and equity. There appear to potentially be

---

21. Discussing Niebuhr's theological interpretation of history lies well beyond the scope of this chapter. Nevertheless, I have been greatly influenced by four principal books. See Niebuhr, *Human Destiny*; *Beyond Tragedy*; *Faith and History*; *Self and the Dramas of History*.

two distinct historiographies. One is created from historical optimism that advocates idealistic human progress, and historical despair, which demonstrates the pessimism of human regression. I am concerned that these two belief systems influence how we dismiss and reject certain historical African-Americans, who do not identify with the dominant contemporary African-American cultural, sociopolitical, and academic trends. With the rejection of these historical African-Americans are the sociopolitical philosophies and evangelical theologies that shaped their identities, sense of belonging, and construction of shared-spaces—all of which were devoid of essentialist, racialized-binary reasoning, and the cycle of dehumanization. From this perspective, I interpret dismissal and rejection as representative of self-dehumanization, self-enslavement, and self-oppression: a fragmentation *within* Blackness.

I am convinced that within these conceptions of illusory optimism and despair lies the unacknowledged pervasive forces of essentialist, racialized-binary reasoning, and the cycle of dehumanization. They existed within the *idea* of America. These principles are grafted within the basic structures of how we socialize with one another.[22] They are employed throughout our academic and political institutions in ways that often escape our conscience, desensitizing us to the perpetual modes of self-enslavement through the enslavement of the human-Other. I am emphasizing the inability to discern how and why we employ these forms of reasoning.

Religion is not devoid of these destructive attributes. Religious people deceive themselves if they claim innocence or are mere participant observers to the corroding aspects of essentialist and racialized-binary reasoning. Recorded history demonstrates how religion and various religious beliefs have been bedfellows with corrupt politics, providing quasi-divine justification for colonial slavery, contemporary wars, and other forms of dehumanization. I am troubled that we are often unaware of how these principles are deceptively normalized within society. There are destructive consequences for employing essentialist, racialized-binary reasoning, and principles of dehumanization. One is that we become

22. An example is observed in Berger and Luckmann's theory of "typification." Typification is the ways we perceive and engage the human-Other. It constructs negotiable identities of the human-Self and the human-Other. The distancing and intimacy that shape our relationships influence how typification is expressed. Typification is not isolated but connected to our habits (habitualization) and institutions. However, I am highlighting how we cease to question the ways we reason and behave. See Berger and Luckmann, *Social Construction of Reality*, 30–34, 53–58.

dependent upon them to construct our identities, sense of belonging, and shared spaces with the human-Other.

Nevertheless, the two poles of historical optimism and despair that generally characterize how we determine human progress and regression, have often blurred the boundaries between fantasy and reality. This skews how we construct and employ the ideologies, philosophies, and theologies that subsequently define our identities, sense of belonging, and shared-spaces. In expressing my thoughts further, I will employ the theories of the influential social-psychologist Erving Goffman (1922–1982) and psychiatrist R. D. Laing (1927–1989). Goffman's theory of *dramaturgy* or *dramaturgical analysis*, and Laing's conception of the *game of collusion*, are informative in discussing what I view as the theatrical and superficial aspects of Western American politics. Their theories assist me in examining aspects of American culture that employ essentialist and racialized-binary reasoning, in ways that create and reinforce a cycle of dehumanization and oppression.

THE MERGING OF FANTASY AND REALITY

Contemporary Distortions of Identities, Sense of Belonging, and Shared-Spaces

The chasm that once divided fantasy from reality is disappearing. This does not stem from some natural occurrence. It develops from the intentional efforts of individuals and groups who are consumed with acquiring their self-interest. Self-interests are representative of the debris, dirt, and rocks that have filled the chasm. Yet, self-interests are never isolated desires and goals. Self-interests are typically attached to identities, a sense of belonging, and shared spaces. The chasm that once separated fantasy from reality is reduced to a boundary. In some cases, this boundary has completely disappeared, and both worlds have merged, creating an ambiguous quasi-reality where fact and truth are pitted against each other to sustain organized ambiguity and confusion. The merging of fantasy and reality distorts how people construct their identities, sense of belonging, and shared spaces. Yet, this merging also extends to how we contextualize politics with forms of entertainment within Western America.

Western America is experiencing excessive *politicizing*, a hyper-politicization of identity politics, and a morbid obsession with entertainment. Aspects of Western American culture have been redefined into ambiguous displays of outcries, venting, and skirmishes between *enemies*. Each group claims to be the oppressed, and siding with other oppressed groups as they collectively seek liberation from the oppressor. These *confrontations* often display a feeling of being staged as they are presented to us like a movie, theatre, or reality television series with complementary color commentary, statistics, and photographic images.

Erving Goffman (1922–1982), one of the most influential sociologists of the twentieth century, articulates this clearly in his theory of *dramaturgy*, or *dramaturgical analysis*. He emphasizes how individuals or groups create *performances*, *fronts*, *masks*, and *settings* that blur the lines between fantasy and reality.[23] Goffman insists that,

> When an individual plays a part he implicitly requests his observers to take seriously the impression that is fostered before them. They are asked to believe that the character they see actually possesses the attributes he appears to possess, that the task he performs will have the consequences that are implicitly claimed for it, and that, in general, matters are what they appear to be. In line with this, there is the popular view that the individual offers his performance and puts on his show "for the benefit of other people."[24]

These performances are enacted in every aspect of society: the academy, politics, religious institutions, and marriages. We uncritically accept what we see and believe to understand, because there is an absence of evidence that demands disbelief. For example, words and garments can be authentic expressions of an individual's confidence and sophistication. However, a person's speech and clothing can be misleading, as they are used to construct an illusion of confidence and sophistication to deceive. In this context, Goffman claims that "an idealized impression is offered by accentuating certain facts and concealing others," and that some performers often "engage in concealed practices which are incompatible with fostered impression."[25] For me, these elements are observed within almost every Western American act of sociopolitical protest. Within this context, how do we interpret contemporary concepts of sociopolitical *liberation*?

---

23. Goffman, *Presentation of Self*, 17, 19, 22, 24.
24. Goffman, *Presentation of Self*, 17, 66.
25. Goffman, *Presentation of Self*, 65, 64.

An example of what I am referring to is witnessed in the feminist-inspired transnational movement called the *Slutwalk*. Slutwalk advocates are presenting an excellent social justice cause to end rape culture, the abuse of women, and victim blaming/shaming. Obviously, these are righteous aims that extend beyond feminism, as every society should promote and conform to these goals. However, certain controversies of the movement involve the hyper-sexualization of its cause, the glorification of promiscuity, random acts of public nudity, and the dramatic display of sexual toys such as dildos/vibrators. Some Slutwalk advocates seek to redeem aspects of the lascivious and promiscuous woman by identifying her to sexual liberation and abused women. In theory, Slutwalk proponents are empowering women through reclaiming or *sanctifying* offensive identities and images of the *slut*, along with other derogatory stigmas. In many cases, Slutwalk protests intentionally create an atmosphere of a theatrical event, as many participants masquerade in flamboyant attire, and behave in ways that are *counter-cultural*, or *oppositional* to the socio-cultural and political norms. Yet, it is difficult to discern who is sincerely there because they truly believe in the cause, and the methods employed to achieve its ends.[26]

This critique is also applicable to aspects of the Black Lives Matter movement, and other forms of contemporary African-American protest. In this context, the questionable elements centre on how peaceful protests can be infused with excessive emotionalism to the extent that it discharges itself through rioting. Protesting for sociopolitical equality and equity is noble, but those moments where individuals resort to the destruction of public property, and/or burglarizing, will always function as counter-intuitive and counterproductive to the initial intent of protesting. It is also interesting that Blue Lives Matter arose as the counter-movement to Black Lives Matter. One of the more striking aspects of Blue Lives Matter involved the problematic if not overtly manipulative rhetoric some members espoused. This is in reference to variants of the slogan, "We have a right to go home," and, "I will make sure that I go home to my family." These statements, and others, were employed in ways that manipulated the legitimate goal of the Black Lives Matter movement: holding police accountable for killing innocent Black people. Various statements by Blue Lives Matter advocates created the illusion that Black Lives Matter proponents disagreed with the fact that police officers have the right

---

26. See Valenti, "SlutWalks and the Future"; McDonald, "Complicated Feminism." See also http://www.amberroseslutwalk.com.

to go home, unharmed. The essentialist and racialized-binary reasoning employed by some Black and Blue Lives Matter members is representative of the blurring between fantasy and reality that concerns me. Certain members of both groups employed oppositional-binary reasoning to stress an us versus them, either or paradigm.[27] In this context, Niebuhr makes a keen observation that, "in every social conflict each party is so obsessed with the wrongs which the other party commits against it, that it is unable to see its own wrongdoing."[28] Moreover, the sharp boundaries of identity politics shielded each group from acknowledging the sympathy and empathy they had for one another.

I am not questioning the legitimacy of these movements, but the means to achieve their goals and how easily they can be corrupted. I am continually troubled by how certain people have concealed their true intentions in joining legitimate movements. They engage in identity politics to achieve shallow notoriety, financial gain, and superficial political power. In this discussion, I am also focusing on the *compulsion* of some people to identify with and become the embodiment of what or whom the *oppositional-Other* fears. This stems from and reinforces essentialism and racialized-binary reasoning. Ironically, the counterintuitive and counterproductive reasoning enslaves individuals, making them dependent upon the fears of the oppositional-Other, to create their identities and overall worldview.

We need our enemies like we need our gods. If they are not present, or to our liking, we deceive ourselves into creating them to justify the procurement of our self-interest. Thus, in many ways, understanding and navigating through Western American culture becomes a game, a spectacle, and often a form of entertainment. From this perspective, aspects of Western American culture lose the necessary authenticity and realism of the masses to garner legitimate sociopolitical equality, equity, and peace. The influential psychiatrist, R. D. Laing (1927–1989), refers to this as the *game of collusion*:

27. In this context, I am highlighting the skewed relationship between the defiance toward authority and the abuse of authority. Some individuals display an irrational level of rebelliousness towards authority structures. The goal is often to confront, and then minimize, if not in entirety transcend the symbol of authority itself. The binary-opposite to these people are obviously those individuals who, whether in single events or as a representative of their character, seek to dominate people through their authority. Chaos ensues when these individuals meet, as essentialist/binary-reasoning influences each person to possible destructive ends.

28. Niebuhr, *Moral Man & Immoral Society*, 248.

> The game *is* the game of mutual self-deception. Whereas delusion and elusion and illusion can be applied to one person, collusion is necessarily a two-or-more-person game. Each plays the others' game, though he may not necessarily be fully aware of doing so. An essential feature of this game is not admitting that it is a game. When the one person is predominantly the passive "victim" (one can be victimized for not playing "victim") of a trick or manoeuvre or manipulation, the relationship will not be called collusive. It will be difficult in practice to determine whether or to what extent a relationship is collusive. But the distinction is still work making in theory. A slave may collude with his master in being a slave to save his life, even to the point of carrying out orders that are self-destructive.[29]

African and Anglo-Americans, who portray themselves as *perpetual* enemies, are locked within a game of collusion. Yet, I am highlighting what Laing expresses as the individual's unawareness to their participation in the game, and the inability to comprehend what this entails. Goffman makes a similar point: "the legitimate performances of everyday life are not 'acted' or 'put on' in the sense that the performer knows in advance just what he is going to do, and does this solely because of the effect it is likely to have."[30] Nevertheless, some African and Anglo-Americans portray themselves as the heroic victims in this narrative of racial conflict. The game of collusion is, in part, created and sustained by essentialist and racialized-binary reasoning, and the cycle of dehumanization. This involves fragments of cognitive dissonance and confirmatory bias. Laing further states that,

> Collusion is always clinched when self finds in other that other who will "confirm" self in the false self that self is trying to make real, and vice versa. The ground is then set up for a prolonged mutual aversion of truth and true fulfilment. Each has found an other to endorse his own false notion of himself and to give this appearance a semblance of reality.[31]

---

29. Laing, *Self and Others*, 90. The German-Swiss psychologist Arno Gruen (1923–2015) referred to a similar relationship as "a game involving mutual validation, in the course of which one partner feels himself powerful and important while the other proves how obedient he can be." See Gruen, *Betrayal of the Self*, 16–17.

30. Goffman, *Presentation of Self*, 73.

31. Laing, *Self and Others*, 93. Goffman refers to this as a "team collusion," and a "performance team." See Goffman, *Presentation of Self*, 79–80, 104–5, 177.

It is here we witness the irony of some African and Anglo-Americans who employ essentialist and racialized-binary reasoning. They portray themselves as heroic victims, locked into a war with one another, and each act of defiance or rebellion from the other group is interpreted as justification for their agenda. In part, facts, truth, and genuine self-sacrificial fulfilment are representative of everything that reveals these illusions for what they truly are, as well as the false conceptions of the human-Self, and the human-Other. Yet, there is difficulty in determining who has established these conceptions of false-Selves and is subjecting us to them. One of the strongest ironies of ironies may be that they stem from those individuals who claim to be enlightened and liberated. The knowledge they claim will bring enlightenment, and the fulfilment they assert will bring liberation, are nothing more than a lock and key to the game of collusion.

Race and the ideology of White supremacy have been severe problems in America. They existed before the idea of America was conceived and provided important contributions to the development of the United States. Most contemporary cultural and sociopolitical dialogues regarding racial equality and equity, the nature of Whiteness, and the developing identities of Blackness, have grown stagnant since the Civil Rights Movement. For some people, African and Anglo-Americans exist in perpetual opposition. They impatiently wait for a racial conflict to occur, using this opportunity to express their general concerns about how America is deteriorating, each side violently gesturing towards one another, the enemy, as the exclusive cause of sin within Eden.

Superficial social justice and its reactionary conservative Anglo-rights (or tyranny, anti-social justice) counterpart, with their complementary protests have become a mockery. They have become a *fetish* that provides emotional stimulation, and pseudo-psychological stability that incites the *actor's* fascination with social justice icons and American patriots of the past. These individuals have a compulsion to not only identify with their icons, but some express a passion to supersede them in popularity, influence, and overall greatness. The narcissistic impulse of the individual is stroked by superficial politics. The individual becomes enamored by desires to be idolized, portrayed as a person of relevance, or the main character of a narrative. The individual feels immortalized, worshiped in a secular sense, as a figure to be discussed within recorded human history. In this context, I am concerned with how we must distinguish the wheat from the tares (Matt 13:24–30). Each is representative of reality and fantasy, along with a set of identities, a sense of belonging, and a conception of shared-spaces, which are situated between the poles of historical optimism and despair.

Contemporary American politics are drastically different from what developed during the Civil Rights Movement. Some individuals and communities often embrace their *performances* and *games of collusion*. However, some people during the Civil Rights Movement were surprisingly unaware of their participation in these deceptive embodiments. This was an era where performances and games were initially coalescing. For me, since the end of the Civil Rights Movement, African-American culture has been enamored by conceptions of historical despair, influenced primarily by Black Nationalism and Black Power. These sociopolitical ideologies permeate African-American academics, culture, politics, and religion. This is to the extent that although many African-Americans may not directly identify with these hyper-liberal sociopolitical ideologies, they nevertheless employ various hermeneutics and methodologies that created them. I also include academic Black theology, as some advocates may not agree with some of Cone's theology, but nevertheless identify with the discipline for sociopolitical, not intrinsic theological reasons. Yet, in reference to African-American culture, I question the intentions or *performances* of people who dismiss and ignore certain conservative evangelical African-Americans during colonialism who do not identify with their agendas. The dismissed and rejected are those African-Americans who did not employ essentialist and racialized-binary reasoning and the cycle of dehumanization.

Moreover, I am skeptical of African-Americans who claim enlightenment and freedom from these destructive attributes, but embody a narrative that is obsessed with race, and cannot conceive of Blackness without being in *opposition* to Whiteness. Collectively, we must question not only if we are truly seeking freedom, but what/whom we are seeking freedom from, and whether we are achieving the proper means to do so. How does authentic emancipation, a mended consciousness, and the ability to construct our identities, develop when we are locked inside a narrative that defines our existence, but also conceals our self-imposed bondage, self-degradation, and how we dehumanize the human-Other?

I pose this question to further examine the *fragmented* nature of Blackness. It is a question that challenges the sensitivity of the African-American collective and individual consciousness. This question elicits and scrutinizes the insecurities, phobias, and paranoia we either avoid, are unaware of, or reluctantly accept. The discomfort and trauma I want us to reassess provide no guarantee of acquiring the answers we claim to want. Rather, the discomfort and trauma provide accessibility to the honesty, transparency, and vulnerability needed to acquire potential answers. I am highlighting the fragmentation of Blackness as it relates to African-American identities, sense of belonging, and conceptualizing of shared-spaces with Anglo-Americans. Where did the initial fragmentation begin, and who is responsible for it? Does Evangelicalism provide a distinct form of liberation from the deteriorating effects of essentialist and racialized-binary reasoning?

2

The Melodrama of Fragmented Blackness

King and Essentialist/Racialized Binary-Reasoning

HISTORICAL REVISIONISM

A Cynical Evangelical Approach

WE CANNOT ADEQUATELY DEFINE our humanity and reality apart from concepts of freedom and power. We need them and often cling to, lust for, and withhold them from the human-Other to alleviate any fears or paranoia of losing it. Freedom and power are deceptive aspects of reality to comprehend, employ, and embody. The potential and manifestation of deception appear to exist within our ignorance, lack of humility, and overconfidence in their purpose and value. Attached to this is the assumption we represent the apex or should epitomize freedom and power over and against the human-Other, all for the benefit of us, them, and the entirety of human existence. There is also an ethical component and complementary dilemma when people mistakenly assume freedom transcends morality because it is intrinsically good. Ideally, at least from a Christian perspective, freedom and power are maximized by grounded people and communities who abide by realistic and humanizing ethical and moral principles, not intending to serve their self-interest, or their communities, but to achieve peace and harmony with everyone, attempting to eliminate the possibilities of oppression, injustice, and dehumanization. Naturally, this is attempted and achieved through principles like self-sacrifice, empathy, and love for God, the human-Other, and the Self.

The Civil Rights Movement in America represents various things to people worldwide. Aspects of it clearly represent freedom and power. There is also equality, equity, justice, self-sacrifice, and love for humanity. Yet, the Civil Rights Movement also represents a heightened self-awareness and actualization of religious freedom in relation to a specific theological conflict, a theological fragmentation within American religiosity, one that was unavoidable and necessary if and only if African-Americans, along with other ethnicities, achieved an increase of genuine freedom and power.

The purpose of this chapter is to examine the awareness of essentialist and racialized-binary reasoning by Martin Luther King Jr. I will explore his thoughts on their usage through his critique of Black Power and Black Nationalism. Although King did not label them as such, he was one of the first African-Americans to acknowledge their existence. I also maintain he inevitably relied upon basic Christian principles that revealed these problematic forms of reasoning, and how to evade and minimize their influence. I will discuss King's theories in relation to Reinhold Niebuhr. King's insight, along with Niebuhr's views, provides a sharp cultural and sociopolitical critique that I feel is greatly neglected. I will examine King's thoughts regarding Anglo-Americans, Whiteness, White Supremacy, and *Black Supremacy*. I emphasize Black Supremacy mostly as a skewed ultimate outcome that was feared, and how precautions were taken to minimize the fruition of that ultimate outcome. I stand in opposition to the current hyper-liberal sociopolitical theory that only White people (Whiteness) can be racist. Racism, for me, is about the fallacy of intrinsic superiority, and this can develop within everyone, based on whatever imaginary concepts they believe to innately hold over the human-Other. This can develop through conceptions of spirituality, intelligence, and athleticism. Racism at its core is *sin* as a psychological distortion that manifests socio-politically.

Nevertheless, King's engagement with Anglo-America represented the discord between races in America, that developed, in part, through essentialist and racialized-binary reasoning. Naturally, this is interpreted as the discord *outside* of Blackness. However, King's disagreement with Black Nationalists and Black Power advocates represented the fragmentation *within* Blackness. This characterized a conflict between two or more sets of *oppositional* Black identities, a sense of belonging, and conceptions of shared-spaces. Moreover, I interpret King as an evangelical theologian and situate him within the colonial African-American Evangelical tradition.[1] He serves as a theological descendent of Jupiter Hammon, John Chavis, Frances E. W. Harper, and Mrs. Julia A. J. Foote.

There is a certain level of cruelty within Whiteness that provides well-meaning but impractical and despair-driven forms of Blackness power equal to or above those forms of Blackness more grounded, proficient, and guided by self-sacrificial hope. The latter form of Blackness must contend with its internal counterpart and the external self-deceived Whiteness in the attempts to assist the emancipation of everyone. In this context we must ask ourselves a series of questions. How do we interpret a person or group who uses their freedom and power to inflict pain upon the human-Other? Likewise, what do we say of the person or group who uses their freedom and power to punish themselves? Can we properly communicate with these people, who for various reasons, cannot see the nihilism within, and the external discord they create in the name of liberation?

KING AND FREIRE

The Imago Christi & The Imago Tyrannus

King opposed many apathetic Anglo-Americans, and White supremacists, but also African-Americans, who identified with Black Nationalism and Black Power. It is confusing to understand why this fact has been ignored and minimized by certain African-American scholars. For example, it is widely known that King advocated principles of sociocultural integration, non-violent protest, and a *non-racialized* Christ. These beliefs were confronted with principles of sociocultural segregation, the permissibility

---

1. There is an enormous amount of scholarship centered on King's life, sociopolitical philosophy, and as a theologian. However, there is little scholarship exploring his theological connection to colonial African-American Evangelicalism. See Baldwin, *There Is a Balm in Gilead*; *To Make the Wounded Whole*; Carson et al., "Martin Luther King Jr.," 99–105; Cone, "America," 263–78; "Demystifying Martin and Malcolm," 27–37; *Martin & Malcom & America*; "Martin Luther King Jr., Black Theology," 409–20; "Martin Luther King Jr. and the Third World," 455–67; "Theology of Martin Luther King Jr.," 21–39; DeWolf, "Martin Luther King Jr.," 1–11; Downing, "Martin Luther King Jr.," 15–31; Fairclough, *Martin Luther King Jr.*, 834; Garber, "King Was a Black Theologian"; "Black Theology," 100–113; Ivory, *Toward a Theology of Radical Involvement*, 35; Rathbun, "Martin Luther King," 38–53.

of violence, and a Black Christ.[2] I interpret this as a representative of essentialist/racialized-binary reasoning *within* Blackness. However, rather than discuss and reinterpret these commonly known paradigms within the context of essentialist/racialized-binary reasoning, I will explore some of the underlying issues that framed this internal turmoil.

King demonstrated that *authentic* liberation had spiritual, psychological, and sociopolitical elements. Liberation, from an Evangelical stance, was deeply influenced by how the oppressed perceived and engaged their oppressors when it came to the principles of repentance, forgiveness, reconciliation, and redemption. We can generally categorize three major paradigms with this issue. First, some people do not believe the oppressor can be redeemed, and reconciliation be obtained between the two eternally oppositional groups. Secondly, other people may be suspicious of whether repentance, reconciliation, and redemption are possible. However, they can be inclined to do their part (forgiveness) if the proper conditions justify it (equality, equity, justice, etc.). A third group will always advocate for the possibility, and gesture towards reality for examples of how it has and is manifesting presently in their context.

Yet, all three groups are susceptible to self-deception and narcissism that are embedded within essentialist and racialized-binary reasoning. From this perspective, I am highlighting the possibility that the oppressed could potentially become the oppressor if there are legitimate opportunities for dramatic shifts in sociopolitical power, and the character of the oppressed is not morally grounded. We view this theory from the Brazilian philosopher and educator, Paulo Freire. Freire's classic text, *Pedagogy of the Oppressed*, presents timeless universal observations within the relationship between the oppressed and oppressor. At this point, I want to focus on the *image* as representative of the *character* of the individual and group. Freire presents a controversial paradox regarding the inner fear of the oppressed as they seek freedom.

> The "fear of freedom" which afflicts the oppressed, a fear which may equally well lead them to desire the role of oppressor or bind them to the role of oppressed, should be examined. One of the basic elements of the relationship between oppressor and oppressed is *prescription*. Every prescription represents the imposition of one individual's choice upon another, transforming the consciousness of the person prescribed to into one that conforms with the prescriber's consciousness. Thus, the behavior

---

2. See Barbour, *Black Power Revolt*.

of the oppressed is prescribed behvior, following as it does the guidelines of the oppressor.³

Freire makes a powerful observation and one African-Americans can understand within the context of American slavery. It is widely known of the skewed codependent relationships which existed between master/mistress and slave, especially regarding the context of the slave acquiring their freedom and faced with the decision to stay with their masters or seek an emancipated life. We must acknowledge the reality that many slaves preferred a life under their master, which they viewed as easier, than a life of freedom after slavery. We also have a scriptural account of this paradoxical phenomena regarding the Hebrews and Egypt. Exodus 14:1 states, "Is this not the word that we spoke to you in Egypt, saying, 'Leave us alone so that we may serve the Egyptians'? For it would have been better for us to serve the Egyptians than to die in the wilderness!" There is also Exodus 16:2,

> But the whole congregation of the sons of Israel grumbled against Moses and Aaron in the wilderness. The sons of Israel said to them, "If only we had died by the LORD'S hand in the land of Egypt, when we sat by the pots of meat, when we ate bread until we were full; for you have brought us out into this wilderness to kill this entire assembly with hunger!"

Nevertheless, Freire emphasizes the influence of fear upon our reasoning and decisions. Yet, the process of how this fear is constructed remains a general mystery. He only assumes two potential paths: to be like the oppressor in their liberation or to remain the oppressed. Freire's statement also alerts us to the psychological element of oppression that transcends our self-awareness. Yet, we must acknowledge that the oppressor is encased within their prison and they too experience it in ways that evade their self-awareness. Thus, there are complementary dualities between the oppressed and oppression, whereby their humanity is intertwined, interconnected, and interdependent. My humanity is dependent upon your humanity equally to how your humanity is dependent upon mine. It is difficult for the oppressed to recognize the complexity of their oppression, especially when they are mimicking the existence of the people they distrust, and possibly hate. Freire continues with another penetrating statement,

---

3. Freire, *Pedagogy of the Oppressed*, 46–47.

> The oppressed, having internalized the image of the oppressor and adopted his guidelines, are fearful of freedom. Freedom would require them to eject this image and replace it with autonomy and responsibility. Freedom is acquired by conquest, not by gift. It must be pursued constantly and responsibly. Freedom is not an ideal locked outside of man; nor is it an idea which becomes myth. It is rather the indispensable condition for the quest for human completion.[4]

The identities, sense of belonging, and construction of shared-space by the oppressed are enslaved and entangled within a complex web of psychological distortion—a complex web that develops from the intentionality of the oppressor, and the natural consequences of dehumanization that transcends the oppressor's self-awareness. Yet, this psychological distortion also skewed concepts of righteousness.

An example of this possibility lies in the skewed belief that the oppression of the oppressed endows them with a certain form of righteousness, self-awareness, and determination that *sanctifies* all or most of their actions toward liberation. This view is sometimes connected with the belief of an existential judgment whereby the oppressed view the oppressor as irredeemable. From an Evangelical perspective, these beliefs are antithetical to Scripture, the Gospels, and specifically the teachings of Jesus. We have examples of this tension between the repentance of the oppressor and the forgiveness of the oppressed within the story of Jonah 4:1–4:

> But it greatly displeased Jonah, and he became angry. Then he prayed to the Lord and said, "'Please Lord, was this not what I said when I was still in my *own* country? Therefore in anticipation of *this* I fled to Tarshish, since I knew that You are a gracious and compassionate God, slow to anger and abundant in mercy, and One who relents of disaster. So now, Lord, please take my life from me, for death is better to me than life." But the Lord said, "Do you have good reason to be angry?"

Yahweh allowed Jonah to wrestle with the contours of his faith in Him over and against his displeasure, if not unacknowledged hatred for the Ninevites. Jonah had judged Ninevah and already declared within himself what he felt was their suitable punishment. This was in complete conflict with his belief that Yahweh honors the sincerity of those who repent. We can interpret Johnah as being influenced by the oppressive Ninevites, not in that he wanted to remain the oppressed, but arguably

---

4. Freire, *Pedagogy of the Oppressed*, 47.

wanted them to experience the same pain and suffering Israel had undergone. For him, liberation was connected to God's judgment upon the Ninevites. Thus, the oppressed was in danger of becoming the oppressor.

King advocated that there was a system of deceptive illusions the oppressed needed to acknowledge and fight against to achieve universal emancipation for them and the oppressor. We can associate some of these illusions with the biblical principle of the wheat and tares, relating to the genuine character of the oppressed group (Matt 13:24–43). In this context, *complete* solidarity and oneness of a group do not exist, particularly when we assess the motives and goals of every participant. The Apostle Paul had to acknowledge that people preached the Gospel for selfless and selfish reasons. Philippians 1:15–18 states,

> It is true that some preach Christ out of envy and rivalry, but others out of goodwill. The latter do so out of love, knowing that I am put here for the defense of the gospel. The former preach Christ out of selfish ambition, not sincerely, supposing that they can stir up trouble for me while I am in chains. But what does it matter? The important thing is that in every way, whether from false motives or true, Christ is preached. And because of this I rejoice. Yes, and I will continue to rejoice.

It is difficult to assess the complexity of attempting to undo the image of the oppressor within the oppressed. The character of the oppressed, at least to a certain extent, is marred and in desperate need of a superior antithetical ideal and embodiment of ethics and morality. From a Christian vantage point, we must imagine the implications of attempting to install, reinforce, and emphasize the Fruit of the Spirit as the ideal template for inner character transformation for those seeking liberation (Gal 5:22–23). Within this context, King once advocated that,

> Every minority and every people has its share of opportunists, profiteers, freeloaders and escapists. The hammer blows of discrimination, poverty and segregation must warp and corrupt some. No one can pretend that because a people may be oppressed, every individual member is virtuous and worthy. The real issue is whether in the great mass the dominant characteristics are decency, honor and courage.[5]

King consistently emphasized that African-Americans, in their attempts to achieve liberation, were susceptible to inheriting the skewed

---

5. King, *Why We Can't Wait*, 41.

logic of White supremacy, conceptualized as *Black supremacy*. Consequently, a mirroring effect would develop, as African-Americans behaved and reasoned in ways they disdained from Anglo-Americans. King attempted to confront the elitism, narcissism, and self-righteousness among African-Americans, because these were unacknowledged hindrances to achieving liberation. For King, it was irrational to assume that oppression necessarily endowed an individual or group with the knowledge and ability to exist within a higher state of ethics/morality. This is the self-deceptive element of essentialist/racialized-binary reasoning. However, oppression subjected the oppressed to a set of knowledge, and ways of existing that were not present among the oppressors.[6]

Sin and immorality affect the oppressed and the oppressor. In this context, Niebuhr makes a wise observation that "the weak will not only sin when they become mighty, but they sin in prospect and imagination while they are weak."[7] King echoes a similar sentiment: "You must come to see that a man may be self-centered in his self-denial and self-righteous in his self-sacrifice. His generosity may feed his ego and his piety his pride. Without love, benevolence becomes egoism and martyrdom becomes spiritual pride."[8] Thus, the *character* and *consciousness* of the oppressed must be emancipated from nihilistic and narcissist reasoning, which typically develop from the fallacy that liberation can be achieved, *by any means necessary*.

When the ends justify the means, the oppressed attempt to subject their oppressors to the same forms of pain and suffering that were inflicted upon them. King was conscious of this, and consistently structured aspects of his program to alleviate the fears and paranoia of many Anglo-Americans: "A guilt-ridden white minority fear if the Negro attains power, he will without restraint or pity act to revenge the accumulated injustices and brutality of the years."[9] In part, this develops by constructing a set of ethics and morality which stem from the self-interest of and desire for retribution from the oppressed. The oppressed are therefore participating in a mirroring of their oppressors. The oppressor creates this vicious cycle in their attempts to obtain their self-interest.

This provides a glimpse into why King emphasized Christian ethics through love, justice, and power. They were central elements to his

6. Niebuhr, *Beyond Tragedy*, 209–10.
7. Niebuhr, *Beyond Tragedy*, 219.
8. King, *Strength to Love*, 153.
9. King, *Strength to Love*, 126.

theories of the Beloved Community, non-violent protest, and social/racial integration. The character and integrity of the oppressed must undergo a transformation, by constructing a different set of ethics and morality that is *devoid* of essentialist/racialized-binary reasoning and does not reproduce a cycle of oppression. Liberation does not exist within the cycle of oppression. For the oppressed and oppressors exist within contextualized forms of enslavement, whereby each views the human-other as an existence that cannot be reconciled with, because of their inherent corruption and inferiority. Thinking otherwise reinterprets liberation into an *idol* to the extent that it becomes a concept of pseudo-worship, consuming the hearts and minds of the oppressed as well as the oppressor. If the means to achieving liberation are counterintuitive and counterproductive, the oppressed will remain locked into the *process* itself, and that process will define their identity. The oppressed will remain in an existence of always seeking, but never quite obtaining, and if there is an element of liberation received, the oppressed are unable to recognize it.

We see aspects of this within contemporary African-American culture, politics, and the academy. There is an *oversaturation* of political views, books, sociopolitical protests, social media activity, and professors who have created an identity of Blackness resigned to primarily speaking about its existence in relation to oppressive-Whiteness. They demonstrate a general cycle whereby they come into a greater awareness of their oppression, the struggle within their oppression, and the acquisition of some form of empowering liberation, which culminates into a prophetic jeremiad calling to deconstruct Whiteness. Aside from my cynicism and sarcasm, my issue is not the legitimacy of a person expressing their views. Nor am I arguing against the annihilation of White Supremacy. Rather, it is the oversaturation of this set of ideologies that I argue is dependent upon a particular interpretation of oppression, our current condition, and Whiteness. A superficial trend has developed mirroring what the Apostle Paule mentioned in Philippians 1:15–18. Some Black people talk about their Blackness out of jealousy, envy, greed, vanity, and financial gain, but also from sincerity, love, and self-sacrifice for the human-Other. Blackness is promoted regardless of the intent, and my cynical side also includes the dismissal of realistic and healthy objectives. Nevertheless, we must continue to ask ourselves what occurs if there is a reversal of sociopolitical power between the oppressed and the oppressor, and the oppressor has not psychologically emancipated themselves from skewed notions of justice and superiority. Will the oppressed become the oppressor?

In this context, Niebuhr questions the sociopolitical reversal of power through a critique of Marxism: "If the poor man is generally trusted as a social force of high destiny in society he will achieve the power to overturn society and build a new social order. He will then cease to be the poor man and will become the powerful man."[10] The new social order will mirror the old order, if, and only if, there is merely a reversal of sociopolitical power between the oppressed and the oppressor. The oppressors are subject to the same pain and suffering the oppressed experience. King echoes Niebuhr's words, but frames them within the context of mirroring the thoughts, emotions, and actions of White supremacy: "But if we will become bitter and indulge in hate campaigns, the old, the new order which is emerging will be nothing but a duplication of the old order."[11] Oppression as a means of righteousness is an illusion and an illusion that the oppressors constructed when they were the oppressed.

Again, I am highlighting situations whereby the *image* of the oppressor is implanted within the oppressed through the inheritance of essentialist/racialized-binary reasoning. Thus, narcissism, self-deception, and self-righteousness are then possibly concealed within the heart, mind, theories, and struggles of the oppressed in achieving liberation. This develops when we deny the possibility that the oppressed can become tainted or corrupt from skewing their conception of liberation and power. Niebuhr elaborates: "All over the world we find the minority groups which once suffered from the arrogance of majorities, quickly adopting the vices of the majority when they attain a dominant position."[12] History testifies to Niebuhr's statement, and this obscure historical fact created a set of boundaries and limitations within King's program.

Throughout American history, and particularly within the Civil Rights Movement, some African-Americans constructed ideologies, philosophies, and theologies that gave the *pretense* of strength, self-sacrifice, enlightenment, and emancipation. Racial and sociopolitical segregation was the complementary *elusion*. Many African-Americans not only desired freedom, but they obsessed over it, and in not knowing how to obtain freedom, they merely acted as if they had—a solid *performance* whereby they believed a fantasy to the extent that it became real to them. This is what Laing described in the relationship between pretence and elusion: "Elusion is a way of getting round conflict without

10. Niebuhr, *Beyond Tragedy*, 130.
11. King, *Call to Conscience*, 51.
12. Niebuhr and Robertson, *Love and Justice*, 122.

direct confrontation, or its resolution. It eludes conflict by playing off one modality of experience against another."[13] We imagine things as we would like them to be, and even if we have achieved or obtained them, we develop a preference for fantasy rather than reality. Thus, the *perception* of strength and liberation we imagine is greater than the level of strength and liberation we concretely have.

King and Niebuhr conceptualized unique ways of achieving psychological and physical liberation. I am highlighting their emphasis that authentic liberation developed through an equilibrium of power, aware that merely reversing sociopolitical power, will sustain a cycle of oppression. King contextualized these principles to how African-Americans perceived and engaged Anglo-Americans, Whiteness, and White supremacy.

KING

Anglo-Americans, Whiteness and White Supremacy

Whiteness has become a consuming entity within parts of African-American culture, politics, and the academy. Whiteness has become a reluctant idol, a skewed symbolism, and a lighthouse that can only direct us into further enslavement to itself. For some African-Americans, Whiteness invokes anger, fear, frustration, paranoia, and even wrath. I argue that Whiteness has come to define many contemporary African-Americans' core sense of value, meaning, and purpose in life. This is in the sense that Whiteness, and/or a reaction against it, constructs African-American identities, sense of belonging, and conceptions of shared-space.

I am not arguing against African-Americans speaking about Anglo-Americans, race, and White supremacy. Rather, I am questioning our ability to determine the *boundaries* and *limitations* of such thoughts and actions. I am concerned that the *process* of exposing White Supremacy, and articulating the Black experience as the oppressed under Whiteness, becomes the norm, the benchmark for expressing Black liberation and Black existence in its entirety. In this context, I am arguing within the framework of Goffman's *performance* and Laing's *game of collusion*. Aspects of African-American politics, cultural development, and academic scholarship that are dependent upon Whiteness to construct their

---

13. Laing, *Self and Others*, 32.

identities, sense of belonging, and shared spaces, exist within the space of ambiguity created by blurring fantasy and reality.

Humans construct their identities, sense of belonging, and shared spaces in relation to one another. This involves elements of compromise and negotiation. To think otherwise is to employ essentialist/racialized-binary reasoning, which creates the illusion that the human-Self can exist independently of the human-Other. From colonialism to the present, Whiteness has been dependent upon Blackness to construct its identity, sense of belonging, and shared spaces. Oppression and dehumanization within the Transatlantic slave trade developed from Anglo-Saxons rejecting the idea of *co-dependency* with the non-Anglo Saxons. I am also concerned about the unacknowledged compulsion and reactionary nature some African-Americans embody toward Anglo-Americans, Whiteness, and White supremacy. I am advocating a loosening, a relinquishing of this compulsion, obsession, and quasi-worship of Whiteness, which thrusts some African-Americans into a *performance* they are not conscious of. What occurs within the mind of the liberated who are deceived into thinking they are enslaved? How do we interpret their attempts at liberation from slaves who have greater sociopolitical power?

Niebuhr habitually discussed the ability of the human-Self to enslave itself within itself. The process of self-enslavement resulted from a matrix of skewed desires, fears, narcissism, and self-deception which corrupted the self-interest of the human-Self.[14] The deviant aspect of this self-entrapment was that it is largely unacknowledged by the human-Self. From a Niebuhrian perspective, this is a *creation* account of the oppressor, oppression, and the oppressed. African-Americans experience self-entrapment when they are completely dependent upon Whiteness to construct their identities, sense of belonging, and shared-spaces. They cannot acknowledge that they exist within the space of ambiguity created by blurring the boundaries between fantasy and reality. Authentic liberation develops when the human-Self acknowledges the potential and legitimate ways they contribute to their own enslavement. One of the crucial elements of African-American liberation involves how we perceive and treat Anglo-Americans, Whiteness, and White supremacy.

King emphasized a distinction between the skewed ideology of White supremacy, the symbolism of Whiteness, and the Anglo-Saxons. Many Anglo-Saxons were and still are White supremacists, and for them,

---

14. See Niebuhr, *Dramas of History*, 43, 237; *Faith & History*, 244.

Whiteness represents White supremacy. However, there are many Anglo-Saxons, who were not and are not White supremacists, and for them, Whiteness does not represent White supremacy. All three are deeply related but are not synonymous. To view all three as synonymous, not allowing for Anglo-Saxons to reject White supremacy, and to not allow Whiteness to represent anything righteous, is a result of essentialist/racialized-binary reasoning.[15]

One of King's most piercing statements against essentialist/racialized-binary reasoning, was formulated in the contexts of psychological liberation and African-American solidarity: "to develop a sense of black consciousness and peoplehood does not require that we scorn the white race as a whole. It is not the race per se that we fight but the policies and ideology that leaders of that race have formulated to perpetuate oppression."[16] The policies and ideologies that Anglo-American leaders perpetuated, and many of their people supported, were creations from and reinforced White supremacy. Nevertheless, King refused to construct a racial identity and form of solidarity that was dependent upon Whiteness and/or a negative disposition towards it. Knowledge of systemic racism was not to influence African-Americans into interpreting Anglo-Americans, Whiteness, and White supremacy as *inseparable* and *irredeemable*:

> The Negro of America is saying he's determined to be free and he is militant enough to stand up. But this new militancy must not lead us to the position of distrusting every white person who lives in the United States. There are some white people in this country who are as determined to see the Negro free as we are to be free. This new militancy must be kept within understanding boundaries.[17]

People create and embody ideologies, philosophies, and theologies. In the context of liberation, there is tension between confronting the

---

15. King was a realist and understood that many African-Americans had distrusted or even displayed hatred towards Anglo-Americans. However, he encouraged African-Americans to understand that some Anglo-Americans had sacrificed themselves in opposing White supremacy. "The oppression of Negroes by whites has left an understandable residue of suspicion. Some of this suspicion is a healthy and appropriate safeguard. An excess of skepticism, however, becomes a fetter. It denies that there can be reliable white allies, even though some whites have died heroically at the side of Negroes in our struggle and others have risked economic and political peril to support our cause." See King, *Where Do We Go From Here*, 52.

16. King, *Trumpet of Conscience*, 9.

17. King, *Call to Conscience*, 68.

human-Other who is interpreted as the *enemy*, and distinguishing them from their oppressive beliefs. Often, this tension remains unresolved.

Nevertheless, attempts of liberation should never involve submitting to bitterness, emotionalism, hatred, undisciplined anger, and general maliciousness towards the human-Other. Whether we are reflecting upon a new Black aesthetic or Black subjectivity, we witness King emphasizing a set of limitations that considers the existence of the human-Other. In part, it is an aspect of African-American consciousness that grafts the human-Other into its self-interest, mitigating and negating the perpetual attempt to redefine Blackness in relation to an irredeemable Whiteness. King consistently maintained that the goal was never to reverse the *roles* or *performances* of the oppressed and oppressor: "We must also avoid the temptation of being victimized with a psychology of victors."[18] Principles of demoralization and demonization were aspects of the psychology of the victors. Therefore, as King conceptualized it, there was a reflexive element of dehumanizing oneself through the oppression of the human-Other. Doing so would only maintain a cycle of oppression and dehumanization.

Psychological liberation and the "equilibrium of power" also involved a transformation of linguistics. These were important elements in expunging essentialist/racialized-binary reasoning from African-Americans, causing them to reflect upon how they perceived, as well as engaged Anglo-Americans: "We do not wish to triumph over the white community. That would only result in transferring those now on the bottom to the top. But, if we can live up to nonviolence in thought, and deed, there will emerge an interracial society based on freedom for all."[19] This is the crucial element to rupturing the cycle of oppression and dehumanization that existed, in part, through essentialist/racialized-binary reasoning. For King, African-Americans were to nurture and love the humanity of Anglo-Americans. Anglo-American humanity was not chattel for purchasing. Nor were they interpreted as an *irredeemable* enemy, deserving unmitigated violence inflicted upon them. *Triumph* was a word that was present throughout colonial literature. The word conjures images of European conquest of the New World and dominance over the non-European.

Negating the reversal of power by creating an equilibrium of power, devoid of essentialist/racialized-binary reasoning, was an aspect

---

18. King, *Call to Conscience*, 53.
19. King and Washington, *Testament of Hope*, 81.

of negating the psychology of the victor. In this context, triumph would be redefined to represent the liberation of the oppressed and the oppressor. Liberation was not dependent on merely exposing the different forms of White supremacy that existed and the systemic racism that subjugated people. Although these were important elements. The salvation, or liberation of the oppressor, was an often-dismissed principle. This has greater relevance within belief systems that emphasize the intertwined and interdependent lives of the oppressed and oppressor. Nevertheless, sociopolitical equality and equity involved separating fantasy from reality, making distinctions between the wheat and the tares, as well as exposing *performances* for what they truly are.

King's attention to Anglo-America was not a sign of timidity, fear, or *Uncle Tom-ism*. In part, it stemmed from the dangerous possibility that African-Americans would become ensnared into the same fallacies that dominated Anglo-American existence from colonialism to the Civil Rights Movement:

> We must not seek to use our emerging freedom and our growing power to do the same thing to the white minority that has been done to us for so many centuries. Our aim must never be to defeat or humiliate the white man. We must not become victimized with a philosophy of black supremacy. God is not interested merely in freeing black men and brown men and yellow men, but God is interested in freeing the whole human race. We must work with determination to create a society, not where black men are superior and other men are inferior and vice versa, but a society in which all men will live together as brothers and respect the dignity and worth of human personality.[20]

The words *defeat* and *humiliate* often characterized the heart, mind, and spirit of the oppressed. These words, like triumph, coerce our conscience into meditating on the unspeakable evils of the transatlantic slave trade to the Civil Rights Movement. King's program of decolonization negated the usage of essentialist/racialized-binary reasoning, but also created critical reflection upon how African-Americans utilized their increasing freedom and power. The increase of freedom brings the increase

---

20. In another context, King makes the statement, "In the process of gaining our rightful place, we must not be guilty of wrongful deeds. Let us not seek to satisfy our thirst for freedom by drinking from the cup of bitterness and hatred" (King, *Call to Conscience*, 53, 83).

of power, and vice versa, both creating a heightened sense of responsibility to utilize them righteously.

This is a significant aspect of King emphasizing Christian love as a psychological and relational element to liberation, via African-American perception of and engagement with Anglo-Americans. *Disciplined* anger is governed by love and justice. King reinforced the importance of critically reflecting upon differentiating the person from the ideology they embraced. We must always scrutinize the actions of the person in relation to the ideology that influenced them. In principle, this is observed in how King viewed Anglo-Americans, Whiteness, and White supremacy. He also contextualized this principle in relation to power, violence, and hate.

> Are we seeking power for power's sake? Or are we seeking to make the world and our nation better places to live? If we seek the latter, violence can never provide the answer. The ultimate weakness of violence is that it is a descending spiral, begetting the very thing it seeks to destroy. Instead of diminishing evil, it multiplies it. Through violence you may murder the liar, but you cannot murder the lie, nor establish the truth. Through violence you may murder the hater, but you do not murder hate. In fact, violence merely increases hate. So it goes. Returning violence for violence multiplies violence, adding deeper darkness to a night already devoid of stars. Darkness cannot drive our darkness: only light can do that. Hate cannot drive out hate: only love can do that.[21]

Thinking otherwise subjects African-Americans to self-deception, maintaining the cycle of oppression, and the continual spirals of *pretences* and *elusions* of freedom. Contextualizing these principles in our contemporary era, the cycle of oppression continues an endless loop of sociopolitical protest that displays a veneer of entertainment. We lose the ability to distinguish the wheat from the tares, and how some tares deceive themselves into thinking they are the wheat. We become captivated by the performances that are televised, and spoken about within newspapers and social media. We fantasize, constructing a fetish of displaying a power performance that bears similarity to those we idolize. Self-deception is a location we can travel to, but never know when we have arrived.

21. King, *Chaos or Community*, 64–65. He also stated that "hate is just as injurious to the hater as it is to the hated." Furthermore, in King's famous speech, "Give Us the Ballot," he argues, "We must meet hate with love. We must meet physical force with soul force" (King, *Chaos or Community*, 66; *Call to Conscience*, 51). Niebuhr argued that soul force could be used to oppress people through the proponent's self-righteousness. See Niebuhr, *Human Destiny*, 271.

Nevertheless, I interpret King's differentiation between Anglo-Americans, Whiteness, and White supremacy as centred upon certain Christian theological convictions. White supremacy was not a secularized concept of immorality. Nor was it a representation of human wickedness that could be defeated entirely through simple sociopolitical programs. Aspects of it were and could be confronted by those means. However, there were religious elements of White supremacy. An underlining issue was making theological principles applicable to the public sphere, without senseless arguments, defensiveness, and rejection that negated necessary progress. King's views of racism and White supremacy bore stark similarities to the theological interpretations of certain Anglo-American ethicists/theologians during his period. Surprisingly, most of them are relatively minimized and ignored, by both African and Anglo-Americans.

KING AND NIEBUHR

The Quasi-Deification of White Supremacy

African-American scholars have demonstrated the reluctance and inability of Anglo-Americans to discuss, as well as confront, White supremacy in America. At this point, I am not concerned with adding to the wealth of literature on this subject. Rather, I am introducing an Anglo-American perspective of White supremacy that informed King's progressive interpretation. The early-twentieth-century Anglo-Americans rarely spoke about the destructive presence of White supremacy relating to African-Americans. However, when they did, some produced interpretations that have gone largely ignored by both African and Anglo-American scholars.[22]

We witness an example of such an interpretation from the Christian ethicist, William Waldo Beach (1917–2001): "In sum, the problem of race is at its deepest level not a factual problem, nor a moral problem, but a theological problem."[23] Beach asserted that racial discrimination was an idolatrous internal conflict between conflicting *faiths*. In this context, faith is interpreted from the Judean Christian narrative. It is an internal war between an authentic religious faith in Yahweh and an inordinate

---

22. Examples of this are viewed by the discourses of George Fox (1624–1691), William Edmondson (1627–1712), Richard Baxter (1615–1691), and other Anglo-Saxons during the seventeenth century.

23. Beach, "Theological Analysis," 208.

amount of quasi-religious faith in oneself, as well as their representative finite communities. Beach argues that,

> From the standpoint of classical Christian thought, of course, racial prejudice is not one of a catalogue of sins, but is a fact or expression of the single sin of "pride," the rejection of the absolute Sovereign Sense of life and the attempt to set up as final some substitute sovereignty derived from the finite. In so far as fallen, man tends to make of himself or some collective projection of himself the center of love and value.[24]

Generally, Anglo-American theologians interpreted racism as excessive group pride.[25] However, this was not a simplistic notion of pride. It was a form of pride that extended to idolatry that mirrored the narrative of the mythic biblical figure, Lucifer. Racial discrimination, in this context, represents the displacement of perfection for the imperfect masquerading as perfection: an aspect of the game of collusion. I am highlighting Beach's emphasis on pride, and humanity projecting itself as the *centre* of how love and value are defined.

One of the destructive elements of essentialist/racialized-binary reasoning is how it redefines and imposes a set of core *meanings, values,* and *purposes* in life upon the human-Other. This process is a normal occurrence within humanity. Every culture or civilization establishes a set of aesthetics, meanings, values, and purposes in life that represent their existence. Anderson's concept of the "European Cult of Genius," and West's "Normative Gaze" are two interpretations of this, and how it formed White Supremacy in America. We also witness this within the breadth of African-American literature that seeks to articulate new forms of Black aesthetics, meanings, values, and purposes in life. Often, they are expressed in tension with one another. Problems occur and intensify from the rejection of natural boundaries and limitations an individual and culture have in relation to the human-Other. The existence of the majority culture and its self-interest define how the minority culture is oppressed and dehumanized. Thus, liberation becomes a conflict via a

---

24. Beach, "Theological Analysis," 211.

25. Niebuhr makes the statement, "Racial prejudice is indeed a form of irrationality; but it is not as capricious as modern universalist assume. Racial prejudice, the contempt of the other group, is an inevitable concomitant of racial pride; and racial pride is an inevitable concomitant of the ethnic will to live." See Niebuhr, *Children of Light*, 139; *Pious and Secular America*, 81.

game of collusion whereby two sets of aesthetics, values, meanings, and purposes in life oppose each other.

From this context, I am reinterpreting the insight of H. Richard Niebuhr (1894–1962), one of the most important Christian ethicists/theologians of the twentieth century, in relation to White supremacy, the European cult of genius, and the normative gaze. Regarding the inner contestation of opposing faiths, H. R Niebuhr states, "When men's ultimate orientation is in their society, when it is their value-center and cause, then the social mores can make anything right and anything wrong; then indeed conscience is the internalized voice of society or of its representation."[26] Essentialist/racialized-binary reasoning and the game of collusion become socialized to the extent its employment escapes the awareness of many people within society. Whiteness as White supremacy recreates many of the important and influential social norms. American ethics and morality, shaped by White supremacy, receive the appearance of universal truth and applicability. Thus, we tragically witness many Anglo-Americans, and other ethnicities, who view society as the *center* of their existence, become enslaved to essentialist/racialized-binary reasoning and White supremacy. This is to the extent that certain forms of Anglo-American reasoning and behaviour may resemble the disposition of White supremacy, but the individuals themselves are not inherently racist.

These destructive effects exist within the religious and secular worlds. Anglo-Americans constructed a competing god from the societal norms that represented their existence and self-interest. Within Western America, many Anglo-American Christians created what some African-Americans scholars refer to as a "White Christ."[27] The White Christ is the religious extension of Anglo-American self-interest and White supremacy. Niebuhr's words are applicable to this view: "He tends to worship a supernatural being who is the collective representation of his own community or who is the principle of its being; to make his center of value that which bestows value or the members of the special society as though it were the ultimate cause."[28] I am highlighting the modes of self-deception through the game of collusion that escapes the awareness of the individual and community. Regarding the idolatry of humanity that taints everyone within society, Niebuhr asserts:

26. Niebuhr, *Radical Monotheism*, 20.
27. See Douglas, *Black Christ*.
28. Niebuhr, *Radical Monotheism*, 60.

> As a rule men are polytheists, referring now to this and now to that valued being as the source of life's meaning. Sometimes they live for Jesus' God, sometimes for country and sometimes for Yale. For the most part they make gods out of themselves or out of the work of their own hands, living for their own glory as person and as communities.[29]

Thus, from the Judean-Christian narrative, any and everything could be interpreted as a quasi-god. This perspective is an important element in how I interpret King's awareness of and attempt to expunge essentialist/racialized-binary reasoning from Anglo-American culture. His critique of the American church, both within its African and Anglo-American contextualisms, displays elements of the quasi-deification that Beach and Niebuhr referenced.

King levied stern and insightful critiques regarding the American church. He revealed the contradictory and hypocritical conflicts within the institution. They represented the consequences of employing essentialist/racialized-binary reasoning and participating in the quasi-deification of the human-Self. Religious White supremacy represents the apex of an identity crisis within Anglo-American culture: the game of collusion that has collapsed within itself. African and Anglo-American cultures, to varied degrees, were apathetic, and inept at opposing White supremacy. They were not equally culpable in participating in and sustaining colonial slavery, as well as its residual effects on the Civil Rights Movement.

For example, King makes a powerful ecclesiastical statement in generalizing the causes which led to the origin of the African-American church: "it is to their everlasting shame that white Christians developed a system of racial segregation within the church, and inflicted so many indignities upon its Negro worshipers that they had to organize their own churches."[30] At this point, I am highlighting the inner conflict within the colonial Anglo-American church that represented opposing religious faiths: Yahweh from Judean Christian texts, and the quasi-deification of Whiteness via White supremacy. Segregation, hate, and the irrational racializing of Christianity had divided the American church.

The conflict between these two faiths had dramatically affected how African and Anglo-American Christians constructed their identities, sense of belonging, and shared-spaces with each other. However, there were individuals who achieved relative freedom from these destruction

---

29. Niebuhr, *Meaning of Revelation*, 40.
30. King, *Strength to Love*, 60.

processes. Certain colonial evangelical African-American Christians achieved a level of freedom, devoid of essentialist/racialized-binary reasoning, and the quasi-deification of their social norms. It is tragic that the lives and literature of Chavis, Harper, and Wheatley have been minimized, neglected, and ignored, simply because they do not support the dominant *norms* of African-American culture, politics, and the academy. King asserted that the inadequacy of the American church stemmed from its development, the principal developers, and their attempts to obtain their self-interest through the institution:

> Honesty also impels us to admit that the church has not been true to its social mission on the question of racial justice. In this area it has failed Christ miserably. This failure is due not only to the fact that the church has been appallingly silent and disastrously indifferent to the realm of race relations but even more to the fact that it has often been an active participant in shaping and crystallizing the patterns of the race-caste system.[31]

Those Christians and aspects of the American church, which supported slavery and the oppression of minorities, by their very nature could not honor the integrity of Christianity's social mission. Silence and indifference represent the internal duality of competing religious faiths: the Christ of Yahweh and the Christ of White supremacy.

King's patience and methodical attempt at reaching the conscience of Anglo-America must be reflected upon from this theological perspective. The quasi-deification of Anglo-American culture enslaved everyone in variant degrees. This required a series of distinct but interlocking programs to reach people where they resided emotionally, psychologically, and spiritually. Self-oppression and self-dehumanization of Anglo-Americans developed through their treatment of African-Americans, as well as other ethnicities. The quasi-deification of Anglo-America led King to question the very object or deity that Anglo-American Christians worshiped:

> I have travelled the length and breadth of Alabama, Mississippi and all the other southern states. On sweltering summer days and crisp autumn mornings I have looked at the South's beautiful churches with their lofty spires pointing heavenward. I have beheld the impressive outlines of her massive religious-education

---

31. King, *Strength to Love*, 105.

buildings. Over and over I have found myself asking: "What kind of people worship here? Who is their God?"[32]

Quasi-gods cannot exist without the employment of essentialist/racialized-binary reasoning, cognitive dissonance, and confirmatory bias. Socializing these attributes within society dulls our awareness of their existence, and how we may employ them within our lives. Participation in the racialized game of collusion, willingly or not, causes us to collapse into an endless loop of self-deception and conflict, as we either justify the worship of our quasi-gods or refuse to bow at the altar. Reinhold Niebuhr briefly references this in his statement that:

> In so far as life, in its individual or collective form, which affronts God by making itself into a perverse centre for the whole of life, also affronts and wrongs the neighbour by reducing him to an instrumentality of the interests of the self, it is subject to punishment and vengeance, whenever the neighbour acquires the power to resist such encroachments upon his dignity.[33]

Dehumanization and oppression have a secular and religious element. A fuller revelation to this occurs when we choose not to worship our oppressors and their deities. The same critique King levied upon the Anglo-American church bears similarity to how he characterized secular society. For example, King employed the word schizophrenic to signify the noticeable split, or collective identity crisis, of Anglo-America through essentialist/racialized-binary reasoning, cognitive dissonance, and confirmatory bias:

> Ever since the birth of our nation, white America has had a schizophrenic personality on the question of race. She has been torn between selves—a self in which she proudly professed the great principles of democracy and a self in which she sadly practiced the antithesis of democracy. This tragic duality has produced a strange indecisiveness and ambivalence towards the Negro, causing America to take a step backward simultaneously with every step forward on the question of racial justice, to be at once attracted to the Negro and repelled by him, to love and to hate him. There has never been a solid, unified and determined thrust to make justice a reality for Afro-Americans.[34]

32. King, *Why We Can't Wait*, 105–6.

33. Niebuhr, *Faith and History*, 145.

34. King also mentioned this duality in reference to Abraham Lincoln (1809–1865). See King, *Where Do We Go From Here*, 72, 82–85.

The illusion of normality and human progress maintained the tension between democracy and slavery, attraction and repulsion, love and hate. King argued that an Anglo-American *schizophrenic* collective mentality created and sustained these illusions. They assisted in creating the mythic hierarchy of human value, and the irrational theories of inherent superiority and inferiority. These were the Anglo-American quasi-gods and their accompanying myths. Aspects of Western American culture, politics, and the academy demonstrate how two or more sets of worshippers are engaged in a Manichaean struggle. Their conflict is representative of *performances*, to determine the superior deity, and how society will worship that deity, conforming to its standards. I often wonder how many quasi-gods exist within African-American culture, politics, and the academy. King was developing a nuanced program, through trial and error, to confront and overturn the influence of global White supremacy. This involved the simultaneous process of liberation, healing, and reconciliation of everyone.

I am highlighting elements of his theories associated with essentialist/racialized-binary reasoning, confirmatory bias, and cognitive dissonance. Surprisingly, they have been largely dismissed, ignored, and rejected as they relate to both Anglo and African-Americans. Dismissing King's theories, and beliefs from other individuals, have nurtured these destructive forms of reasoning to shape the dominant trends within African-American culture, politics, and the academy. Consequently, we are socialized into the endless game of collusion, with its skewed performances, that distort our identities, sense of belonging, and shared space with the human-Other.

Nevertheless, an interesting aspect of King's theories involved the binary-opposite of White supremacy: Black supremacy. Surprisingly, the similarity between these two philosophies is possibly the most ignored, disputed, and rejected of King's theories. He asserted that "black supremacy is as dangerous as white supremacy."[35] King was careful to explain that Black supremacy was not inherently racist.[36] It did not advocate notions of human superiority and inferiority that defined White supremacy.

---

35. King, *Call to Conscience*, 69.

36. King argues that, "Black Power is an implicit and often explicit belief in Black separatism. Notice that I do not call it Black racism. It is inaccurate to refer to Black Power as racism in reverse, as some have recently done. Racism is a doctrine of the congenital inferiority and worthlessness of a people. While a few angry proponents of Black Power have, in moments of bitterness, made wild statements that come close to this kind of racism, the major proponents of Black Power have never contended that the white man is innately worthless" (King, *Chaos or Community*, 49).

KING

Black Supremacy

King characterized the extremist forms of Black Nationalism during the Civil Rights Movement and Black Power as representatives of Black supremacy.[37] The central critique of mine, and how I interpret King's views, is not condemning the entire *system* of beliefs. Nor am I placing irrational skepticism upon the good actions of everyone who identified with and embodied these sociopolitical philosophies. Rather, I am reflecting upon the destructive consequences of certain principles within those sociopolitical philosophies, that not only mirror White supremacy, but influenced the trajectory of certain discourses and trends within African-American culture, politics, and the academy.[38] During the Civil Rights Movement, African-American subcultures competed with one another for the heart, conscience, and soul of the people. Although there was a spectrum, the subcultures typically expressed themselves through the secular and religious aspects of conservatism and their liberal/militant counterpart. I am concerned that earlier warnings from King and other African-American scholars are still dismissed and ignored. African-Americans are either unaware of essentialist and racialized-binary reasoning, or consciously utilize it to construct their cultural, political, and academic views.

Individuals within the Civil Rights Movement magnified these forms of reasoning by exploiting various paradigms. For example, there

---

37. Regarding Black Nationalism, King was adamant that "it substituted the tyranny of black supremacy for the tyranny of white supremacy" (Carson and King, *Autobiography*, 269). Furthermore, I am emphasizing that Black Nationalism within colonialism was different from how it developed principally through the philosophy of Marcus Garvey and the Nation of Islam during the Civil Rights Movement. I interpret Black Nationalism as providing a general philosophical foundation from which Black Power was birthed. Furthermore, I am including aspects of Afrocentrism and Pan-Africanism that share philosophical principles with Black Nationalism and Black Power. See Moses, *Golden Age*; *Classical Black Nationalism*; Deburg, *Modern Black Nationalism*.

38. Victor Anderson makes an interesting statement: "I am not saying that the cultural nationalism of the 1960s and early 1970s and its influence on African-American aesthetics is blameworthy for its identification of black aesthetics with 'revolutionary politics.' What I stress are certain consequences of this aesthetic for the subsequent development of African-American cultural philosophy under today's drastically changed conditions in which neither the protest politics of the 1960s nor the revolutionary rhetoric of the 1970s seem effective." It is difficult to assess how Anderson is defining cultural nationalism, and revolutionary politics. They appear to be in a general sense that consumes both conservative and liberal dispositions. See Anderson, *Beyond Ontological Blackness*, 144.

were the categories of integration and segregation, the social construction of race, and the ambiguity between this and the reification of race. These paradigms also expressed themselves through conceptions of non-purity and purity, no possibility of losing Blackness and the non-being of Blackness, as well as the absence of redefining Blackness with the perpetual redefinition of Blackness. We also witness the polarities of a non-ideal Blackness and an Ideal Blackness, Whiteness as redeemable and Whiteness as irredeemable, or the ambiguity thereof, monotheistic Protestant evangelicalism and the religious syncretism of Christianity and other religions, non-racialized Christ and a racialized Christ. The spectrum of African-American conservatism and liberalism/militancy displayed areas of commonality, but both subcultures typically had distinct sets of Black aesthetics, and Black subjectivity.[39]

Nevertheless, the essence or spirit of Black Nationalism and Black Power remains influential within our culture, political theories, and aspects of Black academia in elusive ways. They influence how we shape our identities, sense of belonging, and shared spaces. I am highlighting the divisiveness of essentialist/racialized-binary reasoning that developed *within* Blackness. It causes us to minimize, dismiss, and ignore the contributions of many colonial African-Americans, who were emancipated from this destructive reasoning, and do not support the agendas of the dominant trends within contemporary African-American culture, politics, and the academy.

LIKE PRODUCES LIKE

White Provocation of Militant Blackness

Anglo-Americans, Whiteness, and White supremacy created the *conditions* and *contexts* that birthed Black supremacy. Black supremacy did not erect itself within a void. It did not originate within the collective conscience of individuals who constructed an imaginary world; whereby systemic dehumanization and oppression were an illusion, stemming from their inherent ineptness. A certain level of cruelty and malice exists within provoking the human-Other to destructive ends. The human-Self then manipulates these destructive ends to quasi-justify inequality and oppression.

---

39. Anderson, *Ontological Blackness*, 86–117.

The selective morality of Anglo-America regarding African-American crime, violence, and the destruction of property is a fruitful example. King argued that "It is incontestable and deplorable that Negroes have committed crimes, but they are derivative crimes. They are born of the greater crimes of the white society."[40] The perception that Anglo-Americans were not culpable for the immorality of some African-Americans, was an illusion. The more immoral sinner is one that uses the lesser sinner's actions as a form of escapism, shifting attention from their destructive nature, which is ironically a sign of their greater wickedness. King revealed the hypocrisy of White supremacist, corrects the misunderstanding of some Anglo-Americans, and rebuked the actions of militant African-Americans through stating,

> The riots are now in the centre of the stage, and are being offered as basis for contradictory positions by whites and Negroes. Some Negroes argue they are the incipient forms of rebellion and guerrilla tactics that will be the feature of the Negro revolt. They are represented as the new stage of Negro struggle replacing the old and allegedly outworn tactics of nonviolent resistance. At the same time some white forces are using riots as evidence that Negroes have no capacity for constructive change and in their lawless behaviour forfeit all rights and justify any form of repressive measures. A corollary of this theory is the position that the outbursts are unforgivable, ungrateful, and a menace to the social order.[41]

Oppression is not a means to righteousness. Nor is it an entity, or force that sanctifies counterintuitive and counterproductive reasoning and action. King was apprehensive of militant African-Americans, who not only justified violence beyond self-defence, but feigned it within ambiguous contexts. This provided White supremacists with an excuse to justify their views, pushing themselves, and everyone ensnared within essentialist and racialized-binary reasoning, into their imaginary world. I am highlighting the way reactionary responses can often mimic the initial act of provocation: "the irony is that the white society ruefully complains that if there were no chaos great changes would come, yet it

---

40. King, *Trumpet of Conscience*, 8.

41. King, *Trumpet of Conscience*, 7. Niebuhr provides a similar critique, stating, "dominant groups indulge in the hypocrisies beside the claim of their special intellectual fitness for the powers which they exercise and the privileges which they enjoy. Frequently they justify their advantages by the claim of moral rather than intellectual superiority. See Niebuhr, *Moral Man Immoral Society*, 118, 123, 140–41.

creates the circumstances breeding the chaos."⁴² King and other African-American scholars affirm that Black Nationalism and Black Power arose within this chaos. However, I suspect many African-American scholars are reluctant to acknowledge the destructive aspect of this Manichaean conflict between these sociopolitical philosophies and White supremacy. I am interpreting King's views within Goffman's concept of performance, Lang's game of collusion, and Niebuhr's theory of the human-Self attempting to progressively deceive itself, by entrapping the human-Other into its imaginary world.

King provided many controversial views regarding Black Nationalism and Black Power, many of which centered on Black Power as an ambiguous philosophy of despair, frustration, and an emotional reaction against White supremacy.⁴³ However, scholars tend to avoid King's association of Black Power as a reaction against the Anglo-American philosophy of the ideal slave. In doing so, King employed the research from the influential historian, Kenneth M. Stampp (1912–2009). This was another way King demonstrated aspects of the schizophrenic duality that permeated within the collective American conscience.

Stampp crafted a realist interpretation of the relationship between the master and slave. In part, his research, within *The Peculiar Institution: Slavery in the Ante-Bellum South*, refuted many myths of American colonial slavery. Stampp presented a well-organized understanding of the economic, emotional, ideological, psychological, and social benefits that Anglo-Americans perceived themselves acquiring. One of the unique qualities of his interpretation was an emphasis on power and the perception thereof within the relationship between master and slave. Stampp ascertained that the philosophy of the perfect slave reinforced five to six general principles:

> Here, then, was the way to produce the perfect slave: accustom him to rigid discipline, demand from him unconditional submission, impress upon him his innate inferiority, develop in him a paralyzing fear of white men, train him to adopt the

---

42. King, *Trumpet of Conscience*, 10.

43. King argued, "Beneath all the satisfaction of a gratifying slogan, Black Power is a nihilistic philosophy born out of the conviction that the Negro can't win. It is, at bottom, the view that American society is so hopelessly corrupt and enmeshed in evil that there is no possibility of salvation from within." He also characterized Black Nationalist as bitter, expressing hatred and despair. See King, *Chaos or Community*, 45, 33; *Why We Can't Wait*, 100.

master's code of good behaviour, and instil in him a sense of complete dependence. This, at least, was the goal.[44]

The foundations of America, White supremacy, and Anglo-American culture were, in part, created from the philosophy of the perfect slave. These principles existed well beyond the moments when the ideas of America were beginning to coalesce. I argue that the quasi-deification of Whiteness, and Anglo-America via the extension of their self-interest, complemented this dehumanizing philosophy.

Nevertheless, King was meticulous in demonstrating the close association of Black Power to White power and aspects of Anglo-American culture. Like produces like through grafting an image of itself within another. Anglo-Americans exaggerated and often obsessed over skewed conceptions of power. This invoked a counter, distorted oppositional form of power *within* the philosophy of Black Power: a fragmentation within a fragmentation.

The essentialist and racialized-binary reasoning are observed in how King articulated Black Power's deep fascination with deconstructing White authority structures. Any and everything that represented Whiteness and Anglo-American culture were vessels of White supremacy. Thus, Black Power sought to confront and deconstruct Whiteness. This represented the Manichaean melodrama between the dehumanized slaves and their quasi-deified masters. Referencing Black Power's aversion to White authority, King stated, "the defiance almost becomes a kind of taunt."[45] King explained that underneath the taunt, was the drive to assert selfhood, and expunge any presence of submissiveness to Whiteness. The presence of Whiteness represented an *intrusion* upon Black space and being.

Second, Anglo-Saxons reinforced the belief of the African's inherent inferiority, in part, by denigrating African civilizations, aesthetics, and subjectivity. We observed this through the theories of Anderson's cult of *European genius* and West's concept of the *normative gaze*. For King, Black Power countered the skewed belief, with a stern "determination to glory in blackness and resurrect joyously by the African past."[46] However, the employment of essentialist and racialized-binary reasoning influenced romanticized interpretations of Blackness and African heritage. Therefore, Whiteness represented America and Christianity, as Blackness

---

44. Stampp, *Peculiar Institution*, 148; King, *Chaos or Community*, 40.
45. King, *Chaos or Community*, 41.
46. King, *Chaos or Community*, 41.

represented Africa and traditional West African religiosity.⁴⁷ This can be interpreted as representative of and the reinforcement of DuBois's double-consciousness. King never rejected what he perceived as healthy articulations of Blackness and conceptions of an African heritage. He never shunned anyone for being proud of their Blackness as Black people within a White Supremacist world. The problem was how they were often dependent upon and reactionary to negative Anglo-American perceptions.⁴⁸

Third, Black power advocates rejected any presence of fear and awe from African-Americans in relation to White authority. Referencing this, King maintained that some Black Power advocates had "encourage[d] contempt and even uncivil disobedience as alternatives to the old patterns of slavery."⁴⁹ This stemmed from the belief that Black liberation exclusively developed through countering White power with Black Power. Principles four and five are deeply related. The "code of good behaviour" was social and religious extensions of Anglo-America, Whiteness, and White supremacy. These standards and social norms influenced the development of the collective identity of African-Americans, their sense of belonging, and conception of shared-space with Anglo-Americans. The oppressive code of good behaviour reinforced conceptions of inferiority, submissiveness, and servitude within African-Americans. Consequently, they established the complete dependency of African-Americans to Anglo-Americans. Thus, to counter these principles, King argued that many Black Power advocates developed an urgent need to establish forms of justice and governance that were exclusively for African-American communities. Racial, religious, and social segregation created perfect independence from Anglo-American influence.

---

47. This interpretation can be witnessed from many Black Nationalist and Black Power advocates. One of the more influential scholars of his time, St. Claire Drake provides an interesting interpretation representative of a racialized-binary reasoning, via Afrocentrism. Drake advocates that it is highly questionable that many African-Americans converted to Christianity between 1619 and 1750. He argues that the African-American slaves feigned conversion. The sole purpose was for cultural and sociopolitical benefits. Drake is situated within a tradition of African-American scholarship that focuses on how the slaves preserved their African heritage and religiosity. See Drake, *Redemption of Africa*.

48. An example can be observed by the father of contemporary Black liberation theology, James Cone. Referencing Black Power, Cone stated, "The black power rhetoric was the only language we had that was both radical and also derived from and accountable to black history and culture." See Cone, *For My People*.

49. King, *Chaos or Community*, 41.

Nevertheless, there were *fragments* of positive emotional, psychological, and physical benefits to the Black Power program. These are partially observed in their binary-oppositional stances against Anglo-America, Whiteness, and White supremacy. However, I am emphasizing how we can be unaware of or intentionally embrace the philosophy of the Victor. Regarding Power, King employed a popular description of how African and Anglo-Americans conceptualized their theories. For him, America never displayed an equilibrium of power between the races: "This has led Negro Americans in the past to seek their goals through love and moral suasion devoid of power and white Americans to seek their goals through power devoid of love and conscience."[50] This perception led to what King claimed as "a few extremists today to advocate for Negroes the same destructive and conscienceless power that they have justly abhorred in whites. It is precisely this collision of immoral power with powerless morality which constitutes the major crisis of our times."[51] Guided by morality and noble intentions, Black Power advocates expressed further positive aims that King acknowledged. He asserted that Black Power was positive when the philosophy advocated more political awareness among African-Americans, strengthening their communities with qualified leaders, and utilizing their vote to achieve freedom and human dignity. Black Power was admirable when it asserted that African-Americans were to unite economically, strengthening the people through financial stewardship and wise investments. Black Power represents empowerment when the individual and community achieve psychological wholeness from the effects of dehumanization and oppression. However, the troubling aspect of King's assessment focused on how Black Power, and the conservative element of the Civil Rights Movement shared these positive attributes. King maintained that,

> Nevertheless, in spite of the positive aspects of Black Power, which are compatible with what we have sought to do in the civil rights movement all along without the slogan, its negative values, I believe, prevent it from having the substance and program to become the basic strategy for the civil rights movement in the days ahead.[52]

---

50. King, *Chaos or Community*, 38.

51. King, *Chaos or Community*, 38.

52. King stated this on at least three different occasions. See King, *Chaos or Community*, 38, 39, 45.

The relationship between principles of segregation and cultural/racial/ethnic purity existed before the emergence of recorded human history. Colonial Anglo-Saxons exaggerated and infused them with the philosophy of White supremacy. For King, the principles of Black Nationalism and Black Power employed these concepts in similar ways. Many people argued then that Anglo-Americans and Whiteness were corrupt and irredeemable. These beliefs permeate among contemporary African-Americans and have shaped much of our culture, politics, and academics. This influences the dismissing, minimizing, and rejection of colonial evangelical African-American literature, that does not represent the dominant trends within contemporary African-American culture, politics, and the academy.

THE MELODRAMA CONTINUES

In this discussion, I emphasized the counter, mirroring, and reactionary principles of Black Nationalism and Black Power that stemmed from essentialist and racialized-binary reasoning. These principles also invoked aspects of cognitive dissonance and confirmatory bias. All three contribute to the unintentional participation in the game of collusion. At this point, King's perception of Black Nationalism and Black Power serves as an axis. Similar beliefs of his are situated within colonial African-American socio-religious traditions. Although labelled differently, there were colonial African-Americans, who were aware of essentialist and racialized-binary reasoning, and the cycle of dehumanization that developed through oppressing the human-Other. However, they chose to reveal and expunge them, not construct mirroring principles that we observed within aspects of Black Nationalism and Black Power.

3

Colonial African-American Self-Awareness, Obliviousness, and Fragmented Whiteness

"For to us God revealed them through the Spirit; for the Spirit searches all things, even the depths of God."

(1 Cor 2:10)

"For they exchanged the truth of God for falsehood, and worshiped and served the creature rather than the Creator, who is blessed forever. Amen."

(Rom 1:25)

AMERICAN HISTORY BECOMES A rather skewed and questionable discipline to study when Eurocentric and White supremacist present their interpretations of events and figures. Especially when we study various colonial Anglo-American accounts. The difficulty for me is to assess the writer's self-awareness and overall comprehension of reality as reality is. My attempts become further interesting when I imagine the writer may have submitted to essentialist and racialized-binary reasoning. They cause the writer to be oblivious to what resides in front of their eyes: Black intelligence and self-awareness. The distorted White conscience cannot search for something it cannot conceive existing. However, within my transparency, I acknowledge these same beliefs regarding Anglo-Americans are applicable to some African-Americans. I often experience frustration and question the agenda of some Black Nationalist historiographies.

Nevertheless, this chapter examines examples of the colonial Black consciousness that has been deeply affected by essentialist and racialized-binary reasoning. I will also explore the testimonies of colonial African-Americans who were knowledgeable of those forms of reasoning, and demonstrated keen self-awareness in articulating how it affected Anglo-American society. This chapter completes our journey backward to demonstrate a subtle tradition, or at the least, the presence of a heightened sense of Black self-awareness, guided by the biblical principles of repentance, forgiveness, reconciliation, and redemption for everyone, including Whiteness, broadly construed. I am challenging the reader to reflect on why these forms of reasoning may not be the predominate attributes of contemporary African-American culture, politics, and academic theology.

Fragmented Whiteness can be observed in the lack of self-awareness from some colonial Anglo-Americans, regarding White self-degradation, initiated from their abuse of African and African-American slaves. Dehumanization, degradation, and other forms of abuse develop initially from within the human-Self. The internal fragmentation of the human-Self eventually extends to the human-Other, creating forms of distortions within them, all of which are concealed, existing beyond everyone's self-awareness. The fragmented conscience of some African-American slaves had developed in various ways. It is important to have a brief understanding of this through the slave narratives. Some narratives provide testimony to the lack of self-awareness some slaves exhibited, in relation to understanding progressive moral and ethical principles, and juxtaposing them upon the institution of slavery and their personal masters. I now present two unique examples of the colonial African-American conscience regarding the effects of slavery.

MRS. MILLIE EVANS & MRS. MALINDA DISCUSS

Two Forms of Black Conscience

During colonialism, there existed a co-dependent relationship between the psyche of a particular Black slave and their White master, that *colluded* to create a skewed perception of reality that justified the institution of slavery and everything it entailed. Mrs. Millie Evans was an African-American slave, born in North Carolina in 1849. Although unaware, Evans presents a testimony that reveals how she was participatory in a co-dependent relationship with her master and mistress. She, like many other slaves, had no recollection of the exact day or time of her birth. Evans recounts a particular event in her childhood that represented happiness and peace. It can also be interpreted as a memory that demonstrates the internal fragmentation within the Black and White psyche, developed through degradation and dehumanization. Evans was roughly eighty-eight years old when she retold this story, and did so under the belief, as did many other African Americans, that life after the Emancipation Proclamation was harsher than being a legalized slave. Evans innocently explains,

> I stayed with my ma every night, but my mistress raised me. My ma had to work hard, so every time Old Mistress thought we little black chilluns was hungry between meals she would call us up to de house to eat. Sometimes she would give us johnnycake and plenty of buttermilk to drink with it. Dey had a long trough for us dat dey would keep so clean. Dey would fill this trough with buttermilk, and all us children would get around de trough and drink with our mouths and hold our johnnycake with our hands. I can see myself drinkin' now. It was so good.[1]

Nostalgia and yearning are two words that describe Evans's articulation of this memorable childhood experience. We witness a displacement and replacement of mother figures in her life. Evans's Black biological mother is absent, tending to her slave duties, and in her stead is the White mistress. The Mistress is an interesting figure. She expresses, at least in appearance, meaningful intent, influenced by a desire to care for and to humanize the slave children. However, this is tainted by the usage of the *trough* and what it represents: unacknowledged self-dehumanization and the dehumanization of the human-Other. The imagery from Evans's recollection is startling. Young children who are hungry and thirsty are provided nourishment through an instrument designed for an animal. This is established through the claim of care and protection. Perhaps, this gesture may also represent love in the mind of the White mistress. Who can imagine the early developments of a slave child's identity construction, sense of belonging, and conceptualizing of shared-space within this context?

1. Yetman, *When I Was a Slave*, 31.

Evans displays the subtle presence of a skewed inversion of morality. This event was deemed good, and by inference, the mistress was good too. The very nature of how Evans defined who and what as good is challenged by its association with an unacknowledged dehumanizing act, initiated by the self-dehumanized mistress, who consequently dehumanizes the Black children she attempts to care for. The mistress blurred the lines between Black humanity and farm animals. Stated differently, the mistress lacked the self-awareness to recognize how she was dehumanized by participating in the institution of slavery, and how participation created a form of self-dehumanization, which distorted her *good* intentions.

Evans, conditioned by slavery, lacked the self-awareness to question the mistress's dehumanizing act. For Evans, her mistress was unquestionably righteous. The mistress, as an Anglo-American who represented Whiteness, was the beneficiary of the illusion of sanctification and love. This was a quasi-religious, sociopolitical articulation of sanctification and love that supposedly cleansed her thoughts and actions from any immoral and dehumanizing taint. Paternalistic White Supremacy distorts genuine empathy and love. There is a secular and religious element of this distortion. These elements are created from an unacknowledged *collusion* between the master and slave who have unknowingly succumbed to the taint of essentialist and racialized-binary reasoning. This too is observed in Evans's account of her Master and Mistress' religious beliefs. Evans explains,

> We had de best mistress and master in de world, and dey was Christian folks and dey taught us to be Christianlike too. Every Sunday mornin' Old Master would have all us niggers to de house while he would sing and pray and read the Bible to us all. Old Master taught us not to be bad he taught us to be good. He told us to never steal nor to tell false tales and not to do anything dat was bad. He said: "You will reap what you sow; dat you sow it single and reap double." I learned dat when I was a little child and I aint forgot it yet. When I got grown I went to de Baptist way. God called my pa to preach, and Old Master let him preach in de kitchen and in de back yard under the trees. On preachin' day Old Master took his whole family and all de slaves to church with him.[2]

The perception of the master and mistress' righteousness is reinforced by Evans's statement that they were Christian. The secular and religious spheres are united, creating a quasi-justification for Evans's

2. Yetman, *When I Was a Slave*, 32.

worldview, and perceived righteous relationship with her master and mistress. Evans is invoking the divinity in her skewed relationship, creating a religious justification for its existence. She attempts to crystalize this claim by stating that she and her family were evangelized into the Christian faith by her master and mistress. Evans is unable to acknowledge their moral contradiction and hypocrisy. She cannot see the need or value in judging their motives. Therefore, she cannot entertain the possibility that these biblical principles, employed by the people she has deep affection for, were framed in a way that reinforced her identity as a slave. They were not intended to cultivate a loving relationship and wilful obedience to her spiritual Master, Yahweh.

Christian ethics, and divine rewards for obedience, were preached to Evans to strengthen her loyalty to a dehumanizing religiopolitical system. Evans does not question the moral legitimacy of slavery. The institution, like her master, is endowed with a form of unquestionable righteousness. With this, the greatest irony is that the righteous master, and mistress, who are situated within their world of cognitive dissonance, and confirmatory bias, lack the self-awareness to understand the divine judgment that they are subjected to, are represented in part by the very reaping and sowing principles they preach to their slaves. Divine judgment, at least for some, occurs from Yahweh simply leaving individuals and communities to their own vices—self-destruction vis-à-vis unacknowledged self-dehumanization. We have a testimony of this by the Apostle Paul in Romans 1:28, "And just as they did not see fit to acknowledge God, God gave them up to a depraved mind, to do those things that are not proper."

In Galatians, Paul outlines the tension between unacknowledged bondage to the Law, which is concealed through the perception of *earning* righteousness from obedience to it, that stands against genuine freedom, only experienced in Jesus as the Christ. His discussion presents a slight parallel to the slave and master's bondage and conceptions of sociopolitical freedom. In this context, I elaborate further on my view that some Eurocentric Christians created a dehumanizing *interpretation* of the Law as a representative of the slave master's and mistress's authority, through the social construction of Whiteness, and the institution of slavery.

The slave's obedience to them endows the slave with the perception of a skewed form of righteousness. Evans articulates such a view by further describing her relationship with her master and mistress, as the Civil War waned: "Old Master didn't want to part with his niggers, and de niggers didn't want to part with Old Master, so dey thought by comin' to Arkansas dey could have a chance to keep dem."³ Sociopolitical freedom is rejected, viewed as an intrusion into the delicate world created through the collusion between Evans, her slave family, and their paternalistic master and mistress. Evans's ultimate allegiance and devotion are to them, not to Christ.

Sociopolitical freedom, to some extent, is reinterpreted as an impending doom that is forced upon the slave and their *loving* relationship to their Masters. From this perspective, *escaping* to Arkansas was a desperate attempt to maintain their skewed perspective of reality, predicated on their co-dependent relationship. However, Evans acknowledges that freedom was in Arkansas too. Her master and three other slaves died during their journey to Arkansas. He was brought back to North Carolina, and Evan's mistress eventually returned to her and the other slaves after his burial.

Evan's testimony displays a startling but common bond between some slaves and their masters. This is epitomized by a statement she recounts, one that many slaves heard from their former masters and mistresses after the Civil War: "Old Mistress begged us to stay with her, and we stayed till she died."⁴ The co-dependency between slave and master typically expressed itself in various ways. For instance, some masters, perceiving the slave to have no intrinsic value, viewed their slaves as *chattel*. These masters did not have any emotional or psychological attachment to their property. Secondly, other masters tended to function in a state of visible contradiction, and confusion, as they were knowledgeable of an emotional and psychological attachment to their slaves but opted to suppress their feelings. With the suppression of their feelings came the unacknowledged suppression of their humanity. These masters refrained from cultivating any form of *healthy* attachment and intimacy with their *property*. Lastly, a third group of masters, aware of their emotional and psychological attachment, could not acknowledge its distortion but attempted to cultivate a healthy relationship with their slaves. These *good* masters expressed obvious affection for their slaves. However, they could not assess to what extent this affection made them completely dependent upon their slaves.

Evans's mistress became self-aware of her eventual loneliness in the world, and impending death, without a loving husband and family of

---

3. Yetman, *When I Was a Slave*, 35.
4. Yetman, *When I Was a Slave*, 35.

slaves to support her. This incited the mistress's begging, or *request*, to keep her slave family intact. The mistress's biological children were adults with their own families. It is interesting to observe how and why many masters and mistresses opted to spend their last years on earth with their slaves, and not their own children. Nevertheless, the mistress's request was forced from acknowledging her *former* slave's current sociopolitical freedom, but it was also a request that was structured to manipulate Evans, according to her identity as a slave, which was cultivated by the mistress's identity as a motherly figure to her. A master and mistress's authority ceases to exist as freedom eradicates the power of obligation. However, coerciveness is continually tainted when it is employed to elicit a certain response from the space of psychological bondage.

Naturally, many slaves did not share the same experiences and sentiments as Evans. We observe an interesting contrast between her account and that of another slave, named Mrs. Malinda Discuss. Discuss provides a concise and direct articulation of the contradiction and hypocrisy many Anglo-American Christians exhibited. She demonstrates a level of self-awareness that wrestles with the fragmentation of colonial Whiteness and the degradation of the White conscience:

> Our Master took his slaves to meetin' with him. There was always something about that I couldn't understand. They treated the colored folks like animals and would not hesitate to sell and separate them, yet they seemed to think they had souls and tried to make Christians of them.[5]

Discuss, as I interpret her, struggled to explain the presence of what we define as confirmatory bias and cognitive dissonance within Anglo-American proslavery Christians. The conflict between, and contradictory nature of dehumanization and humanization, are displayed in Discuss's statement tha, the inhumane treatment of the slaves could not be synthesized with evangelizing them into the Christian faith. Obedience to the Great Commission does not dissolve an individual and community from the sins they have submitted to, which not only distorts the essence of their calling into spiritual service but opposes the God who requests them. Through the testimonies of Evans and Discuss concerning the relationship between slave and master, we may ask ourselves, "Who is the real slave?

---

5. Mellon. *Bullwhip Days*, 190.

An unacknowledged form of slavery is slavery of the mind and spirit, whereby the individual and community relinquish their humanity through choosing to exist in a way that opposes their divine purpose for existing. Gross immorality, which the Apostle Paul articulates, is a broad category of self-dehumanizing thought, reason, and action. Paul is not, nor am I, minimizing or dismissing the dehumanizing nature of physical slavery. I am merely discussing a specific misconception of the colonial masters and mistresses, that they were not emotionally and psychologically damaged through the dehumanization of the human-Other. Physical, psychological, and emotional slavery are deeply connected. This is a neglected, if not entirely dismissed, view in relation to the Anglo-American master and mistress. We have further testimony of this articulated by colonial African-Americans, J. H. Banks (1833–?), Charles Ball (1780–?), and Austin Stewart (1793–1869).

J. H. BANKS (1833–?)

J. H. Banks (1833–?) was an escaped slave from Rockingham County, Virginia, and a friend of an influential ex-slave named, James W. C. Pennington (1807–1870).[6] Banks articulates one of the earliest African-American acknowledgments of how essentialist and racialized-binary reasoning was expressed by some Anglo-Americans. Banks experienced trauma from the loss of his two sisters, Charlotte and Martha, who were purchased by slave masters from differing cities. Banks was close to Charlotte but had a deeper connection to his younger sister, Martha.

Banks was told by his master that Martha was sold to another master who lived in the city of Gardensville. The pain of Martha being sold had triggered a dormant bitterness and resentment towards his master that Banks had relatively suppressed. Yet, for Banks, the potentiality of experiencing a crippling amount of depression and hatred for his master was soothed with the psychological and emotional anesthesia of knowing he could visit Martha once a year. Gardnesville was located within a reasonable traveling distance from Banks. However, with good reason, Banks did not trust his master and sought to verify what was told to him. Devoid of essentialist and racialized-binary reasoning, Banks sought the assistance of a trusted *friend*, an Anglo-American named Mr. Kyte. Kyte knew of Banks's sister, his master, and was quite familiar with the town of

---

6. Pennington, *Fugitive Blacksmith*.

Gardnesville. Kyte later informed Banks that Martha was purchased by a known slave trader in Gardensville, but was eventually sold to a master in Richmond, Virginia. Upon hearing this, anger and confusion saturated Banks's conscious as he wondered "Why?" Why was slavery designed to strip slave families apart, selling brother from sister, daughter from father, and son from mother? Why would Banks's master lie to him? Every conceivable answer Banks reflected upon had hinged on the fulfillment of Anglo-American self-interest, despite the pain and suffering African-Americans experienced:

> He did it all for his own gain and for his own advantage. He did it without regard to my known and expressed feelings; he did it with the full knowledge that it would be like sending a dagger to my heart; he did it knowing that my aged parents would feel the shock. This was injury enough surely? Why then add insult to injury, by telling a bare-faced lie? A useless, mean, unmanly lie, which he must have known would come to light.[7]

For Banks, this unnecessary lie had no rationale for existing other than from a malicious intent to hurt him and his family. Banks confronts his master. Astonished and confused, his master attempted to regain control of the relationship by levying questions to Banks regarding how he became knowledgeable of his sister's whereabouts. After this tense discussion, Banks critically reflects upon an aspect of essentialist and racialized-binary reasoning that permeated within colonial America:

> If a poor coloured man, under some powerful temptation, deviates from the truth it is put down as an evidence of the moral inferiority of the race, and no excuse is admitted in extenuation, But Southern white men may tell lies for the accommodation of their own pockets, and yet it is all well. The slave is his property, and he may deceive him as he likes; there is no law to punish him for defrauding or perjuring himself to his slave. Will the Christian merchants of the world continue to uphold such a system through the medium of the cotton, sugar, or rice trade?[8]

Banks articulated the tension between two opposing moral standards. We witness the totalizing of African-Americans as a perpetual or inherently immoral creature. Lying, and by assumption thievery, were never permissible, even to the extent of slavery creating the contexts

---

7. Banks, *Narrative of Events*, 27
8. Banks, *Narrative of Events*, 27–28.

whereby they were necessary for survival. We witness semblances of this during the Civil Rights Movement. Anglo-Americans created contexts of anger, bitterness, and despair that fostered nihilistic actions from African-Americans. This complemented the binary-oppositional sets of ethics and morality that deceived Anglo-Americans into thinking they were not culpable. Colonial America displayed the rudiments of performances, games of collusion, and endless loops of self-deception that attempted to prostitute the human-Other for the self-interest of the human-Self.

The binary-oppositional sets of ethics and morality were constructed from the basic belief of Anglo-American superiority that justified blatant acts of immorality. Cognitive dissonance and confirmatory bias are important pillars within the structures of essentialist and racialized-binary reasoning. They create sequences of confusion, obsessiveness with power and domination, and self-deception. Banks is keenly aware of this through demonstrating its presence within a common experience among colonial African-Americans. For him and others, the separation of African-American families was a complex ethical and moral issue that influenced how American slave laws were shaped.

The inherent contradiction and hypocrisy of this reasoning lies in the permissibility and justification of inverting ethics and morality, based on the existence and self-interest of the human-Self. It is largely accepted as a historical fact that many proslavery Anglo-Americans lavished on their vices and practiced them to the extent of encouraging their slaves to do so. This is a form of self-dehumanization: the inability of the human-Self to gauge the extent of its oppressive nature, and how this oppresses the human-Other. Banks understood that the slaves existed without legal rights, and the absence of legal defense against injustice was an injustice itself. He concludes this discussion by associating his experiences with global Christianity's influence in initiating and maintaining the transatlantic slave trade. For him, the enslavement of Africans is also a socio-religious and theological issue.

Essentialist and racialized-binary reasoning persisted from colonialism to the Civil Rights Movement. This reasoning continued to saturate Anglo-American culture, influencing sociopolitical discourse, and theological interpretations that maintained a racialized caste system. Aspects of this were discussed clearly by King's confrontation and frustration with the Anglo-American churches. Yet, I assert that this reasoning did not have a strong presence with some colonial African-Americans, and conservative evangelicals throughout the twentieth century. Its popularity increased among the more militant and radical individuals within the culture. There are dismissed, ignored, and forgotten colonial African-American voices. I am merely highlighting some of the African-Americans who were aware of and sought to expunge essentialist and racialized-binary reasoning and the cycle of dehumanization from their lives. However, concern for European-Americans was deeply connected to their lives. J. H. Banks was an influential voice within this context. He rests alongside colonial evangelicals such as Jupiter Hammon, John Marrant, Maria Stewart, Julia Foote, and Francis Harper. I argue that their lives and literature challenge the distorted and perpetual attempts by some African-Americans to construct a mythic *Ideal-Blackness*—an Ideal-Blackness that represents what I believe is a seemingly endless search for a new Black aesthetics, a new Black identity, and a new Black subjectivity completely detached from Whiteness.

We must ask ourselves, how *new* is new when we perpetually seek to answer the same questions that lock us into the cycle of dehumanization and racial bondage. The blurring of fantasy and reality creates a space of ambiguity, deceiving us into thinking that we are nomads, people who lack a coalesced identity, sense of belonging, and conception of shared-space with the human-Other. I am concerned that we look upon our colonial foremothers and forefathers as naïve, unsophisticated, and inept, as if they have not wrestled with our contemporary issues, or even arrived at some relative peace, and conclusion regarding their identities, sense of belonging, and conceptions of shared-space. Nevertheless, Charles Ball provides another account of essentialist and racialized-binary reasoning via the cycle of dehumanization.

CHARLES BALL (1780–?)

Charles Ball was a Maryland slave who served in the US Navy within the Chesapeake Bay Flotilla, during the War of 1812.[9] In his 1837 autobiography, Ball expresses an acute awareness of White supremacist ideology, as he repeatedly references the deceptiveness and ignorance that pervaded proslavery Anglo-American culture. Ball does not employ essentialist and racialized-binary reasoning in his poignant assessment. However, his interpretation of Anglo-American culture develops upon

---

9. Weber, *Deep Like the Rivers*, 35, 101, 109, 158, 239; Baptist, *Half Has Never Been Told*, 1–2, 16–37, 111–31, 167–69; Sterling, *Slave Narrative*, 106–7, 226–27, 230, 232.

the subtle duality or binary-opposition that existed between anti-slavery and pro-slavery Anglo-Americans. This extended to the tension between Northern and Southern America:

> The system of slavery, as practised in the United States, has been, and is now, but little understood by the people who live north of the Potomac and the Ohio; for, although individual cases of extreme cruelty and oppression occasionally occur in Maryland, yet the general treatment of the black people is far more lenient and mild in that state, than it is farther south. This, I presume, is mainly to be attributed to the vicinity of the free state of Pennsylvania; but, in no small degree, to the influence of the population of the cities of Baltimore and Washington, over the families of the planters of the surrounding countries. For experience has taught me, that both masters and mistresses, who, if not observed by strangers, would treat their slaves with the utmost rigour, are so far operated upon, by a sense of shame or pride, as to provide them tolerably with both food and clothing, when they know their conduct is subject to the observation of persons, whose good opinion they wish to preserve. A large number of the most respectable and wealthy people in both Washington and Baltimore, being altogether opposed to the practice of slavery, hold a constant control over the actions of their friends, the farmers, and thus prevent much misery; but in the south, the case is widely different.[10]

Ball expresses an interesting power dynamic in the North. Tension exists between many wealthy Anglo-American antislavery advocates and the proslavery Anglo-American farmer/planter class. Whiteness is articulated as divided or fragmented through a moral and possible theological disagreement regarding the legitimacy of practicing slavery. This extended to *negotiating* a standard of humane treatment for northern African-Americans.

Ball also articulates the wealthy antislavery Anglo-Americans as valuing the humanity of the African-American slaves. He does not provide details explaining why and how this developed. According to Ball, Anglo-Americans used their sociopolitical power and cultural prestige to deter the dehumanization of northern slaves. Cruelty and violence were observed in the North, but the greater presence was witnessed in the South. Yet, the more disturbing issue is the northern antislavery Anglo-Americans' motivation for valuing their slave's humanity and abiding by

---

10. Ball, *Slavery in the United States*, 13.

a loose standard of humane treatment. The desire to acquire their sociopolitical self-interest, the fear of shame, sociocultural and racial pride, as well as wanting approval from wealthy Anglo-Americans, had taken precedence over acknowledging the dehumanizing nature of slavery and using cruelty and violence to maintain authority. Ball's account challenges us to identify who the slaves truly are in this context.

Ball describes the northern proslavery advocates as enslaved by their ignorance and vices. Their morality and ethics were devoid of a healthy understanding of slavery and equality with African-Americans. For him, the northern proslavery advocates were deceived by the belief that the wealthy antislavery Anglo-Americans would fulfill their self-interests. Moreover, the humanity of the slaves was reinterpreted as a narcissistic extension of proslavery Anglo-American cultural and sociopolitical self-interest. For most Anglo-Americans, African-American humanity was devoid of value beyond the existence of servitude. The humane treatment of the slaves was also a narcissistic extension. It was representative of proslavery Anglo-American sociocultural status or prestige. This contributed to the cognitive dissonance that shielded many proslavery advocates from entertaining the possibility that self-dehumanization could occur from dehumanizing the human-other.

Ball continues to emphasize the ignorance and cognitive dissonance of some northern Anglo-Americans. He attempts to penetrate the Anglo-American consciousness, causing them to acknowledge their ignorance of how southern African-American slaves were dehumanized. In this context, I interpret willful ignorance and cognitive dissonances as forms of self-dehumanization. Ball posits a solution to the northerner's ignorance:

> People of the northern states, who make excursions to the south, visit the principal cities and towns, travel the most frequented highways, or even sojourn for a time at the residences of the large planters, and partake of their hospitality and amusements, know nothing of the condition of the southern slaves. To acquire this knowledge, the traveller must take up his abode for a season, in the lodge of the overseer, pass a summer in the remote cotton fields, or spend a year within view of the rice swamps. By attending for one month, the court which the overseer of a large estate holds every evening in the cotton-gin yard, and witnessing the execution of his decrees, a Turk or a Russian would find the tribunals of his country far outdone.[11]

---

11. Ball, *Life and Adventures*, 14.

Ball reinterprets African-American humanity as the means from which to judge the ignorance and naivete of some Anglo northerners. *Excursion* is an interesting word he uses to describe the activity of some northerners visiting the South. The word provokes the imagery of a vacation, pleasure, and leisure. The *purpose* of these trips provides another element of Anglo-American self-interest. Ball supports this by mentioning the locations visited by northern Anglo-Americans, such as popular cities/towns, frequented highways, and large plantations with the intent of indulging in Southern comforts. For Ball, the purpose, and destinations of northern Anglo-American excursions in the South had created their ignorance and cognitive dissonance towards the dehumanization of the Southern slaves. These excursions also deaden the northern Anglo-American consciousness in comprehending how the humanity of the slave and master are interdependent.

Ball's solutions to this problem require a shift in intent, a transformation of consciousness, and a change in social locations. Ideally, he attempts to establish curiosity within the Anglo-American regarding the slave's plight. This would progress to sympathy and mature into the empathy many of the wealthy northern antislavery Anglo-Americans embodied. Ball encourages the reader to reflect upon a greater level of intimacy. We can associate this with principles of humanization. Northern Anglo-Americans must wilfully set aside the narcissistic aspect of their self-interest. Only then can they selflessly graft within their self-interest, the self-interest of the slave. The African-American slave, at one point, interpreted as the *invisible-other*, becomes visible and rehumanized through the process of Anglo-Americans understanding their dehumanized condition.

I use the term *invisible-other* to reference the slave as perceived by the northern Anglo-American visitor. It also connects to the Southern illusion of a sophisticated slave economy, cultural tranquillity, and the slave's complicity to the *peculiar institution*. The humanity of the southern slave is reinterpreted as a hidden, obscure, or transparent *object* that you could sense. The slaves were some *things* easily avoided, dismissed, and ignored. Ball repositions African-American humanity into the northern Anglo-American conscious. He humanizes both groups by advocating intimate interaction among them within specific locations and spaces: the lodge of overseers, remote cotton fields, within rice swamps, and the cotton-gin yard where the overseers exercised their authority over the slaves. Nevertheless, Ball guides the reader to this central issue:

> It seems to be a law of nature, that slavery is equally destructive to the master and the slave; for whilst it stupefies the latter with fear, and reduces him below the condition of man, it brutalizes the former, by the practice of continual tyranny; and makes him the prey of all the vices which render human nature loathsome.[12]

Ball makes anthropological claims regarding the natural developments of the slave and master within the institution of slavery. He challenges us to reflect upon how principles of equality extend to the negative effects of oppression and violence. Principles of immorality and how we practice wickedness are not racialized. The supposed inferior races are not more prone to practicing and embodying them. These principles are non-racialized and universally applicable.[13]

Ball continually emphasizes how the oppressor and oppressed are simultaneously dehumanized through slavery. He insinuates that humans may have the ability to, but are not created to, oppress and dehumanize each other without everyone being tormented. For Ball, the practice of tyranny is a form of self-oppression. It also thrusts the practitioner into excessive debauchery. He is not gesturing to a superficial practice of immorality. He is referencing a level of debasement and perversion that makes visible what we define as evil. Wickedness is viewed within the master's conception of slavery. It is also witnessed in how Anglo-Americans define and treat their African-American slaves.

Ball's usage of the word *stupefy* is relegated to how slavery affects the slaves. The institution negates the natural human development of the individual and group. The slave is forced to embody fear of their master, insecurity regarding their existence, astonishment at their master's authority, and various aspects of shock in relation to the system itself. The Anglo-American philosophy and theology of the ideal slave installed and reinforced these and many more attributes within the African-American slave. Nevertheless, Ball attempts to rehumanize the aloof northerners. He deconstructs and replaces the structures of essentialist and racialized-binary reasoning. This is not an inversion of an inversion. Rather, Ball is

---

12. Ball, *Life and Adventures*, 14–15.

13. J. H. Banks, a fugitive slave from Alabama, had argued that, "I need not tell my reader here that a drunken master is a curse to a slave, as well as a drunken husband is to a wife; but a drunken master is a sevenfold greater curse to a slave than a drunken husband can be to a wife, since he has the power of life, liberty, work, food, and clothing, without any remedy at law. No vice, therefore, that slaveholders has, involves a slave in more evil than drunkenness. I have ever since a deep abhorrence of the habit of drunkenness." See Banks, *Life of Banks*, 16.

seeking to construct an inclusive bricolage of new identities, senses of belonging, and conceptions of shared spaces. Emulation is a subtle theme, as Ball encourages the aloof northerners to redefine themselves like the northern antislavery Anglo-Americans.

Many things must occur and be experienced before an individual acknowledges that self-dehumanization is an extension of dehumanizing the human-Other. Ball's suggestions to the northern Anglo-American sought to place them within contexts that fostered sincere *curiosity* for the southern African-American slave. In this context, curiosity is related to aspects of our human desires. In that, the more questions I have that are answered, the more knowledge I acquire, and this knowledge produces certain *desires* within me *for* the human-Other. This is a cultivated desire to know and build an edifying relationship with the human-Other. It is to set aside our self-interest, and to relinquish our compulsion to be the exclusive self-interest of the human-Other. We observe fragments of these theories within the literature of King, Niebuhr, and also the influential Jewish philosopher, Emmanuel Levinas. Levinas provides an interesting perspective on this issue:

> In Desire for Others—sociality—arises in a being who lacks nothing or, more exactly, arises beyond all that could be lacking or satisfying to him. In Desire the Ego goes out to Others in a way that compromises the sovereign identification of the Ego with oneself whose need is just nostalgia, and that the consciousness of need anticipates. Instead of completing or contenting me the movement towards Others involves me in a contingency that in one aspect didn't concern me and should leave me indifferent: what am I doing in this mess? Where does the shock come from, when I pass by, indifferent, under the gaze of Others?[14]

Levinas's words are what I imagine Ball was attempting to ease the aloof northern Anglo-American into, that a displacement of dehumanizing satisfaction into necessary dissatisfaction. Thus, we can interpret Ball's suggestions as creating an unusual trauma, a disturbance in the northern Anglo-American consciousness through a different form of intimacy with the African-American slave. In Ball's context, the discussion centers on what causes the Anglo-American to experience a sense of discomfort that leads to acknowledging and then reflecting upon a series of problems. One problem was the need to reevaluate how they perceived

---

14. Levinas, *Humanism of the Other*, 29.

the African-American slaves. This connects to how they constructed their identities, sense of belonging, and shared-spaces from those constellations of beliefs about them. These elements contribute to establishing a genuine, self-sacrificial, and loving desire for Others.

In this context, Anglo-Americans are forced to acknowledge that they cannot define their existence through the enslavement of the human-Other. Or, to phrase it another way, Anglo-Americans who identify as Whiteness via White supremacy must question their psychological stability, as well as how they perceive and relate to the human-Other. This questioning is the initial progression towards self-humanization, and humanization of the Other. Levinas remarks,

> The relation with Others challenges me, empties me of myself and keeps on emptying me by showing me every new resource. I did not know I was so rich, but I don't have the right to keep anything anymore. Is the Desire for Others appetite or generosity? The Desirable does not satisfy my Desire, it hollows me, nourishing me somehow with new hungers. Desire turns out to be a bounty.[15]

In Ball's context, the emptying of the human-Self is the relinquishing of White supremacist ideologies that formerly determined how Anglo-Americans constructed their identities, sense of belonging, and shared-spaces with the human-Other. This emptying involves a subsequent opening to new constructions of Anglo-American identities, sense of belonging, and constructions of shared-spaces that develop with the assistance of the African-American slaves and the emancipated. However, this was a process that a few Anglo-Americans underwent. Ball refuted the misconceptions and skewed propaganda that projected slavery as a humane institution. He confronted the ignorance of the pro-slavery northerners, forcing them to reflect upon how slavery dehumanized everyone. Ball was not alone in this assessment as Austin Stewart was another individual who was blessed to see reality as reality was, not how the fragmented conscience of self-dehumanized Anglo-Americans wanted things to be.

---

15. Levinas, *Humanism of the Other*, 29–30.

AUSTIN STEWART (1793–1869)

Austin Stewart was a former slave, teacher, and influential abolitionist.[16] He expressed similar sentiments to Charles Ball regarding Anglo-American society. In his narrative, Stewart recounts a series of abusive and dehumanizing events that expresses the various identities, conceptions of belonging, and shared-spaces between African and Anglo-Americans. One of the striking elements of Stewart's narrative is how he articulates the coldness, callousness, and emotionless demeanor of some Anglo-Americans within violent contexts that rival contemporary notions of sociopathology. Sin does not discriminate and neither does the devastating effects of Eurocentric and White Supremacist reasoning. Anglo-American women were no better than the men. Both exhibited a seared conscience.

Stewart presents an interesting description of his mistress that exemplifies the embodiment of contradiction and hypocrisy, the blurring between fantasy and reality, and the unacknowledged self-dehumanization we create by intentionally dehumanizing the human-Other. One of the consequences is the absence of concern, empathy, and love for the human-Other. The human-Self does not receive a sense of vitality from the care of the human-Other. Instead, it is either completely indifferent to the human-Self or they receive pleasure from their suffering. Regarding his mistress, Stewart explains,

> Mrs. Helm was a very industrious woman, and generally busy in her household affairs—sewing, knitting, and looking after the servants; but she was a great scold, continually finding fault with some of the servants, and frequently punishing the young slaves herself, by striking them over the head with a heavy iron key, until the blood ran; or else whipping them with a cowhide, which she always kept by her side when sitting in her room.[17]

Stewart's words invoke the imagery of a cruel woman who experiences boredom and relative uneasiness when everyone is peaceful with one another. Within her, the principles of morality and immorality are inverted, and a sense of order and stability is achieved partly through the abuse of Black humanity. She may be the cultural ideal of a delicate, pure, and dignified Anglo-American Christian woman, but she is also a

---

16. Weber, *Like the Rivers*, 4, 76, 90, 104, 107–8, 133, 135, 140; Sterling, *Slave Narrative*, 36, 189–93.

17. Stewart, *Twenty-Two Years*, 24.

heartless brute who has lost the ability to genuinely experience compassion, empathy, and love for anyone deemed a slave. On one occasion, Stewart assigns Mrs. Helm as the instigator of his mother's brutal beating by their master. For Stewart, his mother did nothing to warrant punishment, let alone violence that an Anglo-American would not inflict upon an animal.

Another incident involved a severe flogging he received for breaking the lock to his master's shotgun. The traumatizing event involved another slave who was forced to participate in his punishment: "I was commanded to take off my clothes, which I did, and then master put me on the back of another slave, my arms hanging down before him and my hands clasped in his, where he was obliged to hold me with a viselike grasp."[18] This experience triggered Stewart to critically reflect upon how violence affected the slave and the master who enacted it to maintain authority. It is difficult for some people, often myself included, to grasp how the human psyche processes and is affected by the constant trauma of living within contexts of contradiction and hypocrisy. During colonialism, what society deemed abuse and degradation if imposed upon White flesh were reinterpreted as inflicting discipline and installing respect within the Black slave.

Stewart also articulates a common occurrence in the lives of some Black slaves, forced participation in the degradation of Black humanity. In this context, the participatory Black slave who aids their White master, experiences a more complex form of dehumanization, as they are grounded in reality but are forced to obey a corrupt authority figure which is cemented in a skewed Eurocentric inner world. The tension the White master makes between blurring fantasy and reality is the space of contradiction and trauma for the rational Black slave. Stewart continues with his account, articulating his view of reciprocal dehumanization between master and slave:

> Those cruelties are daily occurrences, and so degrading is the whole practice of Slavery, that it not only crushes and brutalizes the wretched slave, but it hardens the heart, benumbs all the fine feelings of humanity, and deteriorates from the character of the slave-holders themselves,—whether the man or woman. Otherwise, how could a gentile, and in other respects, amiable woman, look on such scenes of cruelty, without a shudder of utter abhorrence? But slaveholding ladies, can not only look on

18. Stewart, *Twenty-Two Years*, 25.

> quietly, but with approbation; and what is worse, though very common, they can and do use the lash and cowhide themselves, on the backs of their slaves, and that too on those of their own sex! Far rather would I spend my life in a State's Prison, than be the slave of the best slave-holder on the earth![19]

Within this context, Stewart returns to his critique of his mistress and Anglo-American women. They were the instigators and perpetrators of violence upon Black flesh, including those of Black women. Racial solidarity via Whiteness transcended universal femininity. Violence, cruelty, and dehumanization partly defined the identities, sense of belonging, and shared-spaces between master, mistress, and slave. Stewart's discourse, like Ball's, directly focuses on the degrading effects of slavery upon the master. He gives close attention to how the heart, feelings, and character of the proslavery Anglo-American were transformed. For Stewart, the descent into self-dehumanization occurred when we relinquished compassion, sentiment, and moral and ethical consideration for the human-Other.

Various Anglo-American Christians, churches, and proslavery theology were extremely fragmented because they embraced principles of dehumanization, reinterpreted as divinely ordained means of maintaining God's creative order. Unknowingly, they all embraced continual psychological and spiritual fragmentation, the distortion of their humanity, and their relationship with Yahweh, stemming from a total disregard for non-White humanity. The blurring of fantasy and reality distorted the collective conscience of some Anglo-American Christians who could no longer discern how slavery was antithetical to the essence of Christianity. Stewart provides a poignant account that demonstrates this level of detachment from reality into an idolatrous Eurocentric inner world.

Stewart had a loving sister who was also the mother of a few children. She was also considered a good servant. Stewart recounts an event one Sabbath morning as he was traveling to church to ring the bell, announcing to everyone within a listening ear that it was time to worship the Lord. As he was walking to church he described a horrific event:

> I heard the most piteous cries and earnest pleadings issuing from the dwelling. To my horror and the astonishment of those with me, my poor sister made her appearance, weeping bitterly, and followed by her inhuman master, who was polluting the air

---

19. Stewart, *Twenty-Two Years*, 26.

> of that clear Sabbath morning, with the most horrid imprecations and threatenings, and at the same time flourishing a large raw-hide. Very soon his bottled wrath burst forth, and the blows, aimed with all his strength, descended upon the unprotected head, shoulders and back of the helpless woman, until she was literally cut to pieces. She writhed in his powerful grasp, while shriek after shriek cried away in heart-rending moanings; and yet the inhuman demon continued to beat her, though her pleading cries had ceased, until obliged to desist from exhaustion of his own strength.[20]

The reader is presented with an overwhelming scene. It is difficult to imagine a loving person beating another human to the point they lose consciousness, or at the very least, can no longer express their pain. This is attached to the thought that the victim's pain, suffering, and cries are not adequate signs of the victimizer's boundaries or limitations. Rather, it is the victimizer's energy or endurance that depletes to the point of creating exhaustion. The inability to physically continue the assault is what stops the vicious act. It was not God's voice, a descending angel, the screams of agony from Stewart's sister, or the master's conscience that simply said, "That's enough."

Stewart was caught in a dehumanizing situation. He had to witness the torment of his sister relating to the reality of his sociopolitical weakness, the inability to help stop her abuse. Stewart expresses the difficulty of knowing he was physically capable of defending his sister, but a short-term moral victory would not shield them from the greater reality of both being killed by their master. He continues,

> What a spectacle was that, for the sight of a brother? The God of heaven only knows the conflict of feeling I then endured; He alone witnessed the tumult of my heart, at this outrage of manhood and kindred affection. God knows that my will was good enough to have wrung his neck; or to have drained from his heartless system its last drop of blood! And yet I was obliged to turn a deaf ear to her cries for assistance, which to this day ring in my ears. Strong and athletic as I was, no hand of mine could be raised in her defence, but at the peril of both our lives; nor could her husband, had he been a witness of the scene, be allowed any things more than unresisting submission to any

---

20. Stewart, *Twenty-Two Years*, 96–97.

cruelty, any indignity which the master saw fit to inflict on *his wife*, but the other's slaves.[21]

Stewart crafts a vivid picture of the rupturing of his humanity relating to the inhumanity of his master. God is introduced into this discussion as the only person who can sense and feel Stewart's anger, pain, and helplessness from his sister's abuse. God was participatory in His children's suffering. Yet, He was not the person or force to stop the slave master. For Stewart, the master's authority within colonial America usurped the husband's will and natural rights. Stewart expresses his frustration to the reader that the slave laws in America conditioned Black people to submit to the authority of White people. American culture and its slave laws also elevated mere animals above Black humanity.[22] We must ask ourselves if these forms of violence were within the American Church. Were Black bodies senselessly beaten inside church walls from insignificant or minor infractions according to the White master and mistress' whim?

Conceptions of holiness and sanctification undergo revision within the Eurocentric and White Supremacist conscience. During colonialism, many Anglo-Americans did not believe the Gospel was intended for the slave, and if it was, the slave's salvation did not infer any spiritual or sociopolitical equality. We must take this into consideration within the context of Stewart's sister being viciously beaten on a Sunday morning before Church service. Stewart must struggle with his weakness, helplessness, and vulnerability in the sight of his loved one's pain and suffering. He continues to describe another troubling scene, stating,

> Well, I finally passed on, with a clinched fist and contracted brow, to the church, and rung the bell, I think rather furiously, to notify the inhabitants of Bath, that it was time to assemble for the worship of that God who has declared himself to be "no respecter of persons." With my own heart beating wildly with indignation and sorrow, the kind reader may imagine my feelings when I saw the smooth-faced hypocrite, the inhuman slave-whipper, enter the church, pass quietly on to his accustomed seat, and then meekly bow his hypocritical face on the damask cushion, in the reverent acknowledgment of that religion which teaches its adherents "to do unto others as they would be done by," just as if nothing unusual had happened on that Sabbath morning. Can any one wonder that I, and other slaves, often

---

21. Stewart, *Twenty-Two Years*, 97.
22. Stewart, *Twenty-Two Years*, 98.

doubted the sincerity of every white man's religion? Can it be a matter of astonishment, that slaves often feel there is no just God for the poor African? Nay, verily; and were it not for the comforting and sustaining influence that these poor, illiterate and suffering creatures feel as coming from an earthly source, they would in their ignorance all become infidels. To me, that beautiful Sabbath morning was clouded in midnight darkness, and I retired to ponder on what could be done.[23]

Romans 2:11 is invoked by Stewart. Calling our attention to one of many verses that demonstrated the character of God and how he viewed humanity. The verse also presents itself as a passive critique and judgment of America, a nation claiming to stand for religious and secular freedom yet occupied by Eurocentric and White supremacist Christians and their proslavery theology. Stewart allows the reader the opportunity to feel his anger, frustration, and pain. He demonstrates some of the more intense moments of a slave's life, whereby commonsense and basic comprehension of morality provide keen insight into the skewed psyche of Anglo-American society, but they are relatively socio-politically helpless to stand against it. What occurs within a grounded psyche that is forced to fight against an oppressive worldview of those who have sociopolitical power over them? Does the victim feel a psychological tug or pulling that drifts them from their grounding in reality into the distorted inner world of the oppressor? In this context, how does an individual call upon God, and how does He respond to these types of crises?

Stewart's master exhibits emotional, psychological, and spiritual detachment from our common humanity with one another, and it complements the dismissal of specific verses that support this biblical truth and more. Stewart grows increasingly frustrated and angry by the lack of concern and care from his master towards his mother and sister. This lack of care for the Black-Other influences and in return is influenced by the rejecting and replacement of biblical conceptions of God. The sanctified space of the American Church, at least for some Anglo-Americans, could not be desecrated by their thoughts and actions.

The Golden Rule of Matthew 7:12 is another verse Stewart employs. With it, he continues to passively scrutinize Anglo-American culture and Christianity. It would be completely irrational for a person to desire abuse and to be dehumanized by individuals who do not care for them. If this is accurate, then we are forced to reflect on whether someone can

23. Stewart, *Twenty-Two Years*, 98–99.

dehumanize another person and practice the Golden Rule. Stewart is demonstrating his knowledge of scripture relating to his self-awareness, which is placed alongside those proslavery Anglo-Americans. Yet he, like other African-Americans, can be interpreted as revealing those things that severely impair the maturation of our humanity and love for the human-Other. Stewart also employs in his argument the principle of God identifying Himself with humanity to the extent that what we do for a person, we do for Him too (Mark 9:41; Matt 25:40). This is another way Stewart associates Black existence as a creation of God.

There are elements of dismay and frustration from Stewart relating to why some Anglo-Americans cannot fathom why some African-Americans reject Christianity. Oppression from Anglo-American Christians was a primary reason for some African-Americans to reject Jesus. Yet, within the distorted conscience of proslavery Eurocentric and White supremacist Christians, it was they, as the entirety of the White race, who were the epitome of the biblical principles of the "light of the world," and the "salt of the earth." They convinced themselves there was no contradiction in beating their slaves for insignificant reasoning on a Sabbath day before church service.

Cognitive dissonance and confirmatory bias forces us to no longer see what is directly in front of us. They caused many people during colonialism to ignore the presence of a heightened Black self-awareness that was the assistant for some Anglo-Americans to free themselves from the bondage of racism and return to Christ Jesus.

The institution of slavery stripped humanity from its participants in ways that escaped their consciousness. Many Anglo-Americans were unaware that their supposed economic, psychological, religious, and sociopolitical benefits from the institution were the instruments that corrupted their humanity. For example, many slaveholding families were destroyed because of internal disagreements and conflicts. James W. C. Pennington, an African-American abolitionist and minister stated,

> There is no one feature of slavery to which the mind recurs with more gloomy impressions, than to its disastrous influence upon the families of the masters; physically, pecuniarily, and mentally. It seems to destroy families as by a powerful blight, large and opulent slave-holding families, often vanish like a group of shadows at the third or fourth generation.[24]

24. Pennington, *Fugitive Blacksmith*, 69, 69–73.

It is impossible to eliminate what God has ordained and established as part of His creative order. Humans are dependent upon one another. Our humanity is interconnected and interdependent. We cannot flourish as God intended for us when we deny one another's humanity which consequently has us denying God's creative order. We can make decisions and courses of action that influence us into imprisoning ourselves within an idolatrous inner world. We become quasi-gods with no stability in our inner worlds, and it is only God who can save us. Another layer of difficulty is that God often uses the very things and people we discredit and dehumanize to be the conduits of forgiveness, reconciliation, and redemption.

We must ask ourselves if the same principles that existed within colonialism are influencing us today. If so, then perhaps the colonial Evangelical African-Americans whom God used to transform America then are representative of those who may be currently ignored, dismissed, and rejected because they do not represent the contemporary ideals of progress and freedom, which are at least in part, forms of cloaked self-dehumanization through the dehumanization of the human-Other. I now turn to a dialogue between Jarena Lee (1783–1864) and Old Elizabeth (1766–ca. 1863).

4

Jarena Lee (1783–1864) and "Old Elizabeth" (1766–ca. 1863)

A Dialogue Between the Preacher Who Wrestled with Satan and the Humble Servant of Christ

"For the desire of the flesh is against the Spirit, and the Spirit against the flesh; for these are in opposition to one another, in order to keep you from doing whatever you want."

(Gal 5:17)

JARENA LEE WAS A remarkable woman who shared a unique spiritual and cultural bond with other African-American women.[1] Her life represented a particular normalcy, a disheartening narrative for those who desired to place their ministry within a locally organized church. Yet, the glory Lee and others received was not from a denomination, men, or secular organization. Their glory was from Yahweh, fulfilling His Word to His children who served Him with the entirety of their being. "Old Elizabeth," a ninety-seven-year-old African-American evangelist, is included within Lee's community.[2] Both women were contemporaries of John Chavis (ca. 1763–1838), "Black" Harry Hosier (ca. 1750–1806), and Lemuel Haynes

---

1. Andrews, *Sisters of the Spirit*; *Classic African American Women's Narratives*; Moody, *Sentimental Confessions*; Peterson, *Doers of the Word*; Carter, *Race*; Lindley, *You Have Stept Out of Your Place*, 118, 179, 180–81.

2. Elizabeth, *Memoir of Old Elizabeth*.

(1753–1833).³ Elizabeth was illiterate but refused to allow this to deter her from serving Christ. She defied perpetual opposition, mostly from Christians within her denomination (Methodism), not from atheists, agnostics, or anyone deemed spiritually lost. Perseverance, loyalty, and faithfulness describe Elizabeth's character and relationship with YHWH.

Galatians 5:17 generally describes both women's internal struggle to preserve their lives before salvation.⁴ The conflict appeared necessary and led them to the final confirmation of their salvation in Christ Jesus. The verse also characterizes the strife to understand, confirm, and fulfill their calling from God. Stating this another way, their flesh and spirits warred within them, determining the trajectory of their lives and their potential ceasing via suicide. Lee and Elizabeth display a form of Christian realism that encourages Christians to be transparent, and vulnerable to achieve healing via the Spirit, and progress to glorifying God in their brokenness. I will place Lee and Elizabeth in dialogue with each other. I aim to express their contextualized theologies and embodiments of classical evangelical African-American feminism. The lives of Lee and Elizabeth demonstrate the different forms of Christian spirituality that shaped their identities, sense of belonging, and conceptions of shared spaces with the human-Other rooted in preaching and evangelism.

Historically, Lee is acknowledged as the first African-American woman to preach publicly devoid of a denomination's authority. The uniqueness of Lee's testimony stems from her internal struggles and sheer

---

3. Woodson, *History of the Negro Church*, 44, 46–48, 49–51; Anyabwile, *Faithful Preacher*; Anyabwile and Haynes, *May We Meet in the Heavenly World*; Peck and Haynes, *Descent on the Universal Plan*; Cooley, *Sketches of the Life*; Simmons and Thomas, *Preaching with Sacred Fire*; Othow and Chavis, *African American Patriot*; Kaplan, *Black Presence*, 73–108.

4. African-American scholar Tony Evans focuses on the explicit Pauline view of the "civil war happening in every Christian." For Evans, the conflict also manifests itself biblically between the Torah and God's grace. Submission to God is the sole means to overcoming this internal struggle as, "We are empowered by our relationship with the Holy Spirit." Brad R. Braxton complements Evans's view by emphasizing the communal and social consequences of our internal battle between flesh and spirit. Social injustice vis-à-vis vulture capitalism and racism are two dominant realities within the Western world. Braxton insightfully demonstrates this through his statement, "Similarly, contemporary Christian understandings of salvation or sanctification that do not address social realities misrepresent the truth of the incarnation. Christ was embodied in order to liberate embodied people from embodied problems. Spiritual people do not retreat from 'the world' in order to avoid moral contamination. Rather, the Holy Spirit compels believers to engage the world with the hopes of returning to *holiness* and *wholeness*" (Evans, *Tony Evans Bible Commentary*, 1212). See Blount, *True to Our Native Land*, 344.

will to overcome those struggles. Her efforts centered on inner conflict regarding the self-awareness of her sins, and an external spiritual battle with whom she believed was Satan. Connected to these two conflicts was the overt racism and sexism of colonial American society, regarding her existence as an African-American female evangelist and preacher. These three issues are related and cannot be separated. They were overcome by Lee's strong will to understand her struggles and access her abilities, not in isolation, but through the power of the Holy Spirit within her love and commitment to Christ. Lee's life expressed what she believed was God's desire for her salvation, His reluctance to allow her to suffer alone, and ultimately her willful acceptance of Him as her Lord and Savior.

Elizabeth has a similar testimony. It stemmed from a path of humility and relative obscurity. Her story is seldom mentioned in academic textbooks and liberal historiographies focused on power, emancipation, and distinct ideals of *Blackness*. Elizabeth was simply a woman who loved Christ, committed herself to glorifying Him, and ministered to anyone who desired to hear about Him through her faith. This is the glory and reward of most Christians, which transcends earthly acknowledgments. Like Lee, Elizabeth struggled with her Christian faith, relating primarily to her call to preach and her opposition to skewed patriarchal Christianity. She often expressed sentiments of being unworthy, which was always refuted through the Spirit's voice and presence that confirmed her worthiness. From this vantage point, she and Lee shared a spiritual bond despite never meeting. They struggled to understand the overwhelming presence and healing from God's grace and love, over and against awareness of their sins and the oppression of *man's traditions*.

My interpretation of Lee and Elizabeth emphasizes how they willingly chose their *identities*, created a *sense of belonging*, and established *shared spaces* as evangelical African-American women. Overall, their lives embodied the unavoidable presence of someone greater than themselves, the Judean Christian Godhead, and the increasing desire to experience the fullness of God. For Lee, this included defeating her insecurity and the adversary who attempted to end her life. Elizabeth struggled to understand the fallacy of seeking divine confirmation through human agency. I argue their identities, ministries, and relationships with Christ culminated through experiencing and ministering through their baptisms of *suffering* and of the *Spirit*. Both baptisms were intertwined, not sequential, and further clarified their conceptions of sin (hamartiology), the Holy Spirit (pneumatology), and Christ Jesus (Christology).

Lee's baptisms were experienced as an emancipated African-American female who did not experience the atrocities and dehumanization that countless slave women did. She did not endure oppression under the whip of an enslaver or overseer. Nor did she toil from sunup to sundown within a cotton field or serve a master and his family in the plantation's *great White house*. However, Lee did not have to experience these realities to understand what it meant and felt to be an African-American woman during colonial slavery. She was fully aware of the natural and divine blessings she received from the Lord and dedicated her life to serving Christ with a genuine appreciation of said blessings. Elizabeth's spirituality was slightly different. Her spiritual struggle was deeply connected to the absence of close relationships, and the necessary forms of confirmation we derive from them. She spent much of her early life as a servant. Time away from her family was the conduit of emotional and psychological trauma. Isolation from family, seeking acceptance by a community, and attempts to confirm her divine calling were the contexts from which Elizabeth experienced the baptisms of suffering and the Spirit.

The duality of sociopolitical and religious freedom shaped Lee and Elizabeth's characters. Equality, self-sacrifice, and reconciliation were central principles of their ministries as evangelists and preachers. Like many others, Lee and Elizabeth's narrative begins during their childhood. Childhood for many colonial African Americans served as the genesis for their narrative, which culminated in their salvation within Christ Jesus. These narratives often leave the reader speculating about the unwritten nuances of their life in Christ and fuller explanations of their theologies. Lee exposes the reader to a verse that describes her calling from God and serves as the bridge to retelling her early life.

> The Life and Religious Experience of Jarena Lee,
> A Coloured Lady,
> Giving An Account of Her Call to
> Preach the Gospel
> Revised and Corrected from the
> Original Manuscript
> Written by Herself.
>
> "And it shall come to pass . . . that I will pour out My Spirit upon all flesh; and your sons and your *daughters* shall prophesy"
> (Joel 2:28)

A CALLING THROUGH CHRIST FOR THE HUMAN-OTHER

Joel 2:28 is a verse positioned at the frontispiece of Lee's narrative.[5] It is also an underlining theme throughout her discourse. This verse serves as a scriptural justification of Lee's spiritual calling into Christian ministry and, by extension, alludes to an aspect of her relationship with the Holy Spirit in Christ. However, it is interesting that she does not include the latter portion of verse 28, which reads, "Your old men will have dreams, Your young men will see visions." Another noticeable exclusion is verse 2:29, "And even on the male and female servants I will pour out My Spirit in those days."[6] Lee chooses the original prophetic word over the New Testament fulfillment during Pentecost within Acts 2:17–18. The Old Testament usage may also allude to Lee emphasizing the importance of Joel as the prophet who provided this essential prophecy.

Regarding Joel 2:28, Lee's usage of the text reminds the reader of the biblical fulfillment of God's promise manifested within their present context. The universal declaration of the text transcends gender, race, and social status within colonial America. It is an introductory and subtle corrective against any dehumanizing contextualized theology that reinterprets the verse within excessive Eurocentric, patriarchal, and racialized lenses. Another significance of utilizing Joel 2:28 is within the prophet's character, the act of prophetic utterances, and the assumption of love that empowers the spiritual gift. Lee provides a statement of inference. A knowledgeable biblical reader would naturally understand the New Testament significance of Joel 2:28. Some unaware, if curious, would eventually come to understand the significance of the text, assessing its relevance to Lee's usage.

---

5. Demetrius K. Williams connects the biblical event of Pentecost to the Pentecostal movement initiated by African-American William J. Seymour and the universal participation of people from different ethnicities and races. Interestingly, Williams associates Seymour's belief in the destruction of racial barriers, not speaking in tongues, as the confirmation of the Spirit's presence among people. Williams also references Julia A. J. Foote's being influenced by this same prophecy within Joel. See Blount, *Native Land*, 218–20; Evans, *Tony Evans Bible Commentary*, 1072.

6. "Moreover, I will give you a new heart and put a new spirit within you; and I will remove the heart of stone from your flesh and give you a heart of flesh. And I will put My Spirit within you and bring it about that you walk in My statutes and are careful and follow My ordinances" (Ezek 36:26–27). "'I will not hide My face from them any longer, for I will have poured out My Spirit on the house of Israel,' declares the Lord GOD" (Ezek 39:29). "'For this is the covenant which I will make with the house of Israel after those days,' declares the LORD: 'I will put My law within them and write it on their heart; and I will be their God, and they shall be My people'" (Jer 31:33–34).

Lee's usage of Joel 2:28 possibly relates to the Apostle Paul's message within 1 Corinthians 14. Pursuing genuine love within the context of the two New Testament commandments is the primary aim of all Christians (1 Cor 14:1; Luke 10:27). Paul recites in verse 14:3 the three general goals of genuine Christian prophecy as to edify, exhort, and console. For him, the emphasis, in part, is that a gift received from the Holy Spirit is not intended for the recipient's glorification. Nor, when used for the human-Other, is it to be done in such a divisive, selfish, and non-sacrificial way. Prophetic words edify the Body of Christ within and outside a local congregation and community. In this vein of reason, Lee signals to the reader that her narrative, ministry, and life are called to edify, exhort, and console *everyone*. Prophecy, visions, and dreams represent the relationship and communication between God and the believer, used in the task of edifying, exhorting, and consoling through a Christocentric conception of love. These become the foundation of Lee's identity, sense of belonging, and shared space with the human-Other.

Lee is demonstrating an aspect of her eschatology. The future period of the significant event that Joel spoke of from his present context, is Lee's current context, and she, as well as everyone not identified as the powerful and ideal of society, are living testimonies to God's fulfillment of His Word. They believe in scripture, are transformed by it, and become the embodiment of God's Word. Eschatology and pneumatology are conjoined as the Spirit signifies salvation, the designator of one's gifts (Eph 4), and the individual's performance of their gifts with and through the Holy Spirit. Yet, a subtle attack on misogynistic philosophies, Eurocentric Christianity, and colonial White supremacy is gleaned from Lee's solitary usage of Joel 2:28. Lee avoids an aggressive confrontation against those identifying with distorted contextualized theologies and sociopolitical philosophies by withholding Joel 2:29. For Lee, the Spirit of God is power upon everyone, regardless of gender, race, age, disability, social status, political affiliation, or denominational allegiance. The exclusion of verse 29 does not mitigate the usage of verse 28. Lee's life and ministry demonstrated the example of prophecy, dreams, and vision primarily articulated in the text.

For her narrative, Elizabeth employs another classic verse that signifies equality, harmony, and mutual self-sacrifice within the Body of Christ: Galatians 3:28, "There is neither Jew nor Greek, there is neither slave nor free, there is neither male nor female; for you are all one in Christ Jesus." This verse is couched between two complementary verses that collectively reinforce a central principle of Christianity, Jesus' ministry, and God's creative order through faith in His Son. Elizabeth's usage of Galatians 3:28 alludes to the justification of her ministry and expresses when she has always sought to glorify Christ Jesus.[7] Everyone, regardless of their gender, race, and social status, receives the same baptism into Christ, employing the same salvific faith that grafts them into the fulfillment of the Abrahamic covenant through Jesus.

My interpretations of Lee and Elizabeth are presented through an emphasis on their *Baptisms of the Holy Spirit* and *Suffering*. These are the differential lenses from which we can understand Lee's and Elizabeth's testimony. Their struggles in life, inside and outside of Christian ministry, represent the duality of these baptisms. The genesis of Lee and Elizabeth's testimonies begins at their birth and upbringing; connected to this are the psychologically questionable, ambiguous, and theologically troubling experiences that shaped this early period of their lives.

THE STRUGGLE TO DISCERN THAT VOICE

Suicidal Ideation and the Discovery of Christ

"But you do not believe, because you are not of My sheep. My sheep listen to My voice, and I know them, and they follow Me, and I give them eternal life, and they will never perish; and no one will snatch them out of My hand"[8] (John 10:26)

---

7. Braxton points out that Paul sought "the eradication of dominance, not the erasure of difference. When people enter the Christian community through belief in Christ and baptism, they do not lose the social distinctions that have characterized their lives" (Blount, *Native Land*, 340). Braxton, like others, cherishes human diversity as a part of God's creative order. In our contemporary period, many people categorize this as their complex identities that represent their attachment to various communities. Regardless of categories, we must accept the human-Other's distinctiveness and uniqueness through the Spirit to truly nurture their humanity. It becomes one of many ways to view the human-Other as Christ views them, observing one of the countless reasons He sacrificed His life on the cross. We, in turn, are provided a glimpse of the spiritual family we will live in eternity with at the culmination of our eschatological hope. Evans complements Braxton and this general view by stating, "No one is superior to anyone else before God. We all share equally in our relationship with him through Jesus. Thus, the Galatians didn't have to keep the law and undergo circumcision as the Judaizers insisted. They didn't have to become Jews. The Galatians already belonged to Christ (3:29)" (Evans, *Tony Evans Bible Commentary*, 1207).

8. Blount, *Native Land*, 198–99; Evans, *Tony Evans Bible Commentary*, 1041.

The date and place of Lee's birth and the age she departed from her parents mark the point of departure of her narrative. She was born in 1783 in Cape May, New Jersey. Her parents remain nameless and impersonal to the reader, but her *client* is personalized. His name was Mr. Sharp. The distance from her parents was significant to Lee; sixty miles was considerable for a seven-year-old girl forced by financial circumstances to become a *bondservant*.[9] The reader is left wondering why Mr. Sharp deserved recognition when her parents were seemingly hidden. The importance of Lee's parents, at this point, was concerning their rejection of Christianity and their inability to teach Lee its ethics and morality. Perhaps in principle, this applies to Mr. Sharp and explains why he is personalized to the reader.

Lee creates a unique correlation between the parental moral influence upon a child and the child's moral self-awareness within a context that requires its existence. Lee explained that her parents were not Christian, "being wholly ignorant of the knowledge of God."[10] Thus, they could not instill into her Judean Christian ethics, fulfilling the commandments of scripture such as Proverbs 22:6, "Train up a child in the way he should go, Even when he grows older he will not abandon it."[11] Spiritual and moral self-awareness are intertwined, and central to an individual and community's collective faith in and relationship with YHWH. The rudiments of self-awareness within the individual are essential. The context(s) in which the rudiments are rooted creates the ability within the individual and community to hear a voice they later recognize as from God. Humanity may not designate this voice distinctly from Christ or the Spirit before their salvation, but they will learn to recognize Christ's voice as they grow closer to Him. It is a necessary component of their relationship. Unfortunately, Lee never learned this as a child and soon faced troubling consequences that she struggled to overcome.

---

9. Andrews, *Classic African American Women's Narratives*, 19.

10. Andrews, *Classic African American Women's Narratives*, 19.

11. This biblical principle is expressed throughout scripture (Deut 6:6–7, 11:19; Isa 54:13; Eph 6:4; 2 Tim 3:14–15). Evans does not withhold his belief that, at least in part, God's authority manifests on earth through familial relationships: "A vital way that biblical authority is made manifest in God's kingdom is through the family. That reality, in fact, stands behind one of the most well-known verses in the Bible: *Start a youth out on his way; even when he grows old he will not depart from it.* Child training involves making our teaching understandable so kids can differentiate between wisdom and foolishness as early as possible" (Evans, *Tony Evans Bible Commentary*, 603).

Parental figures were, as they still are, a necessary presence in the early development of African-American slave children. The absence of either parent deeply affected them, like us today, in ways that evaded their self-awareness. Yet, the inner drive for community and family wasn't destroyed during slavery despite countless contexts of familial separation.[12] The family structure of African Americans during colonial America was a fragmented but loving existence for many who crystallized their lives within Judean Christianity.[13] Elizabeth was birthed within an enslaved Christian family. She states,

> I was born in Maryland in the year 1766. My parents were slaves. Both my father and mother were religious people, and belonged to the Methodist society. It was my father's practice to read in the Bible aloud to his children every sabbath morning. At these seasons, when I was but five years old, I often felt the overshadowing of the Lord's Spirit, without at all understanding what it meant; and these incomes and influences continued to attend me until I was eleven years old, particularly when I was alone, by which I was preserved from doing anything that I thought was wrong.[14]

Here we witness the positive influences of Christian parenting and how God honors it, as depicted within His Word. Elizabeth recounts sensing the presence of the Spirit at a young age, devoid of formal theological education or exposure to Christian authorities within a local church. God intentionally revealed Himself, making His presence unavoidable

---

12. The individual and family structure had undergone various types of abuses and trauma that emotionally, psychologically, physically, and spiritually ruptured their humanity. What started on African soil continued on slave ships and progressed in the New World as enslaved Africans started their new life of restoring kinship bonds. Historian Donald R. Wright articulates this by stating, "Even on slave ships they began seeking relatives. Children called friendly adults 'uncle' or 'aunt,' and adults tended to look after younger children whether or not they were related. Where slaves existed in some numbers on the English mainland there developed a broad pattern of slave children addressing all older slaves with kinship titles regarding them as the equivalent of relatives" (Wright, *African Americans in the Colonial Era*, 125). See Wright, *African Americans in the Colonial Era*, 124–29; Blassingame, *Slave Community*; Morgan, *Slave Counterpoint*, 285, 512–19, 553–55; Weber, *Like the Rivers*, 68–70, 113, 114, 224–50; Sterling, *Slave Narrative*, 67, 79, 87; Baptist, *Slavery & Capitalism*, 36–37, 96, 106–7, 148, 171, 180–81, and photos 244, 289, 349.

13. Wright, *African Americans in the Colonial Era*, 131–33, 173. Morgan, *Slave Counterpoint*, 631–38, 644; Irons, *White and Black Evangelicals*; Sernett, *Black Religion & American Evangelicalism*, 17–18, 21, 110, 119, 170, 173–74; Weber, *Like the Rivers*, 43–48.

14. Elizabeth, *Old Elizabeth*, 3.

to a child from ages five to eleven (1 Sam 3:1–18). Human ignorance or the absence of knowledge does not prevent God from speaking to us. Nor does it negate the possibility of us learning about God and experiencing Him in mystical ways. Theologically, human destiny is fulfilled in union with God, and our emotions, intellect, and spirit receive existential stimulation from every revelation from God.

Lee and Elizabeth share testimonies of God's presence among slave children. Some children were ignorant of His Word and others possessed rudimentary knowledge. Yet, God's presence is felt not from the person's intentional actions or involuntary subconscious behavior. Instead, it is initiated by and through YHWH's grace. His *prevenient grace* opens the human-Self's heart and conscience to experience an unavoidable sensing of something unidentified but greater. Existential sensing confronts an overwhelming and inevitable feeling and reflection upon God's presence. This is achieved before the human-Self recognizes them as deriving from God. It is telling that both women expressed ethical and moral self-awareness as children. Their moral conscience was connected to their initial sensing of God's presence and progressive attempts to understand Him. However, comprehension of God was not in the abstract but through intimacy. The human-Self's inner moral conscience serves as the innate space for God and divine revelation to intrude into our lives. Intellect has a continual connection with our emotions and a sharp outward sensation that desperately searches for something or someone greater.

The overwhelming presence of God and attempts to recognize Him are represented in conceptions of the Numen (divinity) and Numenous (the sensing and experiencing of the deity), presented by the German theologian Rudolf Otto (1869–1937). For Otto, the Numenous is an elusive, undefined category of value, a state of mind, and it originates *as sui generis* within the human mind.[15] As I interpret Otto, he advocates that from an emotional and psychological degree, the human-Self assesses the possibility of God's existence through the relationship between its emotional and psychological existence concerning morality. This relationship creates an intricate process of gradually understanding its initial sensing and progressive experience of something greater, attached to the awareness of the human-Self's finiteness. Otto refers to this as *creature-consciousness* or *creature-feeling*.[16] The relationship between intellect and

15. Otto, *Holy*, 7.
16. Otto, *Holy*, 10.

wholistic sensation is defined as an "emotion of a creature, submerged and overwhelmed by its own nothingness in contrast to that which is supreme above all creatures."[17] For Lee and Elizabeth, their creature-feeling was triggered by the profound loss of their parents, the consequential struggle of emptiness, and vulnerability. They experienced their finiteness as much as children could within the dehumanizing institution of slavery. Lee does not articulate how she developed the capacity to hear the Numenous's voice, nor the context(s) from which her abilities to recognize Him were refined. The reader is only given a brief account of Lee's reaction to their existence by the intense guilt she experienced from lying to the woman she served.

Likewise, Elizabeth's event stemmed in part from the Christian tutelage of her parents. Their absence created a debilitating loneliness. She explains, "In the eleventh year of my age, my master sent me to another farm, several miles from my parents, brothers, and sisters, which was a great trouble to me. At last I grew so lonely and sad I thought I should die, if I did not see my mother."[18] Elizabeth eventually runs away from the person she was assigned to serve. Her motive is solely to reunite with her family to experience their love and protection. She cared little for the repercussion of her actions. The restoration of Elizabeth's psyche, emotional stability, and family was achieved by reuniting with her mother and family, albeit temporarily. Elizabeth was forced to return to the individual she was initially sent to serve. However, before leaving, her mother gave her some of the wisest spiritual advice any parent could give their child: "At parting, my mother told me that I had, 'nobody in the wide world to look to but God.'"[19] This advice, a biblical fact embraced by Elizabeth's mother, represents the crystallized faith of her mother. A faith hoped to be embodied by Elizabeth, not by superficial indoctrination, but in the hope that Elizabeth would cultivate a genuine love for Christ, leading to a sincere union between the two. Lee and Elizabeth's early struggle with understanding salvation and sanctification were deeply connected to their understanding of morality, a distorted conception of God's grace, and the natural fear of existing away from their family. The numinous within and outside of them was not comprehended through their loneliness and despair.

17. Otto, *Holy*, 10.
18. Elizabeth, *Old Elizabeth*, 4.
19. Elizabeth, *Old Elizabeth*, 4.

Returning to Lee, she never explained how or who initially introduced her to Christianity. This is a significant event she intentionally withheld. The reader must ponder whether Mr. Sharp presented the Gospel to her, exposing her to the rudimentary knowledge of Christianity. Or, perhaps, the unnamed Lady she served after him. If so, there is a tentative expression between intentionally mentioning Black rejection of Christianity and the inability of Black parents to instill Christian values into their child, over and against White acceptance of Christianity, but the concealment of whether they attempted to instill what her Black parents could not.

Lee's significant moral failure was lying to the woman she served as a child. Possibly still feeling remorse, Lee informs the reader, "Not long after the commencement of my attendance on this lady, she had bid me do something respecting my work, which in a little while after, she asked me if I had done, when I replied, Yes—but this was not true."[20] Lee does not describe Mr. Sharp or the Lady as White supremacists, nor are they portrayed as embodying Eurocentric Christianity. Lee did not fear the Lady, nor was she concerned about any potential punishment for lying. Lee also does not articulate any justification or rationale for lying. Yet, this event sparked an intense moral conviction about the sin she committed: "At this awful point, in my early history, the spirit of God moved in power through my conscience, and told me I was a wretched sinner. On this account so great was the impression, and so strong were the feelings of guilt, that I promised in my heart that I would not tell another lie."[21] Lee's initial theological reflection stems from the relationship between awareness of her sin, reaction to her moral conscience, and recognizing God's voice. The Holy Spirit stimulated Lee's moral conviction by enlightening her to who she was, a "wretched sinner" in need of God. These are strong words to accept by any adult, let alone a sensitive and relatively aloof seven-year-old child. The reader must question why and how, at such a young age, Lee believed the Holy Spirit delivered a frightening message to her. Perhaps, at the time, she didn't and eventually came to this conclusion as a mature woman in Christ.

Lee employs her pneumatology in specific ways. She portrays the Spirit, not Christ or the Father, as actively drawing her to salvation, causing her to eventually accepting Christ Jesus as her Messiah. The Spirit

20. Andrews, *Classic African American Women's Narratives*, 19.
21. Andrews, *Classic African American Women's Narratives*, 20.

is presented within the context of *prevenient grace* relating to the initial process of God choosing a specific moment to intrude upon the sinner's life. The voice of the Spirit convicted Lee to the point of her promising to refrain from lying again. However, she openly admits, "But notwithstanding this promise my heart grew harder, after a while, yet the spirit of the Lord never entirely forsook me, but continued mercifully striving with me, until his gracious power converted my soul."[22] For Lee, the *power* of the Holy Spirit was felt through moral conviction and grace, never violating her free will, but working together to emancipate Lee from the spiritual darkness that consumed her. At this point, the essential elements of her narrative are that God was always present. He revealed Himself and never gave up on her.

From 1790 to 1804, Lee continuously experienced the movement of the Spirit in her life. Not from His *indwelling* but the outer presence of the Spirit devoid of a concrete union with God. Feeling the external reality of the Spirit had incited the internal moral conviction of Lee's heart, not in isolation, but concerning her genuine desire to know God and recognize His voice. Lee struggled to respond to the Spirit's voice as she could not fully recognize Him as God. Yet, she maintained an openness to acknowledge and obey God's voice. For fourteen years, Lee had wandered not so much in spiritual darkness but a deceptive fog, recognizing glimmers of light and sporadic moments of a particular divine voice.

At this point, the unspoken racial aspect of Christian evangelism in Lee's life is intriguing. The assumption holds that Christianity became an unavoidable presence in her life. Its existence was initiated and maintained either by God or through her White *clients*, not her Black parents. In this context, Lee is not demeaning her parents or elevating her White clients. Race does not govern Lee's worldview. It is morality and the pestering sense of something, a divine someone who exists beyond her reach. Yet, she does not invoke a form of escapism to avoid the presence and activity of racialized reason within her reality. Lee possibly spent most of her childhood confronting, questioning, and ultimately rejecting the colonial racialized-binary reasoning that deteriorated colonial conceptions of morality, politics, and religion. Nevertheless, Lee would experience another frightening event in her journey to salvation, a crisis moment of heightened conviction from the Holy Spirit.

---

22. Andrews, *Classic African American Women's Narratives*, 20.

TO WHOM DOES THIS VOICE BELONG?

Crisis Moments of Heightened Conviction.

"Behold, I was brought forth in guilt. And in sin my mother conceived me."
PSALM 51:5

The significance of Psalm 51:5, and by extension, the entirety of the Psalm, functions as an underlining representation of Lee's journey to salvation.[23] From Lee's testimony, she is consistently exposed to her inner moral conviction of her sinful state. Yet, the internal self-awareness of her finiteness also extends outside her immediate context, forcing her to reflect on the human-Other, discerning the possibility of connecting with others through shared experiences. Every person who undergoes a salvific journey comes to the self-awareness of their sin against God. Or they reject the complete revelation of it, consequently pushing away from God, and returning to a state of spiritual darkness. Psalm 51 is attributed to King David, relating to the context of his great sin against God concerning Bathsheba (2 Sam 11–12).[24] Psalm 51 is also categorized with five other Psalms as *Penitential Psalms*.

In 1804, Lee was twenty-one yrs old and still searching for the elusive genuine union with Christ, as she had not yet accepted Him as her Lord and Savior. It was a significant year that manifested a "renewed conviction" within her, during an afternoon church meeting conducted by a Presbyterian missionary. Lee mentions the reading of a Psalm during service and, within her narrative, quotes a stanza from Isaac Watts (1674–1748), the influential hymnist's work titled, "Lord, I am Vile, Conceived in Sin."

> Lord, I am vile, conceived in sin.
> Born unholy and unclean.
> Sprung from man, whose guilty fall
> Corrupts the race, and taints us all.

Watts's inspiration for the hymn is from Psalm 51, but verse five of the psalm serves as the model for the hymn's first stanza. Watts's hymn characterizes an individual as aware of their sinful nature only through

---

23. Evans, *Tony Evans Biblical Commentary*, 534.
24. Allen, *Esther—Psalms*; Cundall, *Psalms—Malachi*; Gaebelein et al., *Psalms, Proverbs*; Williams, *Psalms 1–72*.

exposure to the presence and revelation of God's righteousness. Spiritual self-awareness does not exist apart from God and a divine revelation of His will. Watts describes this individual in a state of humility, regret, sorrow, and desperation to be in union with God. The submitted heart of the individual acknowledges that true salvation is only achieved by and through Jesus Christ:

> Jesus my God, Thy blood alone.
> Hath power sufficient to atone;
> The blood can make me white as snow;
> No Jewish types could cleanse me so.

Psalm 51 also demonstrates David's unique heart for God. His writing expresses his freedom from the deceptive veil of the sins he committed that encapsulated his conscience. David epitomizes a broken and contrite heart. A unique expression of Psalm 51 is the genuine faith of David in God that He has the ability, desire, and love for him to cleanse David of his sins, restoring him to union with God.[25] David's faith in God's grace and acceptance of God's judgment, if given, represents an exceedingly mature version of Lee's confused conscience as she seeks union with Christ. Donald M. Williams succinctly describes the central theme of Psalm 51 as focused on renewal. For him, spiritual renewal is intertwined with moral self-awareness and acknowledgment of one's broken finite existence that is revealed concerning divine revelation:

> The deepest renewal is spiritual, and it has a moral base. Since God is holy and since He has given us a conscience, we cannot be renewed apart from dealing with our moral failure before Him. Try as we may, we cannot remove sin by rationalization or denial. At some point our intellectual and psychological defense mechanisms will be broken. In that moment of truth when we face our own despair, God promises to come to us.[26]

---

25. Arthur E. Cundall's brief synopsis of Psalm 51 discusses the importance of God's justification. This Old Testament example can be interpreted as a foreshadowing of the New Testament's principle of justification through faith in Christ. Cundall articulates God's justification as the central purpose for David's repentance. David was devastated by the self-awareness obtained concerning his sins relating to Bathsheba. To a certain extent, the revelation of his sins may have developed from understanding the initial conception of his sins within his heart and how he physically manifested those sins through his will and abuse of his God-given authority, Cundall, *Psalms—Malachi*, 49–50.

26. Williams, *Psalms 1–72*, 362. Williams makes another insightful remark relating the conviction of our moral conscience and genuine renewal to the experience of pain:

Certain guarantees are established within scripture relating to cause-and-effect principles. Predictability, in this context, is a righteous principle included within the relationship between human faith and divine desire. For example, God forgives everyone who sincerely repents for their sins. Connected to this is the reality of pain and suffering an individual experiences prior to and after salvation. The difficulty for humanity is believing the experiences of pain and suffering could be undergone within a righteous cause. We often hesitate and refuse to view them as neutral consequences of our moral decisions. Shame, guilt, and embarrassment are unavoidable when we scrutinize the depths of our moral conscience. Lee was searching for and desperately needed someone she could relate to, someone who had or was undergoing similar issues. Without someone to help her, Lee would endure the pain and suffering few people have experienced. She was identifying with Psalm 51 and Watt's hymnal and, by extension, to David, in seeking to convey the desires of her heart in the gradual awakening of who God is, concerning her finiteness and affection for Him.

For Lee, the event during the afternoon church meeting created a crisis moment within her. The daunting burden of Lee's self-awareness of her sinful nature, finiteness, and detachment from the Lord was overwhelming. It was a reality she was unable to handle in isolation from Christ. She felt ashamed, not from any experience of sociopolitical oppression or the extreme dehumanization from colonial slavery. Culture, gender, race, or any other social construction had no bearing on her conscience and spirit. Rather, it was being exposed to the ultimate reality of persistent dread from the Spirit's presence around her, the genuine desire to know God for who God truly is, and not having obtained the wishes of her heart. After listening to the reading of Psalm 51, Lee remarks, "a ray of renewed conviction darted into my soul."[27] Lee is making a theological point that informs her sociopolitical and racial realities by locating sin within her, before she entered the world through her mother's womb. She prioritizes her spiritual acknowledgment of sin being the root cause of human wickedness, over any conception of socially constructed systemic

---

"But most of all, we need personal renewal—deep inner conviction of our own sin and poverty—followed by a fresh cleansing and infilling of God's Spirit. There is no renewal apart from pain. This pain may come in a moral crisis. It may come when the placid order of life is broken by illness, economic reversal, or an upheaval in relationships. It may come when we reflect upon the pace with which life passes and upon our haunting need for meaning" (361).

27. Andrews, *Classic African American Women's Narratives*, 20.

forms of oppression. Societal patriarchal systems, White Supremacy, and Eurocentric Christianity did not make her a sinner. This is personalized by her decree: I am a sinner.

Lee believed everyone was born sinful and immoral and humanity in its entirety was *tainted*. Her acknowledgment of sin and her fallen nature do not develop in isolation. They are connected to the presence and voice of the Holy Spirit that leads the individual to Christ and demonstrates Him as the Messiah. Lee is experiencing the prophetic fulfillment of Jesus's words in John 16:8, "And He, when He comes, will convict the world regarding sin, and righteousness, and judgment."[28] Regarding Psalm 51, she explained, "This description of my condition struck me to the heart, and made me to feel in some measure, the weight of my sins, and sinful nature. Not knowing how to run immediately to the Lord for help, I was driven of Satan in the course of a few days, and tempted to destroy myself."[29] The reader must know that Lee is recounting this as a *pre-salvation* event, a former state of ambiguity and confusion regarding her perception of obtaining salvation. Like countless people before her, Lee's unsaved state represented a deep wandering in psychological darkness. She attempts to feel the presence and hear the faint resonance of a voice not yet recognized as from God. At this point, her experiences can be interpreted as grasping at salvation, seeking to be immersed within God's love, and affirming Christ's voice.

Suicidal ideation is connected to Lee's ignorance of turning to Christ when experiencing a severe spiritual and psychological crisis. The absence of Christ at this crucial point had left Lee vulnerable to her sinful conscience, and a voice she perceived as Satan. The reader is not given the explicit reasons for Lee's suicidal ideation. We are merely given the extreme consequence of experiencing the gradual self-awareness of her sin and being unable to cling to Christ. The voice within her conscience encouraged her to leave this earth unsaved and through sin, not through salvation and God's will. The dehumanizing and demonic voice suggested the forfeiting of her life, the voice, we are left to assume, was a subtle, persuasive, and almost convincing voice that could elicit willful obedience: "There was a brook about a quarter of a mile from the house, in which there was a deep hole, where the water whirled about among the rocks; to this place it was suggested, I must go and drown myself."[30]

28. Evans, *Tony Evans Biblical Commentary*, 1053–54.
29. Andrews, *Classic African American Women's Narratives*, 20.
30. Andrews, *Classic African American Women's Narratives*, 20.

Satan used a peaceful and unassuming place to coerce Lee into suicide. It was a familiar place that invoked feelings and emotions that were used to create the deceptive illusion of safety and normality. Suicide was the means to will herself into the presence of God. Theologically, this imagery bears similarity to the Genesis account of Satan engaging Eve and Adam. The goal, in part, is to deceive one into thinking they can usurp God's sovereignty, distorting their free will to oppose Him, not willfully love and submit to Him.

Lee experienced a counter-mirroring of Jesus relating to His being led into the wilderness by the Holy Spirit, to be tempted by Satan, and His water baptism by John the Baptist, the wild man of the wilderness. The imagery of Lee's experiences produces thoughts of demonic mockery, first against Jesus' ministry, and secondly upon Lee's divine calling into Christian ministry, which Satan attempts to thwart. Lee was undergoing her wilderness journey, wandering about for clarity, purpose, and identity established within Jesus. As I interpret her, Lee recounts this event as a battle between Satan and Jesus over her life. The demonic voice within her conscience attempts to lead Lee to a body of water to end her life, not employ the event as the representation of the conversion that occurred in her heart, and faith in Jesus that establishes a new life in Christ.

At this point, it is ambiguous whether Lee eventually submitted to the demonic voice, but for unknown reasons, she appeared to comply with its wishes. Days have passed since she first heard its words, and on a Sabbath morning, Lee wanders to the potential place of her demise. The reader is forced to wonder if she entertained suicidal ideation, or merely tempted the Tempter within her immediate context of temptation. Regardless of these hidden, unnamed causes, Lee finds herself sitting at the edge of the brook, possibly reflecting upon her life, and then,

> It seemed as if some one was speaking to me, saying put your head under, it will not distress you. But by some means, of which I can give no account, my thoughts were taken entirely from this purpose, when I went from the place to the house again. It was the unseen arm of God which saved me from self murder.[31]

Lee's physical salvation foreshadowed her future spiritual union with Christ Jesus. During that moment at the brook, Lee depicts herself as engulfed in a catatonic state. Satan seduces Lee but the then-current force, later revealed as "The Arm of God," mysteriously intervenes in a

---

31. Andrews, *Classic African American Women's Narratives*, 20.

way that transcends Lee's self-awareness (Ps 98:1; 44:3; Deut 7:19; 5:15; Matt 5:11; 24:9). She cannot explain how and why she was freed from suicidal ideation. Lee can only attribute this emancipation to the power of God. God is depicted as employing and moving through prevenient grace.

Lee survived her traumatic moment at the brook, but she continued to experience the duality of struggling with obtaining a sense of value and identity for her existence in ways that cultivated a sense of vitality and passion for enjoying life in every capacity. Through her struggles with suicidal ideation, Lee found herself between a fragmented self-conscience with a torn spirit, and a legitimate but skewed fear of God's judgment. She attributes an extreme illness as the result of these experiences, from which she recovered in roughly three months. Nevertheless, Lee was cognizant of her then-current spiritual wandering amidst the battle for her mind and spirit. She recounts, "But as yet I had not found him of whom Moses and the prophets did write, but extremely ignorant: there being no one to instruct me in the way of the life and salvation as yet."[32] The absence of spiritual guides and natural mentors may be related to the absence of her parents in life. Up to this point in her narrative, Lee has not mentioned her parents, nor has she referenced any parental figures or siblings. Her theology presents Jesus Christ, and by inference, the Father, and Holy Spirit, along with the Body of Christ, as the ultimate replacement for her missing natural relationships. Lee portrays herself as an individual, one whom the reader may assume was forced, like other African-American children during colonialism, to primarily raise themselves with the secondary support of various people they met throughout their lives.

Suicidal ideation may have been a normal part of life for many African-American women. Elizabeth experienced it, and on the surface, her struggles may appear more passive, or less dramatic than Lee's experiences. However, Elizabeth's struggles were just as severe. Her thoughts of despair and loneliness were accompanied by visions and the dread of punishment via alienation from God. She was trapped in a cycle of irrationality and confusion as the extreme loneliness created desires to leave this punishing world, but to do so through sin would be an offense to God.

Like Lee, Elizabeth demonstrated the paradox of exhibiting strong faith in God as she was subsequently reaching the transformative moment

---

32. Andrews, *Classic African American Women's Narratives*, 21.

of salvation. This journey is ambiguous as the reader cannot determine the precise moment of both women's salvation, and evidently neither could they. Yet, the important element of their early journey was experiencing what they viewed as the concrete crystallizing of confirmation of salvation: the inner peace of certainty that they are children of YHWH, sealed by the Holy Spirit (Eph 1:13).[33] Were Elizabeth's visions from God, the devil, or merely figments of her imagination?

Elizabeth's love for her mother was extremely strong, and she influenced Elizabeth in ways the narrative did not express. Elizabeth used her mother's wisdom as support, sustaining her through oppressive periods. An example is witnessed in Elizabeth's recollection of her mother stating that God is always with her and He is someone she could always rely upon. Elizabeth was not liberated from suicidal ideation, loneliness, and despair, but established a conduit for divine healing from YHWH, through a sincere faith in Christ Jesus. She recounts a representative moment in her life by stating,

> One evening, after the duties of the day were ended, I thought I could not live over the night, so threw myself on a bench, expecting to die, and without being prepared to meet my Maker, and my spirit cried within me, must I die in this state, and be banished from Thy presence forever? I own I am a sinner in Thy sight, and not fit to live where though art. Still it was my fervent desire that the Lord would pardon me.[34]

Elizabeth is provided with a disturbing vision that represents her miserable condition, fear of alienation from God, and attempts to achieve forgiveness from Him. She provides a general picture of a gulf of misery experienced through a vision: "Just at this season, I saw with my spiritual eye, an awful gulf of misery. As I thought I was about to plunge into it, I heard a voice saying, 'rise up and pray,' which strengthened me."[35] Misery describes Elizabeth's existence as someone isolated from her family. Fear of falling into the gulf represents the potential finality of her fears, the inability to receive salvation, and the embracing of Christ as Lord and Savior. However, Elizabeth receives strength from YHWH, a direct fulfillment of her mother's words. YHWH instructs Elizabeth to pray for forgiveness, another sign of God's presence in her life, and Elizabeth's

---

33. Blount, *Native Land*, 351; Evans, *Tony Evans Biblical Commentary*, 1219.
34. Elizabeth, *Old Elizabeth*, 4–5.
35. Elizabeth, *Old Elizabeth*, 5.

ability to recognize His voice. The difficult consequence of her obedience was being brought to the gulf of misery by a mysterious figure dressed in *white raiment*, likely from YHWH. Again, Elizabeth is overtaken with fear of isolation from a rejection by YHWH as she is brought to another fiery gulf: "Still I felt all the while that I was sustained by some invisible power."[36] The Lord's voice was heard amid Elizabeth's fear of divine judgment. This becomes another form of confirmation of her mother's advice years prior to this vision. Crying for mercy and salvation was given from sincerity. The reader is never given a description of why Elizabeth was experiencing this level of moral and spiritual intensity, regarding her unworthiness in relation to Christ Jesus. The climax of Elizabeth's vision ends in the confirmation of seeking Christ since her early childhood:

> I then renewed my struggle crying for mercy and salvation, until I found that every cry raised me higher and higher, and my head was quite above the fiery pillars. Then I thought I was permitted to look straight forward, and saw the Saviour standing with His hand stretched out to receive me. An indescribably glorious light was in Him, and He said, "peace, peace, come unto me." At this moment I felt that my sins were forgiven me, and the time of my deliverance was at hand. I spang forward and fell at his feet, giving Him all thanks and highest praises, crying, Thou hast redeemed me—Thou hast redeemed me to thyself. I felt filled with light and love.[37]

Elizabeth's spiritual guide takes her to what could be interpreted as heaven, whereby "I saw millions of glorified white robes." The glorious element of Elizabeth's vision does not end at her salvific confirmation but progresses to an eschatological reality that turns to her calling into ministry. For Elizabeth, divine purpose and election are intertwined. She is saved, not to lavish in imaginative spiritual blessings, but to be a servant of Christ in the vision to assist other people into the family of God. This becomes her identity, sense of belonging, and intent of sharing space with the human-Other.

God eventually revealed Elizabeth's inner conflict. She was attempting to obtain salvation by her own means. She was attempting to redefine her identity, sense of belonging, and conceptions of shared space with the human-Other through deception, clothing her self-interest and pride within the garments of obedience to God, and the magnitude of

---

36. Elizabeth, *Old Elizabeth*, 5.
37. Elizabeth, *Old Elizabeth*, 6.

His righteousness. Three times the Lord spoke to Elizabeth, stating, "Art though willing to be saved in my way?" This alludes to the Apostle Peter's rejection of Christ Jesus, and fulfillment of His prophetic word at the Last Supper. The imagery of Peter is crystallized by Elizabeth's weeping from receiving God's grace, mercy, forgiveness, and love. Reconciliation is finalized at salvation, and with this comes a new identity, sense of belonging, and the possibility of sanctified shared space with the human-Other. The counter mirroring of Peter walking away weeping bitterly is seen with Elizabeth spiritually walking towards God in her weeping.

In returning to Lee, her search for Christ allowed her to engage and fellowship with Christians from various denominations. She never discriminated against people based on class, ethnicity, gender, nationalism, or race. At this point in her life, it was about acceptance and peace. She desired to feel the peaceful confirmation of being loved by a family and returning said love to those within her presence. Yet, it is a mystery to comprehend how the seeds of racial reconciliation, forgiveness, and love were implanted within Lee at a young age. The reader can only presume these beliefs and traits were presented to her through Christianity, and through them, Lee cultivated a desire to be with Christ Jesus. From this, she desperately sought someone to help implant, water, and cultivate her Christian faith. Eventually, Lee's wishes will be granted, but her struggles will continue.

LEE, THE BONDSERVANT OF CHRIST JESUS

Finding a New Identity & Sense of Purpose in Life.

"That if you confess with your mouth Jesus as Lord, and believe in your heart that God raised Him from the dead, you will be saved"

(ROM 10:9)

Lee's search for God was not hampered by the external forces of White Supremacy and Eurocentric Christianity. Nor was her developing theology contextualized by them. Surprisingly, Lee did not exhibit any internal hatred or suspicion of White Society amid questionable actions of certain Anglo Americans toward her. In large part, Lee's search for God was encouraged and empowered by Him. She continued to seek God by visiting churches and working for Christians from different denominations, regardless of race.[38] Racial reconciliation existed in small part during her period, and the realism or genuineness of its existence within colonial America had strengthened her search for God. Reconciliation between her and God was the ultimate goal, and the necessary step towards achieving this was to reconcile with the human-Other. The early implications of Lee's theological comprehension are that the Father, via the Holy Spirit and Jesus, has identified with humanity to the extent that, to abuse, dehumanize, and oppress the human-Other is to do so to God.

Lee's journey eventually brought her to an English (Anglican) church in Philadelphia. She labored with them for three months. For various reasons, unknown to the reader, Lee viewed the English church as one she could not call home, and a voice within her conscience stated, "This is not the people for you." It is difficult to imagine what triggered or pushed Lee away from relating to this group. She acknowledges there was a "wall" between her and them. The creation of this psychological and spiritual barrier is undetermined in Lee's narrative. It merely exists as a stumbling block, a deterrent to Lee achieving her goals of bonding with a spiritual family and God. The reader is left wondering if this voice was from Lee's sinful nature, Satan, or God.

Salvation for Lee was not detached from a loving community, as the community functioned as an essential conduit for union with Christ. Salvation involved the revelation of and relationship between sin and forgiveness of sin but situated within a communal bond of love and acceptance. The discovery and glory of salvation, Lee accepting Christ as her risen Lord and Savor manifested through the preaching and altar call of Richard Allen, the future Bishop of the African Methodist Episcopal Church (AME).[39] Before attending a service, Lee questioned a Methodist co-worker about the character of her denomination, and agreed to worship with them, despite her apprehension from prior knowledge. Lee mentions that,

> During the labors of this man that afternoon, I had come to the conclusion, that this is the people to which my heart unites, and it so happened, that as soon as the service closed he invited such as felt a desire to flee the wrath to come, to unite on trial with them—I embraced the opportunity.[40]

38. Anglican, Methodist, Presbyterian, and Roman Catholic.

39. Woodson, *Negro Church*, 54–55, 58–60, 65, 66, 116; Sernett, *Black Religion*, 116–26, 128, 137–39, 148–50, 155, 157–58, 167–70; Sterling, *Slave Narrative*, 101–4, 296, 309.

40. Andrews, *Classic African American Women's Narratives*, 21.

Allen's preaching was used by the Lord to continually reveal the condition of the human heart to Lee. His preaching also convinced Lee that the Methodists were her people. An emphasis should be placed on the word *unite*. The reader is given a glimpse of an important goal and experience Lee sought. Peace of mind and spirit would only come through a deep connection, a genuine bond with her spiritual-congregational family, and through them, a heightened connection with Christ is achieved. The presumption holds that the Spirit conditioned Lee's heart, spirit, and mind to hear God's voice confirming her new family and home.

Yet, at this point, it is helpful to discuss and scrutinize Lee's conception of salvation, as it appears fragmented throughout the early parts of her narrative. Lee is roughly twenty-three years old around 1806 and is not a Christian. She is still searching for that salvific moment where salvation is confirmed within herself spiritually, psychologically, and externally through a declaration, one representative of Romans 10:9, "that if you confess with your mouth Jesus *as* Lord, and believe in your heart that God raised Him from the dead, you will be saved." Lee's retelling of her journey toward salvation is deeply affected by false notions of sanctification, and relative confusion of biblical testimonies of ways people come to the full awareness of Christ. The interesting element of Lee's religious faith before salvation is the deep self-awareness of her sinfulness in relation to God, and how this is impossible without communication and connection with God. To a certain extent, one could interpret her as already embracing Christ as her Lord, but completely unaware of the simplicity of salvation, because it is interpreted within an immature and distorted theology. God repeatedly spoke with Lee throughout these years, saving her from suicidal ideation, and honoring her heart's desire to come to an authentic union with Him. Theologically, we must ask ourselves if any non-Christian can undergo the same, or similar experiences. Or are these experiences relegated to immature Christians whom God is walking alongside, aiding them toward the culmination of their spiritual awakening, but devoid of faulty theological presumptions?

The reader is forced to reflect on why Lee is struggling to come to the full knowledge of Christ. Up to this point, her effort has been entirely self-directed, impulsive in its zealousness to know the truth and experience the union with God. Lee eventually accepts Christ. In part, it was a culminating experience through a penetrating sermon by Allen and a vision presented by God: "Three weeks from that day, my soul was gloriously converted to God, under preaching at the very outset of the sermon."[41] The verse God used to reach Lee was Acts 8:21, "You have no part or share in this matter, for your heart is not right before God." The power of forgiveness was taught to Lee. Connected to this was the revelation of her heart. God revealed the inner malice Lee held toward a person who intended to harm her. This revelation was given among her congregational family, and she immediately reflected on how she needed to forgive this person, not embrace the inner desire to harm the individual. Lee describes this by stating,

> At this discovery I said, *Lord* I forgive *every* creature. That instant, it appeared to me, as if a garment, which had entirely enveloped my whole person, even to my fingers' ends, split at the crown of my head, and was stripped away from me, passing like a shadow, from my sight—when the glory of God seemed to cover me in its stead.[42]

Forgiveness brought freedom to Lee. Gone was the sin of malice that consumed her. God provided Lee with the self-awareness to recognize how she previously redefined her sin as a form of necessary righteousness to legitimize its unnecessary existence. Complete cleansing of her sins was perceived by Lee. She expresses the practice of Romans 10:9 to substantiate her claim. Salvation, confirmation, and calling were displayed as Lee depicted her new power to encourage people. The scene bears similarity to providing a prophetic message to the congregation through speaking in tongues. Everyone, including the minister, observed Lee's outward expression of joy without interrupting her.

The imagery of the torn curtain is presented by Lee described from Matthew 27:51, "At that moment the curtain of the temple was torn in two from top to bottom. The earth shook, the rock split."[43] Lee articulates the reality of an individual's intentional and unintentional isolation and detachment from people to protect themselves from severe trauma. These attempts are often in binary opposition to psychological, spiritual healing, and liberation from God. She demonstrates the psychological and spiritual bondage we can encase ourselves in through the principle of being covered, relating to the shredding of that unrighteous covering, by the righteousness of God that eventually replaces it. Lee explains, "That instant, it appeared to me, as if a garment, which had entirely enveloped

---

41. Andrews, *Classic African American Women's Narratives*, 21.
42. Andrews, *Classic African American Women's Narratives*, 21.
43. Evans, *Tony Evans Bible Commentary*, 917.

my whole person, even to my fingers ends, split at the crown of my head, and was stripped away from me, passing like a shadow, from my sight—when the glory of God seemed to cover me in its stead."[44] Yet, her peace within the Lord was temporary, and Lee never adequately describes how it waned and eventually ended.

Confusion and doubt resurfaced within Lee. The reader is never given a detailed explanation as to why or how it developed. We are only told that she lapsed into a life of vanities, which exposed her to the debilitating emotions of her past. Divine freedom was forfeited for self-imposed bondage, and the natural excuse of Satan as the hidden orchestrator of her torment:

> For four years I had continued in this way, frequently labouring under the awful apprehension, that I could never be happy in this life. This persuasion was greatly strengthened, during the three weeks, which was the last of Satan's power over me, in this peculiar manner; on which account, I had come to the conclusion that I had better be dead than alive.[45]

Suicidal ideation returns, accompanied by demonic oppression and a sense of God's remoteness. The reader is given a spiritual-psychological view of the irrationality and confusion that sin places upon us. Lee experiences thoughts of drowning and hanging herself to escape her current torment. She states, "Here I was again tempted to destroy my life by drowning; but suddenly this mode was changed, and while in the dusk of the evening, as I was walking to and fro in the yard of the house, I was beset to hang myself, with a cord suspended from the wall enclosing the secluded spot."[46] Lee fought these disturbing thoughts but was eventually overwhelmed by their return. Suicidal ideation and the demonic voice in her head created irrational thoughts of ending her life, to the point of tempting her to plunge her head into a vessel of water holding roughly a gallon of water. However, divine liberation comes to Lee, as she explains that God freed her from such thoughts. Theologically, Lee associates her struggle and the potential consequence of succeeding in ending her life with the ending portion of 1 John 3:15, "and you know that no murderer has eternal life abiding in him."[47] Thus,

---

44. Andrews, *Classic African American Women's Narratives*, 21.
45. Andrews, *Classic African American Women's Narratives*, 22.
46. Andrews, *Classic African American Women's Narratives*, 22.
47. Evans has an interesting perspective of 1 John 3:15. He places an emphasis on

it can be argued that suicide is interpreted as murder and the murderer escapes the possibility of repenting for such sin.

Lee describes a vivid image of a gulf within hell that bears similarity to Elizabeth's visions. Accompanying Lee's visions is the dread of falling into it, crystallizing her eternal separation from Yahweh. The reader is forced to ponder why two conflicting accounts of Lee's struggle to confirm and embody her salvation appear in the narrative. Perhaps they are a consequence of her understanding of scripture, which creates tension with the skewed aspects of her underdeveloped theology. At this point, we need to reflect on the possibility of whether her former church family was aware of her backsliding and struggles with suicidal ideation. Perhaps they were also aware of her spiritual immaturity as she consistently attended church and sought ordination within the Methodist church. The perception of Allen's supposed misogyny may be inappropriate if, and only if, he was able to discern Lee's spiritual state.

Lee, by her admission, was unsaved but deeply seeking her salvific experience. Her description of her salvific journey is confusing and troubling, representing a form of Christian realism that accurately articulates the human condition apart from God. However, in other areas, Lee's perspective of events is confusing as it is difficult to discern the chronology of events, and there are times when her understanding of situations is questionable. For example, Lee consistently articulates her inner spiritual conflict in seeking Christ, but she does not articulate the causes of the issues she experiences. She can only express a genuine fear of punishment from God, but not the reasons for believing He exists, or why the biblical testimony is credible to her. Perhaps these elements are intentionally withheld. A darker but transparent view is simply that she does not understand the causes of her emotions and inner turmoil, but somehow believes healing comes solely through Christ Jesus.

Nonetheless, Lee recounts the final stages of her salvific journey after a particular event when she heard Richard Allen preach. She discusses the inner angst that randomly arose within her. The experience caused her to be honest with herself, stating that she was completely ignorant of the Gospel. Perhaps she is exaggerating this claim, or, if telling the truth, provides a glimpse into the condition of an unbeliever who truly seeks to comprehend the harmony of scripture and the Gospel that leads to Christ. Lee states,

---

the Christian's present life of enjoyment and intimacy with Christ. He dismisses the belief that the verse is referencing salvation. Evans, *Tony Evans Bible Commentary*, 1375.

> Although at this time, when my conviction was so great, yet I knew not that Jesus Christ was the Son of God, the second person in the adorable trinity. I knew him not in the pardon of my sins, yet I felt a consciousness that if I died without pardon, that my lot must inevitably be damnation. If I would pray—I knew not how. I could form no connexion [sic] of ideas into words; but I knew the Lord's prayer; this I uttered with a loud voice, and with all my might and strength. I was the most ignorant creature in the world; I did not even know that Christ had died for the sins of the world and to save sinners.[48]

Lee's primary concern and motivation derive from self-preservation, not entirely from intentional selfishness, but natural ignorance through a sincere search for God. The climax of Lee's liberation came at the shredding of ignorance regarding the cause of her angst or inner turmoil. They existed not because of a greater sin she committed, or a skewed love of the world and its pleasures. Lee's inner turmoil was a product of divine intervention, discipline, and preparation. God's love for Lee manifested in her life before salvation and her awareness of His existence. Lee's biblically untrained mind and spirit reinterpreted righteousness as unrighteousness and, in part, subconsciously ignored the voice of God and His activity in her life, only perceiving Him distinctively in moments God determined His presence unavoidable. The beauty of Lee's acknowledgment is connected to her acceptance of things through faith in Christ. Aspects of discomfort, pain, and suffering are viewed as acceptable, continuous, and necessary for God's creative purpose regardless of her present condition. Lee's present faith and love for Christ, relating to her eschatological hope led her to state, "Every circumstance, however, was so directed as still to continue and increase the sorrows of my heart, which I now know to have been a godly sorrow which wrought repentance, which is not to be repented of."[49] Lee's identity, sense of belonging, and conception of shared-space were transformed by the enlightenment of the Holy Spirit. The natural laws of life, for example, death, were no longer feared once juxtaposed with the reality of God's presence, activity, and voice in her life before salvation—comprehending that it was He who protected her throughout her traumatic events, enduring the struggle of suicidal ideation brought about by Satan. Authentic salvation drifted Lee to a verbal

---

48. Andrews, *Classic African American Women's Narratives*, 24.
49. Andrews, *Classic African American Women's Narratives*, 24.

and physical confirmation of it via baptism, and accepting her genuine call into ministry.

The attractiveness of Lee's testimony lies in her ability to be transparent to her readers. She is intentionally vulnerable as a means to glorify YHWH and minister to those who engage her narrative. Lee perpetually works out her theology. She is a young woman at this point of the narrative, saved but desperately seeking to comprehend her existence in the world. The Lord sends Lee another teacher named William Scott, a mature African-American Christian. Scott gauges Lee as to her experiences in the Lord, obtaining the spiritual realities of salvation, justification, and sanctification. Lee states her ignorance of sanctification, unbeknownst to her that she was undergoing it. She explains,

> He told me the progress of the soul from a state of darkness, or of nature, was threefold; or consisted in three degrees as follows—First, conviction of sin, Second, justification from sin. Third, the entire sanctification of the soul to God. I thought this description was beautiful, and immediately believed in it. He then inquired if I would promise to pray for this in my secret devotions. I told him, yes. Very soon I began to call upon the Lord to show me all that was in my heart, which was not according to His will.[50]

Scott's teaching functioned as a double-edged sword. He rightly conveyed necessary biblical truth to Lee, but her unacknowledged obsessiveness towards eradicating sin from her life was further intensified. If obsessive is a strong word, perhaps skewed distractions best describe Lee's preoccupation with the traumatic effects of sin, above and beyond the grace, love, and forgiveness of YHWH. Lee appears to place an overwhelming amount of attention on obtaining God's affirmation, yet fails to see, accept, and experience the full liberation of God's forgiveness. Lee is fighting a spiritual-psychological war with herself, distorted theological beliefs, and traumatic human relationships that affect her perception of God.

> Now there appeared to be a new struggle commencing in my soul, not accompanied with fear, guilt, and bitter distress, as while under my first conviction for sin; but a labouring of the mind to know more of the right way of the Lord. I began now to feel that my heart was not clean in his sight; that there yet remained the roots of bitterness, which if not destroyed, would

50. Andrews, *Classic African American Women's Narratives*, 25.

ere long sprout up from these roots, and overwhelm me in a new growth of the brambles and brushwood sin.⁵¹

Lee's struggle bears similarity to many great Christians throughout history. Salvation for Lee was not a sociopolitical issue via gender or racial oppression administered through White supremacy and convoluted patriarchy. Salvation was spiritual, a battle between the worship of the human-Self and the worship of YHWH. Lee was cognizant of how her sociopolitical issues influenced people's perception of God. However, sociopolitical issues should not determine people's relationship with God. Rather, they can inform them, as they are submitted to scripture secondly, but primarily to the presence, activity, and voice of YHWH.

ACKNOWLEDGING SANCTIFICATION & THE NATURE OF FAITH

There were certain unacknowledged things that hindered Lee's self-awareness, her ability to perceive and accept what is common sense to other people. Scott was a conduit of information from God, a distinct voice besides His own, to steer Lee to a heightened sense of awareness. Lee struggled to grasp or embody her concept of sanctification, because it was predicted from a concealed view of human perfection. For her, the presence of sin and the continual temptation of the flesh, presupposed her unfaithfulness to Yahweh. She retreated to a spiritual refuge, her "secret place." There she received a command from YHWH,

> When I rose from my knees, there seemed a voice speaking to me, as I yet stood in a learning posture—"Ask for sanctification." When to my surprise, I recollected that I had not even thought of it in my whole prayer. It would seem Satan had hidden the very object from my mind, for which I had purposely kneeled to pray. But when this voice whispered in my heart, saying, "Pray for sanctification," I again bowed in the same place, at the same time, and said, "Lord *sanctify* my soul for Christ's sake."⁵²

Satan is again viewed as the culprit by withholding a natural thought and action relating to human desires. Lee subsequently receives her interpretation of sanctification. I emphasize interpretation because the act of desiring and attempting to physically achieve it stems from

---

51. Andrews, *Classic African American Women's Narratives*, 25.
52. Andrews, *Classic African American Women's Narratives*, 26.

sanctification. The genuine desire to love and worship God is a byproduct of sanctification. Thus, Lee was sanctified as she sought sanctification but needed divine confirmation that elicited her self-awareness to acknowledge its provision. The reader is free to grapple with their conception of sanctification, whether they embrace entire sanctification in our present earthly life, or the maturation of it, only being completed after death, once we reside in the full presence of God.

Years would pass before Lee received her call to preach. Reconciliation would be a pillar of her ministry and theology. To a certain extent, a foreshadowing of this comes from the voice of God speaking to Lee, stating, "Preach the Gospel; I will put words in your mouth, and will turn your enemies to become your friends."[53] In recording this, Lee combines two influential verses as they collectively present to the reader two aspects of her divine calling and the biblical figures that are associated with said scripture. First, there is Isaiah 51:16, "And I have put My words in your mouth and have covered you with the shadow of My hand, to establish the heavens, to found the earth, and to say to Zion, 'You are My people.'" Secondly, we have Proverbs 16:7, "When a person's ways are pleasing to the LORD, He causes even his enemies to make peace with him." Verbal confirmation from YHWH provides reassurance of who will empower her for ministry and the manner in which it will develop. I highlight the emphasis on Lee's enemies becoming her friends. This allows Lee's character to transcend her racial, gender, and sociopolitical status/identities, not in a way that displaces them, but employs them in a way that exposes the corrupt human-Other to their immorality and inner hatred. Yet, doubt resurfaces within Lee regarding the genuineness of her divine calling. Like salvation and sanctification, her ministerial calling was doubted to the extent she needed to retreat once again to her "secret place." Within a few days of receiving a dream that confirmed her calling to preach, Lee attempts to visit Bishop Richard Allen, to receive *denominational* permission to exercise her call to preach. Lee recounts that,

> I now told him, that the Lord had revealed it to me, that I must preach the gospel. He replied by asking, in what sphere I wished to move in? I said, among the Methodists. He then replied, that Mrs. Cook, a Methodest lady, had also some time before requested the same privilege; who it was believed, had done much good in the way of exhortation, and holding prayer meetings; and who had been permitted to do so by the verbal license of the

---

53. Andrews, *Classic African American Women's Narratives*, 27.

preacher in charge at the time. But as to women preaching, he said that our Discipline knew nothing at all about it—that it did not call for women preachers. This I was glad to hear, because it removed the fear of the cross—but no sooner did this feeling cross my mind, than I found that a love of souls had in a measure departed from me; that holy energy which burned within me, as a fire, began to be smothered. This I soon perceived.[54]

Allen rejected any notion of a female preacher within the denomination. Not so much in teaching or presenting the word of God, but more so within the title or position of an authorized pastor/minister. It is interesting that this rejection is associated with losing fear of the cross and a genuine love for people. To a certain extent, Lee could be interpreted as establishing an unhealthy association and an inordinate amount of value upon positional authority. Perhaps God used this connection to express the central purpose of her ministerial calling, which resided in serving and loving people. Another curious observation is Lee's lack of awareness of the Methodist stance with women preachers. This also applies to her prior lack of knowledge of Allen's stance on gender equality with the church. A grounded reader would assume these issues would be something Lee would be aware of prior to receiving her divine calling.

Nevertheless, Lee employs sound reason and biblical interpretations to justify her divinely authorized ministry. Her critique of denominational and patriarchal authority progresses from centering on the biblical testimony of gender equality within the sovereignty of God and women as the first to proclaim the resurrection of Christ, thus, stating in her own way that women were the first to preach the resurrection of our Savior. Lee also unashamedly brings to the reader's attention in her concluding statement, that God also elected uneducated men to be His apostles. Therefore, her gender and educational level had no bearing upon her divine calling and relationship with Christ Jesus.

Christian history testifies to the tension between authorized denominational vocation and divine calling outside of the organized church. Women, in varied degrees, have focused primarily upon their divine calling regardless of whether organizational authority figures chose to recognize it. Lee is within this tradition and proudly proclaimed, "As for me, I am fully persuaded that the Lord called me to labor according to what I have received, in his vineyard. If he has not, how could he consistently bear testimony in favor of my poor labors in awakening and converting

---

54. Andrews, *Classic African American Women's Narratives*, 27.

sinners?"[55] Lee reverts to her past struggles and God's protection during those moments as confirmation of her calling. Yet, a relatively equal set of confirmation resides upon the righteous fruit her ministry produced:

> In my wanderings up and down among men, preaching according to my ability, I have frequently found families who told me that they had not for several years been to a meeting, and yet, while listening to hear what God would say by his poor colored female instrument, have believed with trembling—tears rolling down their cheeks, the signs of contrition and repentance towards God. I firmly believe that I have sown seed, in the name of the Lord, which shall appear with its increase as the great day of accounts, when Christ shall come to make up his jewels.[56]

At this point, it must be acknowledged that Lee's insecurity and disbelief is met with God's reaffirming presence and love. Divine confirmation is patient and never ceases to send itself in relation to human weakness. Much of Lee's narrative at this point had been focused on her struggle and relative torment towards accepting Christ Jesus as Lord. Within it, we witness the underlying issue of acceptance and love from a community. She attended and rejected the Anglo church but eventually found a home among African-American methodists, confirmed by who she believed was God. The issue of an accepting and loving community arises again later in her narrative but within the context of her marriage.

MARRIAGE & THE IMPORTANCE OF COMMUNITY

Lee does not provide much detail about her marriage. She provides her husband's name, occupation, and call to ministry. The character of her husband and his love for Jesus are not important issues for Lee, at least relating to the reader's knowledge. We are also denied how they met and the attributes that attracted her to him. His importance is connected to her obedience as a Christian wife and the sacrifices she made for him to maintain his calling. Lee explains that,

> In the year 1811, I changed my situation in life, having married Mr. Joseph Lee, Pastor of a Coloured Society at Snow Hill, about six miles from the city of Philadelphia. It became necessary therefore for me to remove. This was a great trial at first, as I

---

55. Andrews, *Classic African American Women's Narratives*, 28.
56. Andrews, *Classic African American Women's Narratives*, 38.

knew no person at Snow Hill, except my husband; and to leave my associates in the society, and especially those who composed the *band* of which I was one. Not but those who have been in sweet fellowship with such as really love God, and have together drank bliss and happiness from the same fountain, can tell how dear such company is, and how hard it is to part from them.[57]

Lee's Christian community provided her with a strong sense of family. She hadn't mentioned her biological parents or extended family since the beginning of her narrative. Lee's Christian Philadelphia community was apparently unique and provided deep emotional, psychological, and spiritual intimacy that was rare for many African Americans. Her early struggles with understanding and experiencing salvation, sanctification, and her call to preach the Gospel were established within the African-American church. It's only reasonable to assume Lee had many moments of confession, prayer, and times of happiness and joy within her supportive community.

The community of Snow Hill was the antithesis of Lee's Philadelphia church family. Tension developed between her inability to assimilate or accommodate Snow Hill's culture and the subsequent denial of her needs being met, relating to her husband's obedience to the Lord and his commitment to serve the people entrusted to him. The reader cannot ignore the possible irony and hypocrisy of Lee in this issue. She has spent years trying to grasp the finality of complete obedience to YHWH and the trauma associated with it through the perception of failure. It is surprising that empathy wasn't projected onto her husband's calling and desire to please the Lord. Yet, once again, the beauty of Lee's relationship with YHWH and His desire to strengthen her reveals themselves in a vision:

> I dreamed that as I was walkin [sic] on the summit of a beautiful hill, that I saw near me a flock of sheep, fair and white, as if but newly washed; when there came walking towards me, a man of grave and dignified countenance, dressed entirely in white, as it were in a robe, and looking at me, said emphatically, "Joseph Lee must take care of these sheep, or the wolf will come to devour them." When I awoke, I was convinced of my error, and immediately, with a glad heart, yielded to the right way of the Lord. This also greatly strengthened my husband in his care over them, for fear the wolf should by some means take any of them away.[58]

57. Andrews, *Classic African American Women's Narratives*, 29.
58. Andrews, *Classic African American Women's Narratives*, 30.

Christ ignited Lee's empathy from two areas: first, her experiences and the confirmation of her husband's calling. Lee spent the entirety of her youth without a consistent shepherd. She struggled to discern the voice of God with the guidance of random Christians she engaged prior to her conversion. She, like others, could empathize with those who lacked a Christian leader in their lives and subsequently were left vulnerable to their sinful desires and the voice of Satan. Secondarily, the man whom she married was a spiritual shepherd whose life conformed to the image of Christ. Lee was faced with the difficulty of exercising self-sacrifice of her desires to the will of Christ and the call of her pastoral husband. In many ways, her calling into ministry developed through pain, suffering, trauma, and extreme loss. She experienced physical illness, and divine vision and healing of said illness. Lee's perpetual Baptism of the Spirit was experienced even through the tragedy of losing her husband. The only bright spot throughout this period was the two children they bore. Surprisingly, the death of her husband reinstituted her individual freedom to serve Christ in a ministerial capacity.

We can imagine how much Lee grew spiritually and psychologically during her husband's ministry, and the initial period after his death. Prior to marriage, Lee occasionally demonstrated a persistent naiveness to understanding her sociocultural and religiopolitical contexts. Yet, through her personal struggles and success, she eventually grew to a mature understanding of the extreme denial, rejection, and persecution that women endured who wanted to be pastors or ordained preachers. I also imagine she came to understand the importance and spiritual authority of an exhorter and prayer warrior within the Christian church. Lee exclaims,

> It was now eight years since I had made application to be permitted to preach the gospel, during which time I had only been allowed to exhort, and even this privilege but seldom. This subject now was renewed afresh in my mind; it was as a fire shut up in my bones. About thirteen months passed on, while under this renewed impression. During the time, I had solicited of the Rev. Bishop Richard Allen, who at this time had become Bishop of the African Episcopal Methodists in America, to be permitted the liberty of holding prayer meetings in my own hired house, and of exhorting as I found liberty, which was granted me. By this means, my mind was relieved, as the house was soon filled when the hour appointed for prayer had arrived.[59]

59. Andrews, *Classic African American Women's Narratives*, 31.

There is often confusion and negligence in understanding and practicing genuine equality within the Body of Christ. A testimony of Lee's ministry as an exhorter and prayer warrior came in part through the conversion of a narrow-minded young Black man, whose sister desperately sought his salvation.

Lee succeeded when men within their church had failed; she established a connection with the sister, which merged with the brother, who learned to rely upon her to the extent of his sister calling Lee to minister to him on his deathbed. The deep connection between these two women served as a conduit of communication and love for God to reach the heart of this dying, yet stubborn young man. Lee recounts a surreal moment of enlightenment and salvation for the young man amid spiritual warfare. Lee, the prophetess, receives a genuine vision of Christ at the waning moments of the young man's life, taking this opportunity to lead him to the open arms of Christ Jesus. Lee exclaims,

> Now, while I thus continue importuning heaven, as I felt I was led, a ray of light, more abundant, broke forth among us. There appeared to my view, though my eyes were closed, the Saviour in full stature, nailed to the cross, just over the head of the young man, against the ceiling of the room. I cried out, brother look up, the Saviour is come, he will pardon you, your sin he will forgive. My sorrow for the soul of the young man was gone; I could no long pray—joy and rapture made it impossible. We rose up from our knees, when lo, his eyes were gazing with ecstasy upward; over his face there was an expression of joy; his lips were clothed in a sweet and holy smile; but no sound came from his tongue; it was heard in its stillness of bliss, full of hope and immorality. Thus, as I held him by the hand his happy and purified soul soared away, without a sign or a groan, to its eternal rest.[60]

This is what kingdom work is all about. It is the constellation of selfless acts and words that speak of and direct the listener to the Gospel message. Lee did not preach racial solidarity nor ignore the suffering of the man because of his gender. She did not interrogate the young man to discern his political disposition and allegiance to Black society. Lee was only concerned with his perception of YHWH, and the establishment of a relationship with Him during the final moments of his waning breath. Eventually, the young man died, but the observers within the room obtained peace that he indeed embraced Christ as his Lord and Saviour.

---

60. Andrews, *Classic African American Women's Narratives*, 33.

CALLING REAFFIRMED WITHIN THE CONGREGATION

Lee's congregational church confirmation occurred during a moment when a guest speaker apparently stumbled with his words, noticeably distracted. Lee interpreted this as him losing the Spirit. As he lost him, Lee was empowered by this same Spirit. She described herself as Jonah to the congregation, running from her calling for roughly nine years after she initially approached Bishop Richard Allen to preach. Lee never expounded to the reader the specific reason why she ran from her calling. We are only briefly provided with the suspicion and compromise of Allen as a *relative excuse*.

In this context, Allen must be freed and vindicated from a hyperfeminist projection and critique of his supposed misogyny. Lee, in her own words, validates Allen's initial concerns relating to her sincerity, discipline, and spiritual maturity. Nonetheless, Lee has grown in nine years. She was married to a pastor, served within his congregation, and had two children. Yet, she is focused on the role or profession of a preacher: "During the exhortation, God made manifest his power in a manner sufficient to show the world that I was called to labour according to my ability, and the grace given unto me, in the vineyard of the good husbandman."[61] Allen confirmed Lee's calling to the congregation on that day. She initially feared punishment for being filled with the Spirit, preaching to the congregation when the visitor could not. Perhaps this was divine intervention. Lee mentions that,

> The Bishop rose up in the assembly, and related that I had called upon him eight years before, asking to be permitted to preach, and that he had put me off; but that he now as much believed that I was called to that work, as any of the preachers present. These remarks greatly strengthened me, so that my fears of having given an offense, and made myself liable as an offender, subsided, giving place to a sweet serenity, a holy joy of peculiar kind, untasted in my bosom until then.[62]

Yet, the fear of those things we desire is common for many people. Allen verbally confirmed what the Lord was already doing within Lee. Her fear was later revealed to be centered on the sacredness of the church building and preaching in front of the congregation: "The next Sabbath day, while sitting under the word of the gospel, I felt moved to attempt to speak to the people in a public manner, but I could not bring my mind to

---

61. Andrews, *Classic African American Women's Narratives*, 33.
62. Andrews, *Classic African American Women's Narratives*, 33–34.

attempt it in the church. I said, Lord, anywhere but here."[63] Lee's congregation was within the homes of willing women who opened their lives to her and the Gospel message through the heart of a Black woman.

Lee's ministry represented reconciliation, obedience, and perseverance. Her preaching circuit allowed her to preach to Black and White congregations. Many people from various social professions attended her services, and were blessed by her words. One powerful example is her recounting an interesting story of an elderly seventy-year-old White supremacist who was a slaveholder. He had disdain for Christianity and believed "blacks had no souls." The elderly Anglo man connected to Lee's sermon initially, but eventually was moved morally and spiritually. Lee ascertains he accepted Black people as having souls and, with great zeal, proclaimed the genuine spiritual presence of God within Lee and her ministry. Yet, this brief but powerful story does not end here. Lee mentions eventually seeing this same elderly man at another time during a revival. He apparently walked a total of six miles to hear her preach again. Yet, Lee admits she never heard definitively of whether he truly accepted Christ as his Saviour, rejecting slavery and White supremacy.[64] Another touching event presented by Lee is viewed through the conversion of a young Anglo woman. She explains that,

> Ten years from that time, in the neighbourhood of Cape May, I held a prayer meeting in a school house, which was the regular place of preaching for the Episcopal Methodist; after service, there came a white lady of the first distinction, a member of the Methodist Society, and told me that at the same school house, ten years before, under my preaching, the Lord first awakened her. She rejoiced much to see me, and invited me home with her, where I staid [sic] till the next day. This was bread cast on waters, seen after many days.[65]

---

63. Andrews, *Classic African American Women's Narratives*, 34.

64. Conservative colonial Evangelical Black Christianity did not discriminate according to race, gender, or any other earthly identity. One of the principles that characterizes this broad group of Christians is advocating the Kingdom of God, which includes people from different nations. Ruby F. Johnson summarizes this by stating, "To the converted Negro preacher, it was a sacred obligation to share an abundant religious life with the uninformed in his group, and with other racial groups, for that matter, inasmuch as Negro preachers expounded the Scripture to mixed racial audiences" (Johnson, *Negro Religion*, 33). See also Johnson, *Negro Religion*, 34–35.

65. Andrews, *Classic African American Women's Narratives*, 36.

Lee's ministry was gender inclusive and embraced openness to serve people whenever they were in society. Rich, poor, female, male, old, young, White, Black, and Indian, their identities did not matter.[66] She only sought to serve those who reminded her of herself as a spiritually staggering young lady, desperately seeking to shepherd. Lee was a preaching shepherd to anyone who thirsted for the Word of God, and desired to grow in their union with Him. We witness similar experiences by Old Elizabeth, another pioneering evangelist and preacher of the Kingdom of God.

ELIZABETH'S STRUGGLE & FREEDOM

Like other people, Elizabeth's salvation and call to preach are conjoined, as if the moment she is grafted with the Body of Christ, she automatically receives a secondary confirmation of her ministry. Yet, she is without a supportive Christian community and any relative opportunity for discipleship. The reader must acknowledge she is a young lady at this point, roughly twelve years old, when she experienced the overwhelming realities of salvation and ministerial call. Insecurity, self-doubt, or perhaps the voice of Satan distorts Elizabeth from continuing certain Christian practices. She is accustomed to solitude with the Lord:

> I lived in a place where there was no preaching, and no religious instruction; but every day I went out amongst the haystacks, where the presence of the Lord overshadowed me, I was filled with sweetness and joy, and was a vessel filled with holy oil. In this way I continued for about a year; many times while my hands were at work, my spirit was carried away to spiritual things. One day as I was going to my old place behind the haystacks to pray, I was assailed with this language, "Are you going there to weep and pray? What a fool! There are older professors than you are, and they do not take that way to get to heaven; people whose sins are forgiven ought to be joyful and lively, and not be struggling and praying." With this I halted and concluded I would not go, but do as other professors did, and so went off to

---

66. Historian Christina Dickerson-Cousin provides a brief but insightful account of Lee's ministry among the Native Americans. Dickerson-Cousin articulates the contexts and Indian communities that existed throughout Lee's preaching circuit, along with the Indian communities she served, and worshiped along. See Dickerson-Cousin, *Black Indians & Freedman*, 5, 13, 24–30.

play; but at this moment the light that was in me became darkened, and the peace and joy that I once had, departed from me.[67]

Elizabeth's dialogue with this mysterious voice demonstrates her uncertainty about her salvation and call to preach. The reader is unsure why the previous divine confirmation is followed with submission to a voice of doubt. Prior to this moment of doubt, Lee maintained the discipline of a confessional spirit, one that feels connected and obedient to God when acknowledging their sins. I am referring to genuine spiritual submission whereby the individual's genuine acknowledgment is strengthened by sincere repentance and a desire for full immersion in the Spirit of Christ.

Yet, Lee is now somehow convinced mature Christians do not behave as she does, and by stopping her practice, she experiences the consequence of losing a sense of God's presence around her. The waning of sensing God's presence in and around her is connected to the waning of her sense of joy and happiness. Elizabeth had longed for those previous thoughts, emotions, and feelings of vitality that only stem from YHWH. She admits that returning to her former practices eventually restated her intimacy with Christ: "But by watching unto prayer, and wrestling mightily with the Lord, my peace gradually returned, and with it a great exercise and weight upon my heart for the salvation of my fellow-creatures."[68] Elizabeth received her emancipation at thirty years old, after service to a Presbyterian man who rejected a slave's lifetime service. Sociopolitical freedom created new spiritual experiences as she was able to attend church. The call to preach was unavoidable as she admits to feeling the desire or passion to edify God's people and those curious about Him. Yet, her insecurity and self-doubt deterred her: "As I now lived in a neighborhood where I could attend religious meetings, occasionally I felt moved to speak a few words therein, but I shrank from it—so great was my nature."[69] Elizabeth eventually revealed the source of her doubt: the societal oppression of women and her illiteracy as a former slave. She could not fathom how God could use her in a powerful ministry if she could not adequately read the Bible. It is here also where the lives of Lee and Elizabeth are connected. God is strengthening them to conquer something greater than society and someone greater than ignorant men and their internal insecurities, doubts, and fears that stop them from being a blessing in someone's life.

67. Elizabeth, *Old Elizabeth*, 7–8.
68. Elizabeth, *Old Elizabeth*, 8.
69. Elizabeth, *Old Elizabeth*, 9.

In this context, Elizabeth bears similarity with Job regarding doubt and questioning God's will upon her life. Likewise, God responds to her in a way displayed in Job 38:3, "Now tighten the belt on your waist like a man, And I shall ask you, and you inform Me!" The awesome beauty of God's love for humanity is displayed in this discourse. YHWH does not reject or punish Elizabeth for her doubt but openly acknowledges it and determines that she prepares herself to debate/argue with Him. Ultimately, Elizabeth would come to realize God only desired her to embrace what He had determined for her. Her relationship with YHWH, and the ministry that developed from it were of only importance. Whether she was persecuted or died during ministry was irrelevant. Elizabeth eventually conducted a home Bible study at a fellow church member's home, momentarily deterred by some outside and inside her church. She states that,

> Our meeting gave great offence, and we were forbid holding any more assemblies. Even the elders of our meeting joined with the wicked people, and said such meeting must be stopped, and that woman quieted. But I was not afraid of any of them, and continued to go, and burnt with a zeal not my own. The old sisters were zealous sometimes, and at other times would sink under the cross. Thus they grow cold, at which I much grieved. I proposed to them to ask the elders to send a brother, which was concluded upon.
>
> We went on for several years, and the Lord was with us with great power it proved, to the conversion of many souls, and we continued to grow stronger.[70]

She and those who supported her had experienced alienation and isolation from the surrounding churches. Oppressed because of her gender had brought about inner struggle, and questioning aspects of her ministry.

The intriguing element of Elizabeth's theology expressed the awareness of the relationship between fantasy and reality, self-awareness and obliviousness, enlightenment and self-deception, sheep and wolves, as well as genuine children of God with the children of Satan who think they are of God. Elizabeth had to interpret the reality of oppression within and by the church as the dehumanizing consequence of their disconnect from YHWH. Elizabeth particularly states that,

> Thus we see when the heart is not inspired, and the inward eye enlightened by the Spirit, we are incapable of discerning

---

70. Elizabeth, *Old Elizabeth*, 12.

the mystery of God in these things. Individuals creep into the church that are unregenerate, and after they have been there awhile, they fancy that they have got the grace of God, while they are destitute of it. They may have a degree of light in their heads, but evil in their hearts; which makes them think they are qualified to be judges of the ministry, and their conceit makes them very busy in matters of religion, judging of the revelations that are given to others, while they received none themselves. Being thus mistaken, they are calculated to make a great deal of confusion in the church, and clog the true ministry.[71]

Elizabeth's humility is exposed as she questions why and how Yahweh could use a woman like her. Despite this questioning, she was determined to persevere and consequently developed a positive reputation as a preacher. Black and White men traveled to hear her sermons, some from cynicism, others from doubt, and those of curiosity. She was aware of their various motives and paints a picture of her condition as that reversal mentioned by the Apostle Paul in Philippians 1:15–18. However, Elizabeth was not a spectacle nor a fraud. People from Maryland, Virginia, Canada, and Michigan were blessed by her presence and relationship with YHWH. She started a school in Michigan and ended her journey in Philadelphia. Elizabeth was ninety-seven years old when she departed to spend eternity with her Lord and Savior.

The Spirit of God does not rest within illustrious physical buildings or beautifully handmade objects. He is not concerned with empowering or investing Himself in the lives of deluded men who are preoccupied with their sinful self-interest. The Holy Spirit resided then, as He does now, within those who love God and confess Christ as their Savior. We witness the tension between these two realities within the lives and ministries of Elizabeth and Lee. The greater blessing for everyone who reads their narratives is to be exposed to the triumph of those who dedicate their existence to the Kingdom of God, not humanity's limitless castles of religiopolitical illusions. Elizabeth and Lee embodied a level of transparency and realism that were conduits to authentic life in and through Christ. They overcame their inner struggle with themselves with God's guidance and love, and from this, the external threats of power-hungry men were insignificant obstacles they routinely dismissed, even to the extent of helping redeem them.

71. Elizabeth, *Old Elizabeth*, 15.

5

Maria W. Stewart (1803–1879)
The African-American Evangelical Prophetess

"The fear of the LORD is the beginning of wisdom, And the knowledge of the Holy One is understanding."

(Prov 9:10)

INTRODUCTION

Maria W. Stewart was a discerning, intelligent, and faithful evangelical African-American woman who integrated and emphasized the relationship between ethics, politics, and Christian doctrine. I interpret her as pioneering an introductory but impressive colonial African-American evangelical political theology via ethics and conservative feminism. She demonstrated an interesting assortment of identities that represented her intelligence, passions, and commitment to glorifying Christ Jesus. Stewart, at least for me, is representative of a true prophet of God reminiscent of the Old Testament prototype. In 1832, Stewart delivered a speech titled, "Why Sit Ye Here and Die?" She makes an interesting statement during her introduction that represents the prophetic imagery she presented. The context then is similar to the current text of 1831, the edification of African-Americans. Stewarts proclaims, "Methinks I heard a spiritual interrogation—'Who shall go forward and take off the reproach that is cast upon the people of color? Shall it be a woman?' And my heart made this reply—'If it is they will, be it even so, Lord Jesus!'"[1] Stewart's words invoke thoughts of the character, obedience, and ministries of the prophets Debra and Isaiah. Her words from this speech are likely influenced by Isaiah 6:8, "Then I heard the voice of the Lord, saying, 'Whom shall we send, and who will go for us?' Then I said, 'Here am I. Send me!'"

Regarding her Character, identity, ministry, and theology, I believe each element must be understood together to comprehend her genuine Christian faith and passion for African-Americans. For example, Stewart carefully blended her critique of the sins African-Americans practiced, God's awareness of said sins, and His impending judgment if they do not repent. We cannot minimize the fact that she desired and promoted African-American emotional, intellectual, psychological, sociopolitical, and spiritual edification through education, morality, and Christianity. Stewart's vision for African-Americans stems from her relationship with God, and how God had eviscerated the callousness from her conscience, heart, and spirit that once kept her in debilitating ignorance. I argue that she perceived this multidimensional form of ignorance as the very thing that suffocated African-American intellectual, sociopolitical, and spiritual advancement. Her perspective does not originate from compartmentalizing various beliefs but from understanding the deep association of her Christian faith, sociopolitical views, and passion for intellectual maturation. Collectively, they demonstrated the nuances of her relationship with God, her love for African-Americans, and her important ministry.

My aim in this chapter is not to provide commentary on every article by Stewart. I will focus on one of her major works as the foundation of my interpretation of Stewart's discourses, gaining insight into her heart and character. "Religion & the Pure Principles of Morality, The Sure Foundation On Which We Must Build," is the primary text I will explore. In it, we will see aspects of Stewart's vision for African-Americans, her evangelical faith, and how both are related to and are fulfilled through intellectual, moral, and spiritual grounding within Christ Jesus.

> "Religion and the Pure Principles of Morality,
> the Sure Foundation on Which We Must Build."

There are specific issues that have collectively troubled Stewart's heart and conscience. In part, we can glean aspects of her character and

---

1. Lecture delivered at the Franklin Hall, Boston, September 21, 1832, in Richardson, *Maria W. Stewart*, 45–49.

spirit from what disturbs and ignites her for ministry and social change. It appears as if everything is centered upon the enslavement of African Americans and the nihilistic consequences of the dehumanizing institution. The anguish, pain, and suffering African-Americans experienced through slavery struck at the core of Stewart's being, and this is partially expressed by her stating the purpose for writing: "Feeling a deep solemnity of soul, in view of our wretched and degraded situation, and sensible of the gross ignorance that prevails among us, I have thought proper thus publicly to express my sentiments before you."[2] Stewart employs inclusive language, identifying with African-Americans, whom she believes in part, suffer from unjustifiable ignorance. However, at this point, Stewart has not assessed who is primarily responsible. She is only compelled to express her feelings as if an unavoidable presence, inclination, or voice drives her into action.

The initial motivation is internal, as she has "merely written the meditations of my heart as far as my imagination led; and have presented them before you in order to arouse you to exertion, and to enforce upon your minds the great necessity of turning your attention to knowledge and improvement."[3] Stewart's focus is empowerment vis-à-vis education, morality, and Christianity. She is not influenced by, or promoting a divisive conceptualizing of empowerment and power that create and is dependent upon discrimination, injustice, and oppression. Stewart's conceptions are complementary, whereby a community strives for and obtains a heightened expression of their humanity, allowing them to contribute to the nation and humanity's advancement.

Interestingly, Stewart provides a brief depiction of her life as a child up to the present context of delivering her lecture. It may have been helpful for the listener then, like it is helpful for us today, to understand how certain people, beliefs, and ideologies shaped her views.

STEWART'S CHILDHOOD & THE DESIRE FOR KNOWLEDGE

Stewart had a peculiar childhood. She was born in 1803 and became an orphan at five years old (1808). She was raised in a clergyman's home as

---

2. Andrews, *Classic African American Women's Narratives*, 55; Walters, *Maria W. Stewart*.

3. Andrews, *Classic African American Women's Narratives*, 5.

a bondservant but did not claim salvation or any unique righteousness from her religious upbringing. She merely expresses how the "seeds of piety and virtue early sown in my mind, but [I] was deprived of the advantages of education, though my soul thirsted for knowledge."[4] This is a subtle glimpse of her childhood identity and character prior to salvation and receiving a divine calling in her life. She developed a desire for intellectual growth but never explained the origin of this hunger. Stewart's mentioning of this is abrupt and brief, which creates a sense of mystery as to how and why this hunger for maturation developed. Connected to this is a very generalized understanding of her Christian household. The clergyman and his family apparently cared enough about her to instill Christian principles within her, regardless of whether she entertained embracing Christ Jesus as her Savior. An important point is that a European-American Christian family planted the seeds of the Gospel in her heart and embodied some or most of the Christian ethics that shaped Stewart's life. Interestingly, the testimony of her early life bears similarity to Jarena Lee (1783-1864). In both women, we witnessed the roots of Christianity planted within them by humanizing evangelical European-American Christian, none of whom, as far we are told, demonstrated Eurocentric or White Supremacist ideologies. Associated with this fact is the absence of Black parentage.

For Stewart, the important aspect of her childhood is to express how it aligned with specific biblical principles despite her unnatural and dehumanizing situation of being an orphaned bondservant to a European-American Christian family. We witness this with certain Christians throughout history. For example, there is St. Cyprian of Carthage (ca. 210-258), St. Marcellina (ca. 327-379), and St. Macrina (ca. 327-397). We know very little about their upbringing in comparison to others, but the information disclosed to their readers primarily sought to direct attention to glorifying God. The absence of a detailed account of Stewart's secular, or *worldly* life before conversion is common for colonial African-Americans. Some simply did not have any memories of their families. Yet, others may have had memories, but their new life as a new creation within Christ was the chosen starting point to introduce to their readers.

Regardless of this fact, Stewart's childhood represents a particular testimony of scripture regarding distilling the Word of God into children from the parents. We see a picture of this from Proverbs 22:6, "Train up

---

4. Richardson, *Maria W. Stewart*, 29.

a child in the way he should go, Even when he grows older he will not abandon it."[5] Conceptions of race did not distort her childhood and the way she contextualized her Christianity. The Christian family she served may have withheld secular education from Stewart, but they did not seek to extinguish the fiery desire for knowledge and comprehension of the complexities of life. Stewart was not alone, as countless African-Americans were denied a proper education.

Stewart experienced an interesting dichotomy as a child. First, there is the issue of race and gender, being a young African-American girl raised in a household of Anglo-Americans. Secondly, there is the issue of spirituality, being a child who was honest with herself regarding genuine belief in Christianity. She did not mimic her guardians or seek to construct a deceitful image of being a Christian. It is difficult to imagine life for young Stewart, abandoned by her biological Black parents, but experiencing the non-discriminatory *parentage* of White guardians. We should refrain from demeaning or viewing the White Christian family from a negative perspective. Lemuel Haynes (1753–1833) is another African-American who was a bi-racial child rejected by his parents, only to be raised as a bondservant by a White family. Perhaps this was more common than we realize, a hidden subculture of subversive love and empathy.

The Anglo-American clergy family provided Stewart with what they deemed was best, a solid biblical understanding through Christian education. Furthermore, when she did critically reflect upon Christianity, it ultimately brought her to a genuine faith in Christ Jesus. Stewart resided with her Christian *family* for roughly ten years (1818) and attended Sabbath schools for five years after she left them (1823). We can imagine she obtained some segments of spiritual and intellectual growth during this period. However, she did not obtain salvation. Stewart stopped attending school at twenty years old and was married three years later to James W. Stewart (1826). Unfortunately, he died three years later in 1829. One year later she accepted Jesus as her Lord and Savior, revealing to the world her spiritual identification with Him, in large part expressed through her central narrative. How did young Stewart perceive and construct her identity, sense of belonging, and conceptions of shared-space with the

---

5. The implications of these principles are also displayed in verses like Deuteronomy 5:29, "If only they had such a heart in them, to fear Me and keep all My commandments always, so that it would go well with them and with their sons forever!" Ephesians 6:4 is more succinct, "Fathers, do not provoke your children to anger, but bring them up in the discipline and instruction of the Lord."

human-Other? How radically did her identity, sense of belonging, and conception of shared-space change once she converted and sought to live an authentic Christlike life?

> "Religion and the Pure Principles of Morality,
> the Sure Foundation on Which We Must Build."

There are specific issues that have collectively troubled Stewart's heart and conscience. In part, we can glean aspects of her character and spirit from what disturbs and ignites her for ministry and social change. It appears as if everything is centered upon the enslavement of African Americans and the nihilistic consequences of the dehumanizing institution. The anguish, pain, and suffering African-Americans experienced through slavery struck at the core of Stewart's being, and this is partially expressed by her stating the purpose for writing, "Feeling a deep solemnity of soul, in view of our wretched and degraded situation, and sensible of the gross ignorance that prevails among us, I have thought proper thus publicly to express my sentiments before you."[6] Stewart employs inclusive language, identifying with African-Americans, whom she believes in part, suffer from unjustifiable ignorance. However, at this point, Stewart has not assessed who is primarily responsible. She is only compelled to express her feelings as if an unavoidable presence, inclination, or voice drives her into action.

The initial motivation is internal, as she has "merely written the meditations of my heart as far as my imagination led; and have presented them before you in order to arouse you to exertion, and to enforce upon your minds the great necessity of turning your attention to knowledge and improvement."[7] Stewart's focus is empowerment vis-à-vis education, morality, and Christianity. She is not influenced by, or promoting a divisive conceptualizing of, empowerment and power that creates and is dependent upon discrimination, injustice, and oppression. Stewart's conceptions are complementary, whereby a community strives for and obtains a heightened expression of their humanity, allowing them to contribute to the nation and humanity's advancement. We must remember that Stewart had accepted Christ Jesus into her life before ministering to the world.

---

6. Andrews, *Classic African American Women's Narratives*, 5. Cultural ignorance is a central theme in Stewart's discourse, "Why Sit Ye Here and Die?"

7. Andrews, *Classic African American Women's Narratives*, 5.

A NEW IDENTITY & PURPOSE TO LIVE

"Therefore if anyone is in Christ, this person is a new creation; the old things passed away; behold, new things have come."

2 Corinthians 5:17

Scripturally, a person's acceptance of Christ Jesus as their Lord and Savior rewards them in part with a new identity and purpose on earth. Stewart experienced this genuine transformation, explaining to her readers that, "From the moment, I experienced the change, I felt a strong desire, with the help and assistance of God, to devote the remainder of my days to piety and virtue, and now possess that spirit of independence that, were I called upon, I would willingly sacrifice my life for the cause of God and my brethren."[8] Her wording elicits thoughts of scripture such as Isaiah 61:1, "The Spirit of the Lord God is upon me, Because the Lord has anointed me to bring good news to the afflicted; He has sent me to bind up the brokenhearted, to proclaim liberty to captives and freedom to prisoners." There is also 2 Corinthians 3:17, "Now the Lord is the Spirit, and where the Spirit of the Lord is, *there* is freedom."

Stewart's new identity is a self-chosen identity that embraces the predestined identity that Yahweh created before Creation. Identity and purpose are intertwined and interdependent. Stewart expresses to her reader early in her narrative that the only thing worthy of discussion is her salvation in Christ and how she is empowered to dedicate her life to His glory. This glory, in part, is derived from her sacrificial service and embodiment of Christ as her Lord and Savior. Stewart is also alluding to the biblical principle of God identifying with His greatest creation by holding Him and humanity together as the primary focus of her existence. This attempts to practice, endorse, and fulfill the two New Testament commandments (Matt 22:36–40).

Christian ethics is inferred in Stewart's introductory explanation for writing her discourse. She does not suddenly arrive at this moral self-awareness and zeal to confront the societal and spiritual problems she perceives. It results from Stewart's experience of divine revelation connected to an implanted ethical-spiritual conscience that scrutinizes herself and those within society. It is here that the spirituality of Christianity through her relationship with God, informs her sociopolitical self-awareness in

---

8. Richardson, *Maria W. Stewart*, 29.

recognizing how "All the nations of the earth are crying out for liberty and equality."[9] This statement is followed by the acknowledgment and rejection of global oppression, followed by direct questioning of the sons of Africa's responsibility to confront and subdue this oppression. For her, the genuine inner transformation of the individual and community will inevitably assist in creating a world of sincere equality and equity. Stewart asserts both women and men of Africa are endowed with the ability to excel culturally and morally. She demonstrates this view within most of her discourses, but within this particular discussion, Stewart succinctly expresses it through the poetic phrase, "Though black your skins as shades of night, your hearts are pure, your souls are white."[10] Nevertheless, She is frustrated by the complacency of many African-Americans and the consequential immorality and ignorance some embody from not fulfilling their full potential as creations of God.

Stewart completely acknowledges that the ignorance of some African Americans, representing aspects of their culture, stems from their dehumanizing existence within society, and this creates an unavoidable discomfort, anxiety, frustration, and repulsiveness that reaches into the depths of her soul.[11] Yet, Stewart's moral crisis is intensified by the complacency and immorality of some African Americans regarding their disavowal of the necessary means for genuine sociopolitical and spiritual emancipation.

She demonstrates an authoritative stance created from humility and uncertainty within the early parts of her lecture. Again, the aim is to encourage the betterment of African-Americans, not through impressive rhetoric and philosophical discourse. Nor is she concerned with issuing a harsh critique of African-American culture. She merely desires to speak from her heart regarding the pain she receives from witnessing African-Americans suffer. Stewart's Christian faith understands the reality of divine healing, but this does not occur apart from turning to Christ Jesus. Stewart explains,

> I have not calculated to display either elegance or taste in their composition, but have merely written the meditations of my heart as far as my imagination led; and have presented them before you, in order to arouse you to exertion, and to enforce

9. Richardson, *Maria W. Stewart*, 29.

10. Stewart, *Collected Meditations*, 79. See also Phillis Wheatly's poem, "On Being Brought From Africa To America" (1768) in Wheatley, *Collected Works*, 18.

11. Stewart, *Meditations*, 79–80.

upon your minds the great necessity of turning your attention to knowledge and improvement.[12]

God is not forced upon the reader through the text as the ultimate authority, overpowering the reader's free will to think critically about her views. Stewart confronts the reader with herself, and the reader's imagination regarding how they conceive an African-American Christian woman undertaking ministry and theological ethics. She attempts to cultivate the self-awareness of their ignorance, and responsibility in understanding the importance of knowledge, and sociocultural advancement that subsequently leads to spiritual salvation and sociopolitical emancipation.

For Stewart and others, the institution of slavery imposed a heightened knowledge and practice of sin upon everyone, especially slaves and masters. The immoral and dehumanizing taint of slavery deeply affected society regardless of one's participation and disavowal. Stewart alludes to this in a particular published prayer, one that I view as a prayer of *empowerment*. In reference to European and European American enslavers, she states, "And thou hast caused the daughters of Africa to commit whordoms and fornications; but upon thee be their curse."[13] Slavery did not create the sinful nature of the enslaved. Yet, the enslaved were often forced to participate, practice, and exist within the perpetuation of sinful lifestyles according to their human master's desires. Examples of this are observed through forced sexual interaction with one or multiple people to produce offspring as labor, and the experiences of many enslaved as sexual objects by their masters.[14] Adultery, fornication, homosexuality, and general hedonism were reinterpreted as morally acceptable, or secretly permissible according to the master's will, fulfilling scripture such as Isaiah 5:20, "Woe to those who call evil good, and good evil; Who substitute darkness for light and light for darkness; Who substitute bitter for sweet and sweet for bitter!" Black flesh became a distorted sexual fetish in the minds and hearts of many Anglo-Americans.

Stewart expresses genuine faith in the abilities of African-Americans to uplift themselves by creating practical avenues to equality and

---

12. Andrews, *Classic African American Women's Narratives*, 5.

13. Stewart, *Meditations*, 45. Critique of Pharisees. "Woe to you, scribes and Pharisees, hypocrites, because you travel around on sea and land to make one proselyte; and when he becomes *one*, you make him twice as much a son of hell as yourselves" (Matt 23:15).

14. Reference to slaves as sexual objects.

equity in America. She states, "I am of a strong opinion, that the day on which we unite, heart and soul, and turn our attention to knowledge and improvement, that day the hissing and reproach among the nations of the earth against us will cease."[15] There is a deep religiopolitical eschatological hope from Stewart that demonstrates a form of racial solidarity. It is not from conceptions of racial purity or segregationist racialized nationalism. Rather, it is shaped by biblical principles of ecumenical openness, and racial inclusion within the Body of Christ (Kingdom of God). We view a form of racial uplift from Stewart, which was present among other African-American evangelicals, that stemmed from the notion of the image of God (Imago Dei).[16] Ultimate human value stems from God and it is God who endows each culture, nation, gender, and race with gifts to fulfill their full potential as human beings created in His image. Slavery skews and opposes this principle, allowing some to become who God desired them to be partially, but withholding others from this, shaping them into the image of servants (Imago-Servitus) and the images of their masters (Imago-Humano Domini). There is another aspect of Stewart's Christian faith that requires attention, and this area is reminiscent of persecuted Christians within the first-century persecuted Church.

A MARTYR'S FAITH

Stewart connects the illusory significance of skin color, morality, and martyrdom within a specific context. She makes a universal statement, one that is repeated in different ways throughout African-American history: "It is not the color of the skin that makes the man, but it is the principles formed within the soul."[17] The biblical implications stem from Jesus' words in scripture such as Matthew 15:18–20,

> But the things that come out of the mouth come from the heart, and those that defile the person. For out of the heart come evil thoughts, murders, acts of adultery, other immoral sexual acts, thefts, false testimonies, and slanderous statements. These are things that defile the person; but to eat with unwashed hands does not defile the person.[18]

15. Stewart, *Meditations*, 43.
16. Stewart references Gen 1:26; Ps 8:5.
17. Cooper, *Word, Like Fire*, 46.
18. Prov 4:23; Matt 15:11; Mark 7:5.

Through a brief discussion of martyrdom, Stewart associates her calling with the various Christians who have willfully died for the sake of the Gospel. The knowledgeable reader of Christian history is forced to reflect on figures such as the Apostle Peter and Paul, St. Ignatius of Antioch, and St. Cyprian of Carthage. Stewart proceeds, making a moral and spiritual connection between sociopolitical and spiritual oppression that are intertwined:

> Many will suffer for pleading the cause of oppressed Africa, and I shall glory in being one of her martyrs; for I am firmly persuaded that the God in whom I trust is able to protect me from the rage and malice of mine enemies, and from them that will rise up against me; and if there is no other way for me to escape, he is able to take me to himself, as he did the most noble, fearless, and undaunted David Walker.[19]

Confirmation and empowerment of Stewart's calling do not derive from financial prosperity and being a religious icon within the culture. They stem from knowing she is fulfilling the will of God and that her service to Him may culminate in her death. It must be noted that Stewart's relationship with Christ and her theology inform her sociopolitical activism. Christ calls her to this task. The humility and selflessness of Stewart are also expressed in the vindication and acknowledgment of her teacher's sacrifice, David Walker (ca. 1796–1830), an influential African-American abolitionist.

Naturally, for Stewart, the legitimacy of violence for sociopolitical emancipation is not an issue. Violence is avoided and is not viewed as a virtue within her conceptualizing of freedom, particularly within Colonial America. We view similar thoughts expressed within the early Christian church before Constantine the Great (ca. 280–337). The assumption is that liberation, equality, and equity through morality exceed anything obtained through forced coercion, deceit, manipulation, and violence. To a certain extent, Stewart is employing a form of *Christian realism* regarding the sociopolitical disadvantages of African Americans related to a basic non-violence tradition within Christianity. There is also alluding to the interplay between Black skin and White hearts to the binary-oppositional White skin and dark hearts that created colonial slavery. The issue was not to replicate the immorality and anti-Gospel religiosity that sought to justify colonial slavery through a pseudo-divine decree.

---

19. Richardson, *Maria W. Stewart*, 30.

Stewart, in general, infers that the reality of sociopolitical victory was not equated to spiritual maturity, divine blessing, and the authenticity of one's relationship with Christ. A society of genuine equity and equality can only be achieved from the collective power of the Christian's faith in Christ and fulfilling their responsibility. Stewart's discourse has specific themes, and the current lecture examined displays foundational principles of what I view as ethics within conservative evangelical feminism.

EVANGELICAL FEMINISM

Faith & Responsibility

> Never Will Virtue, Knowledge, and True Politeness Begin To Flow,
> Till the Pure Principles of Religion and Morality Are Put Into Force.

Stewart's character and personality bore similarity to the initial insecurity of Moses with the spiritual empathy of Jeremiah. The heart of Stewart's ministry is partially revealed as she shifts her discourse to concern regarding African-American women. She repeats Jeremiah 9:1 after an acknowledgment of her supposed inadequacy:

> I feel almost unable to address you; almost incompetent to perform the task, and at times I have felt ready to exclaim, O that my head were waters, and mine eyes a fountain of tears, that I might weep day and night (Jeremiah 9:1). Truly, my heart's desire and prayer is, that Ethiopia might stretch forth her hands unto God. But we have great work to do.[20]

Her wording is also inspired by Jeremiah 8:21, "I am broken over the brokenness of the daughter of my people. I mourn, dismay has taken hold of me." Stewart's self-awareness and grounding relating to the condition of African Americans is attributed solely to Yahweh. The empathy Stewart has for her people is intensified by the divine revelation she experienced, and the calling on her life that derived from that interaction. These provided further significance to Stewart's eschatological hope that through faith in Yahweh comes complete restoration and reconciliation. Yahweh will fulfill His Word and promises to those who love Him.

Yet, the striking element of Stewart's view is her focus on the responsibility of African-American women. Stewart is not elevating one

---

20. Richardson, *Maria W. Stewart*, 30.

gender above the other, nor scrutinizing the way men have dehumanized women. She is invoking the relationship between spiritual edification and divine calling that creates practical and righteous Christian sociopolitical activity. Stewart is gesturing to the reality of a specific calling upon African-American women that can only manifest through accepting Christ as their Lord and Savior. This comes in complete opposition to the state of African-American women that Stewart mentions, regarding their immersion into sinful lifestyles, making them beneficial for male sexual gratification and the institution of slavery.

Stewart's conceptualizing of racial and Black solidarity is rational and inclusive, but cannot be detached from her Christology and eschatology. I would argue that her stance was common among other conservative Evangelical African-American Christians, and should not be reinterpreted solely within a contemporary Black Nationalist ideology. Nor should it be grafted within a Black Nationalist historiography that has been imposed upon Colonialism, secularizing Black Christian texts, or "radicalizing" them in ways that infer hyper-liberal sociopolitical beliefs. Many educated colonial African-Americans were cognizant of European cultural development. They understood that from an internal cultural view, each nation focused on cultural development via the arts, politics, religions, philosophy, and ethics. For these African Americans, they believed their race was equipped to do the same, yet devoid of segregationists principles and notions of racial purity. In this context, Stewart issues a litany of questions for African-American women.

> O, ye daughters of Africa, awake! Awake! Arise! No longer sleep nor slumber, but distinguish yourselves. Show forth to the world that ye are endowed with noble and exalted faculties. O, ye daughters of Africa! What have ye done to immortalize your names beyond the grave? What examples have ye set before the rising generation? What foundation have ye laid for generations yet unborn? Where are our union and love? And where is our sympathy, that weeps at another's woe, and hides the faults we see? And our daughters, where are they? Blushing in innocence and virtue? And our sons, do they bid fair to become crowns of glory to our hoary heads? Where is the parent who is conscious of having faithfully discharged his duty, and at the last awful day of account, shall be able to say, here, Lord, is thy poor, unworthy servant, and the children thou has given me? And where are the children that will arise and call them blessed?[21]

21. Richardson, *Maria W. Stewart*, 30–31.

Responsibility and accountability are central issues within these statements and questions. They are held together through Stewart's faith in Christ and concern for African-American women. Stewart implies that God has provided them with innate abilities and a uniqueness that will harmonize with the rest of the world. However, generally speaking, African-American women in various ways have not begun to uncover or unleash their full potential as creations of God. Thus, Stewart shouts for African-American women to awaken to their divine responsibility, not in isolation, but together as a family, in relation to men and children, all united within Christ.

The first three questions elicit reflection on salvation and their potential Christian legacy that unites with progressive cultural development. These elements in turn can form conduits of sociopolitical and religiocultural uplift for the current generation, but empower following generations to build upon the legacy they have received. The imagery presented is one of a ripple effect of positive progressive traditions and spiritual legacies of which the Spirit can use to enact God's will upon the earth. Stewart's fourth and fifth questions focus on the relationships of African-American women: "Where are our union and love? And where is our sympathy, that weeps at another's woe, and hides the faults we see?" The implications of Stewart's words suggest internal confrontation, and divisiveness among African-American women that contribute to the oppression they receive from African-American men and European American society. The issue is not the *absence* of, but the *usage* of one's freedom to create self-oppression and self-dehumanization through the oppression and dehumanization of the Black-Other.

Stewart rejects the notion of exposing someone's weakness to subdue them. She promotes the belief in healing and protection from such abuses. The Christian emphasis on self-sacrificial love influences Stewart's discourse. In part, Stewart is creating self-awareness within African-American women, issuing moral judgment upon their self-centeredness, forcing them to extend beyond themselves to the human-Other—not alone as individuals, but together through the Spirit's power. She also gestures towards a strong presence of apathy connected to ignorance and selfishness among African-Americans. I interpret this as Black nihilism through self-degradation and degradation of the Black-Other, the antithesis of the Gospel, cultural, and sociopolitical development.

Stewart then focuses on the state of African-American families by discussing young daughters and sons. Daughters and sons are largely influenced by their parent's character, discipline, and love. The basics of socializing are ingrained within the child by their parents. For Stewart, there exists a form of reciprocity of representation relating to glorification. The child is the parents' glory, as the parents represent a form of God's glory, especially to the world.

Stewart then poses a rhetorical question regarding the presence of African-American daughters on a physical, emotional, psychological, and spiritual level: "And our daughters, where are they?" Stewart uses inclusive language to express shared experiences, and shared responsibility, although she did not have a biological daughter. Sarcasm within her critique is inferred by Stewart's statement possibly interpreted as a potential answer to her previous question. The implication is that the daughters of Africa have lifestyles that are the antithesis of innocence and virtue. Responsibility is reinforced through questioning the state of the sons of Africa, and how their lives represent the love and guidance of their parents. Stewart is reminding all parents that they will reexamine their lives when becoming elderly, and consequently seek to understand and confirm themselves as faithfully embracing and fulfilling their responsibilities. Yet, a testimony, if not an indication of their progress, is often seen in the character of their children. As with the parents, Stewart articulates genuine faith in the children's abilities if they are committed to a life of moral excellence and sociopolitical development through Christ. She attempts to refute typical excuses for maintaining a life of immorality, sin, and detachment from God by stating,

> Do you say you are too far advanced in life now to begin? You are not too far advanced to instil these principles into the minds of your tender infants. Let them by no means be neglected. Discharge your duty faithfully, in every point of view: leave the event with God. So shall your skirts become clear with their blood.[22]

Stewart provides a rather sharp criticism of African-American women who neglect their divine responsibility to care for their children. Beauty and sexual appeal will always fade. Likewise, the physical ability to enjoy and maintain a hedonistic lifestyle will eventually wane. Yet, the moral instruction and guidance of children and young adults will never end. The tragic irony then, as it is applicable now, is that many immoral people seldom cease the activities that please their flesh, but typically

---

22. Richardson, *Maria W. Stewart*, 32.

find excuses to dismiss the call to righteous living. Parenthood is a divine blessing that is attached to divine responsibility.

For Stewart, the rejection of parenthood for hedonistic pleasure is a sin that is representative of killing, or rather sacrificing one's child to the idol(s) within our lives. She references Jeremiah 2:34, "Also on your skirts is found the lifeblood of the innocent poor; you did not find them breaking in. But in spite of all these things," and to understand the broader context, we must acknowledge verse 35, "You said, 'I am innocent; surely His anger is turned away from me. Behold, I will enter into judgment with you because you say, 'I have not sinned.'" The context of Jeremiah 2:1–33 demonstrates the prophet issuing the Lord's rebuke of Judah for rejecting Him. The dark reality of this rejection back then, as it is today, was Judah embracing an illusory concept, a deity that did not exist, and this illusory concept represented for them the justification for their sinful desires. The acquiring of one's sinful desires dehumanizes them and subsequently creates a false sense of righteousness and justification. Yet, in God's eyes, Judah was not innocent. They sinned and the reference to hands being stained with blood articulates their culpability regarding the devastating consequences people experienced.

In this context, Stewart is juxtaposing colonial African-Americans with the biblical testimony of Judah within Jeremiah 2. The immorality of African-Americans, which stems from their rejection of Christ, created devastating consequences, one of which is directly and indirectly teaching the youth to live nihilistic and hedonistic lives. A flock may eventually aimlessly wander, being relatively scattered and becoming easy prey without a shepherd. Likewise, African-American youth will inevitably contribute to their intellectual, moral, and spiritual demise without the love and guidance of their parents. Yet, Stewart's sharp critique of African-American culture, expresses her view that certain African-Americans unknowingly aided slavery by choosing to satisfy their self-interest and worldly desires at the expense of their children.

In a general sense, the prophetic Word of God is faithful from the aspect of universal morality, and the consequences of rejecting God. The effects of immorality and sin are transferred from one generation to another in terms of socializing. For whatever reason, Stewart assesses the past eight years from the then-current situation and expresses the nihilistic demeanor of some Black youth. They have rejected intellectual, moral, and spiritual improvement. Stewart's primary audience is Black adults and parents. In this context, she is seeking to elicit self-awareness and empathy from those who are callous or oblivious to their situation. They reject intellectual, moral, and spiritual maturity, but have also blinded themselves to the fact that these elements are necessary for true liberation. Stewart is unapologetically Christian, and she does not deviate from an emphasis on the Gospel and salvation as a necessity for true empowerment. Her faith is connected to political views in a way that stresses the importance of correct living when we are young and able-bodied, not physically deteriorating from years of hedonistic pleasure. Stewart somewhat chastises these particular individuals by stating, "Do not presume to offer him the very dregs of your lives, but now, whilst you are blooming in health and vigor, consecrate the remnant of your days to him."[23] For her, there is a connection between sociopolitical despair, the disavowal of genuine religion, and lapsing into an obsessive life of pleasure.

Stewart seems to imply that the desire for greatness and satisfaction must be sanctified, stripped of a person's self-glorification of the individual and community. They need to be revived and reinterpreted by Christ through the Holy Spirit: "Do you wish to become useful in your day and generation? Do you wish to promote the welfare and happiness of your friends, as far as your circle extends? Have you one desire to become truly great? O then become truly pious and God will endow you with wisdom and knowledge from on high."[24] Stewart employs an external discourse to solidify her views. She employs a poem for children called, *A Dialogue Between Christ and A Youth, and The Devil*. In it, there are three central people: a youth, the devil, and Christ. The context of the poem complements Stewart's discourse to this point, as she introduces the initial words of Christ as He intrudes upon an ongoing discussion between the youth and the devil. The youth, in all their immaturity, chooses to dedicate their life to enjoying worldly pleasures, and the devil pleasantly approves as if he were in complete support of this decision.

The devil and the youth determined it best to spend one's existence not in following God, but in discovering the limitations of happiness. We, as the readers of Stewart's text, can see how she has established a general connection between the Black youth of her period to the poem. In Stewart's eyes, both have rejected God, opting to denounce any legitimacy of religious, moral, and intellectual pursuits. For her, and other African-Americans within her period, the precious years of human existence are

---

23. Richardson, *Maria W. Stewart*, 32.
24. Richardson, *Maria W. Stewart*, 32.

within our youth, and it is in that general age range that we should ideally turn to Christ. Yet, this is not the norm for those within Stewart's context and ours as well. Selfishly, some of us know firsthand how it is tempting to intentionally spend our youth practicing reckless hedonism, thinking we can simply turn to God once we have grown bored, tired, or completely satisfied with pleasing ourselves. A person entrenched in this belief has deceived themselves and, for Stewart, it complements the deception from the devil.

Religion is not interpreted in the traditional sense. Stewart employs the term as a primary reference to Christianity and Christ Jesus. She consistently directs the listener and reader to the Gospel narrative. The central goal is to glorify Christ, and a part of this glorification is being an obedient and faithful child of God, assisting others to the awareness and acceptance of Christ as their Lord and Savior. Stewart explains,

> Religion is pure; it is never new; it is beautiful; it is all that is worth living for; it is worth dying for, O, could I but see the church build up in the most holy faith, could I but see men spiritually minded, walking in the fear of God, not given to filthy lucre, not holding religion in one hand and the world in the other, but diligent in business, fervent in spirit, serving the Lord, standing upon the walls of Zion, crying to the passers by, "Ho, every one that thirsteth, come ye to the waters, and he that hath no money; yea, come and buy wine and milk without money and without prince [Isaiah 55:11]."[25]

Stewart's reasoning alludes to Matthew 6:24, "No one can serve two masters; for either he will hate the one and love the other, or he will be devoted to one and despise the other. You cannot serve God and wealth." Her words at this point spread throughout the secular sociopolitical and religiopolitical worlds. African-Americans, Christian or atheist, have the moral responsibility to better themselves and others within their communities. There is no excuse, especially as an enslaved class, to submit to despair in a self-contradictory way, aiding the very wicked force that has placed them in their current situation, White Supremacy.

Stewart shifts her discourse to the prayer portion of her thoughts and beliefs. The prayer portion of Stewart's work is a rather lengthy discussion with the reader and God. The initial portion is a continuance of her expressing concern for the character of African-Americans. She

---

25. Richardson, *Maria W. Stewart*, 33.

expounds on the aspects that demonstrate their self-deception and immorality.

Prayer

Stewart initiates her section on prayer with a judgment on the watchmen of Zion, those Christian leaders within and outside the Black community. The scripture she employs becomes increasingly disturbing once assessed upon enslaved African-American leaders, who we assume, desire nothing but freedom for their people. Yet, deception is revealed when their lives are representative of a group of people entrenched in despair and the idolatrous allure of fleshly pleasure that opposes their divine calling from God. We witness this view from Stewart's words,

> O, Lord God, the watchmen of Zion have cried peace, peace, when there was no peace [Jeremiah 6:14]; they have been, as it were, blind leaders of the blind [Matthew 15:14]. Wherefore hast thou so long withheld from us the divine influences of thy Holy Spirit? Wherefore hast thou hardened our hearts and blinded our eyes?[26]

In this context, Stewart is not attaching the immorality and rejection of God primarily upon the people, but she includes the ineptness and unfaithfulness of certain African-American Christian leaders. Stewart also presents rhetorical questions, as God Himself has not caused the immorality and unfaithfulness of these Christian leaders. It was them who rejected the genuine divine revelation and experience with God through the Holy Spirit, and the tragic consequence was their actions assisted people in practicing sin. Stewart may also be influenced by John 12:40 which is repeated as the prophetic fulfillment of Isaiah 6:10. Stewart is scrutinizing the false assumption by many people that all or most leaders are trustworthy, morally grounded, and intelligent people whose primary aim is to care for the people entrusted to them. Colonialism was a period where this was not the case. Some Black leaders were not chosen by the people but by White masters or members of White society. Black puppet leaders were common, especially within the Southern plantations and churches, and their leadership was merely the social control of African-Americans per White Supremacist self-interest.

Stewart perceives false leaders as intentionally misleading their people. In this context, they may have possibly minimized the barbary

---

26. Richardson, *Maria W. Stewart*, 33.

of colonial slavery, and implemented ways to continually eviscerate the potential for the slave obtaining their freedom. Matthew 15:14, if applied realistically, tends to emphasize the self-awareness of the people as they intentionally follow these false leaders, both colluding with each other to obtain their self-interest.

A questionable aspect of Stewart's theology is the perception of a distorted conception of God's sovereignty. She portrays Him as withholding the Holy Spirit from her people and hardening their hearts/blinding their eyes. At this point it is not determined that God is involved in punishing African-Americans in any way. Stewart is merely applying biblical principles onto contemporary contexts which she believes is appropriate. For her, God's judgment is justified because of the gross immorality and intentionality of African-Americans to reject Him, ultimately projecting themselves to be who they truly are not, genuine Christians. Stewart continues to clothe herself within the imagery of an OT prophet condemning Israel for their rejection of Yahweh and idolatrous obsession with their self-interest. With this imagery, how can we interpret, at least from Stewart's perspective, the nature of African-American identity, sense of belonging, and conceptions of shared space with the human-Other?

The listener and reader of her text must confront the imagery she presents of African-Americans. In part, they are presented to us as an enslaved class of people who talk about freedom but seldom did things of substance to achieve it. An identity of an ideological nomad of sorts is constructed, as African-Americans represent a pseudo-Israel, wandering in the wilderness called America. The collective sense of belonging is also skewed in the sense of complacency and submission to an Anglo-American determination of Black existence as unwanted foreigners, and this includes conceptions of shared-spaces.

Stewart continues to evaluate African-Americans, expressing the consequences of their dark decisions through rejecting the Lord and refusing to be grafted into the royal priesthood of the global body of Christ. Yet, Stewart does not express despair for the potential and future of African-Americans. She emphasizes principles of reconciliation, redemption, and glorification for her people as she pleads to the Lord:

> Return again to us, O Lord God, we beseech thee, and pardon this the iniquity of thy servants. Cause thy face to shine upon us, and we shall be saved. O visit us with thy salvation. Raise up sons and daughters unto Abraham, and grant that there might come a mighty shaking of dry bones among us, and a great

ingathering of souls. Quicken thy professing children. Grant that the young may be constrained to believe that there is a reality in religion, and a beauty in the fear of the Lord. Have mercy on the benighted sons and daughters of Africa. Grant that we may soon become so distinguished for our moral and religious improvements, that the nations of the earth may take knowledge of us; and grant that our cries may come up before thy throne like holy incense. Grant that every daughter of Africa may consecrate her sons to thee from birth. And to thou, Lord, bestow upon them wise and understanding hearts. Clothe us with humility of soul, and give us a becoming dignity of manners; may we imitate the character of the meek and lowly Jesus; and do grant that Ethiopia may soon stretch forth her hands unto thee.[27]

Empowerment and complete transformation occur within Christ if, and only if, sincere repentance is given by African-Americans. Repentance should not be given from a façade of genuine faith in Christ, concealing the primary goal of obtaining one's sociopolitical and cultural self-interest. A possible assumption of Stewart is that genuine faith in Christ transforms the believer through intellectual, moral, spiritual improvement, being a conduit of God's will to deconstruct the influence of White Supremacy within American society. Stewart articulates a present-centered and eschatological hope from African-Americans who willfully turn away from their hedonistic lives and into Christ, freely dedicating their children and themselves to the spread of the Gospel. For Stewart and others during her period, genuine uplift and empowerment begins and ends within Christian ethics, deeply embodying a rich Christology. Moral and religious improvement edified the Black community through empathy, love, and self-sacrifice. An interesting aspect of Stewart's discourse is her ability to present the positive attributes of Anglo-American society carefully. She does not employ essentialist or racialized-binary reasoning that perceives Whiteness as irredeemable.

THE WHITE IDEAL

Up to this point, Stewart has not spoken ill of Anglo-American society. A harsh critique has not been warranted. Instead, she has positioned the positive attributes of Anglo-American society as the things for African-American society to replicate. To a certain extent, Whiteness is

---

27. Cooper, *Word, Like Fire*, 62–65.

established as a *temporary* ideal of progress and social uplift. We are given an early image regarding her observations of Anglo-American society she deemed good and worthy of replication, especially regarding the care of White youth:

> I have been taking a survey of the American people in my own mind, and I see them thriving in arts and sciences, and in polite literature. Their highest aim is to excel in political, moral, and religious improvement. They early consecrate their children to God, and their youth indeed are blushing in artless innocence. They wipe the tears from the orphan's eyes, and they cause the widow's heart to sing for joy [Job 29:13]! And their poorest ones, who have the least wish to excel, they promote! And those that have but one talent they encourage.[28]

An alternative perception may interpret Stewart as employing hyperbole or perhaps even sociopolitical charisma in avoiding the possibility of offending Anglo-American society. Another view may perceive her as a racial assimilationist, catering to both races, concealing a genuine belief that African-Americans, as enslaved people, have sinned more than Anglo-America.

Nevertheless, these brief thoughts are immediately set aside, as Stewart states, "But how very few are there among them that bestow one thought upon the benighted sons and daughters of Africa, who have enriched the soils of America with their tears and blood: few to promote their cause, none to encourage their talents."[29] Violating humanistic and Christian ideals is the underlining assumption in Stewart's critique of Anglo-American society's focus on itself. Unjustified discrimination and White Supremacist reasoning cause Anglo-American society to exist within a state of contradicting the Gospel message and basic secular humanistic ideals. Kernels of righteousness and moral grounding exist within Anglo-American society, but the genuineness of these expressions can only be assessed by how they are employed upon the human-Other. The difficulty of fully embracing Stewart's view is connected to the statement that, "Tis on account of sin," is established as the partial reason for the calamity African-Americans endured. For Stewart, it is the blatant sins of willful ignorance, self-worship through hedonism, the church turning away from its first love, and maintaining a collective black conscience that

---

28. Richardson, *Maria W. Stewart*, 34.
29. Cooper, *Word, Like Fire*, 67.

embodies the principle of "I can't which develops into you can't because we can't," that aids White Supremacy, contributing to Black enslavement.

However, Stewart does not leave the listener and reader in a state of frustration. She is consistent with the central messages of her discourse, presenting the blessings of salvation, in part, through a new evangelical identity, sense of belonging, and conception of shared spaces, predicated on the embodiment of intellectual, moral, and spiritual redemption through Christ. She appears hopeful and acknowledges the glimmer of potential among African-Americans, "And I am rejoiced to reflect that there are many able and talented ones among us, whose names might be recorded on the bright annals of fame. But 'I can't,' is a great barrier in the way I hope it will soon be removed, and 'I will,' resume its place."[30] Religious optimism from a strong faith in Christ, not in what He has not accomplished, but from what He has and is currently doing within the world is what empowers Stewart's life and love for African-American society.

Stewart demonstrates keen insight into African and Anglo-American culture, and this causes the reader to reflect on the possible events and people that helped Stewart avoid, or resist the despair and defeatism she witnessed within African-American culture. Naturally, in a general sense, we can assume her faith and relationship with Christ was the primary reason. However, realistically, there still exist the unknown factors and people who taught her. The curious mysteriousness lies in the details of God's presence and communication within certain pinnacle events.

Moreover, within her discourse, there is the continuous alluding to a collusion between some African and Anglo-Americans, in the sense that some African-Americans constructed a false sense of empowerment by using their freedom to satisfy their self-interest at the expense of cultural uplift. In this context, Stewart calls for collective repentance from African-Americans, as everyone is still considered a sinner in the eyes of the Lord, "O, then let us bow before the Lord our God, with all our hearts, and humble our very souls in the dust before him; sprinkling, as it were, ashes upon our heads."[31] Stewart shifts her moral critique toward African-American males. Her words allude to the possibility many mothers neglected their responsibility which contributed to other aspects of immorality within the community:

---

30. Richardson, *Maria W. Stewart*, 35.
31. Cooper, *Word, Like Fire*, 68.

> O, ye mothers, what a responsibility rests on you! You have souls committed to your charge, and God will require a strict account of you. It is you that must create in the minds of your little girls and boys a thirst for knowledge, the love of virtue, the abhorrence of vice, and the cultivation of a pure heart. The seeds thus sown will grow with their growing years; and the love of virtue thus early formed in the soul will protect their inexperienced feet from many dangers. O, do not say, you cannot make any thing of your children; but say, with the help and assistance of God, we will try.[32]

The beauty of parenthood is partially revealed through Stewart's words. Motherhood is a gift of God, in that women are representative of God's creative power in creating humanity. To be a creator is to be endowed with the ability to mature the creation that was created in your image. Mothers have the powerful responsibility to teach children to be healthy adults, and to instill the Word of God within them in a way that enhances their intelligence, morality, and spiritual sensitivity. Stewart also makes a powerful declaration from her heart. Connected to it is her noticeable disdain for those African-Americans who glorify their sins rather than each other in a positive way: "Finally, my heart's desire and prayer to God is that there might come a thorough reformation among us. Our minds have too long grovelled in ignorance and sin."[33] This is eventually complemented by another principle of exhortation. She provides an optimistic appraisal of Black society and questions the collective character of White society:

> I am of a strong opinion that the day on which we unite, heart and soul, and turn our attention to knowledge and improvement, that day the hissing and reproach among the nations of the earth against us will cease. And even those who now point at us with the finer of scorn, will aid and befriend us. It is of no use for us to sit with our hands folded, hanging our heads like bulrushes, lamenting our wretched condition; but let us make a mighty effort, and arise; and if no one will promote or respect us, let us promote and respect ourselves.[34]

Interestingly, this was probably a common assumption by various African-Americans. For them, progress vis-à-vis genuine intellectual,

---

32. Cooper, *Word, Like Fire*, 70.
33. Richardson, *Maria W. Stewart*, 36.
34. Richardson, *Maria W. Stewart*, 36.

moral, and spiritual improvement consequently elicited repentance and possible admiration from the former oppressive class. The imagery presented is that the contours of racial discrimination through White Supremacist ideology will inevitably be shattered by Black people's impressive contribution to humanity. For me, the troubling element of this form of Black optimism is it does not embrace a biblical concept of human sinful nature. Nor does this view demonstrate historical evidence to legitimatize its claims. The reader is left to wonder if Stewart truly believes this view, or simply posits it to pacify the very things she wishes to defeat: Eurocentric and White supremacist reasoning.

Nevertheless, she continues to elevate Anglo-American women as the ideal for African-American women to mimic and be encouraged by. Stewart is likely using broad generalizations at this point of her narrative in a disarming manner. Yet, her approach can be questionable as it may invoke manipulation and deceit in catering to the arrogance of Anglo-American society in her attempts to invoke, or stimulate the Black conscience to betterment. For example, at one point in her discourse, Stewart asserts,

> The American ladies have the honor conferred on them, that by prudence and economy in their domestic concerns, and their unwearied attention in forming the minds and manners of their children, they laid the foundation of their becoming what they now are. The good women of Wethersfield, Conn., toiled in the blazing sun, year after year, weeding onions, then sold the seed and procured enough money to erect them a house of worship; and shall we not imitate their examples, as far as they are worthy of imitation? Why cannot we do something to distinguish ourselves, and contribute some of our hard earnings that would reflect honor upon our memories, and cause our children to arise and call us blessed? Shall it any longer be said of the daughters of Africa, they have no ambition, they have no force? By no means.[35]

There is power in womanhood and motherhood. Stewart is not concerned with articulation principles of domination but rather principles of responsibility and the ability to influence children to become healthy adults. These women were strong and superseded societal expectations for them, as their interests extended beyond the home and into the workforce. Stewart makes the statement that these same Anglo-American

---

35. Richardson, *Maria W. Stewart*, 37.

women embodied a form of solidarity that benefited their community. They created a church. Then there is the question why African-Americans cannot mobilize in similar ways. Stewart is not ignorant of opposition from Anglo-American society. We can assume she either believes Black solidarity and social mobility can be obtained to a certain extent, or whether opposition comes or not, African-Americans have the responsibility to be the best they can within society. They must use their freedom for intellectual, moral, and spiritual improvement. The attempt itself opens the Black conscience to a greater understanding of its potential within its immediate context, and possibly beyond.

To another extent, Stewart continues to avoid, what some would argue, the obvious influences of Black despair, laziness, and focus on pleasure. In many ways, by doing so, she is eliminating any and every excuse to avoid betterment. Oppressed people tend to collapse upon areas that represent control and freedom. The practice of sin was partially controlled by Anglo-America and the institution of slavery, but the ability to do and say what one wanted apart from them may have created spaces of intellectual, moral, and spiritual stimulation. However, for some, sin, broadly construed, had defined their identities, sense of belonging, and conception of shared-space. These African-Americans exist in a state of contradiction whereby they are not motivated by anyone, including empathetic Anglo-Americans.

Yet, the craftiness of Stewart's presentation is that the White ideal that she presents is not the limitation or boundary of Black potential, although White Supremacists and the collective Eurocentric conscience may have thought so. Rather, Stewart employed White society, at least the positive aspects, as the goal to supersede. Stewart may have positioned the White ideal as an achievable benchmark, but held their existence in tension with Black advancement and Christ Jesus who existed beyond Whiteness. Stewart progresses her argument to express the segments of dissonance within White society via slavery. For her, some Anglo-Americans displayed laziness but also achieved a skewed sense of pride and superiority by taking advantage of a group. The perception of superiority and possessing distorted power over the Human-Other indeed influenced how they constructed their identity, sense of belonging, and conceptions of shared spaces with each other. Attached to these were thoughts of representing the epitome of human intellectual strength, moral uprightness, and spirituality.

Nevertheless, Stewart does not prioritize her critique of Anglo-American society above and beyond that of African-American culture. She demonstrates a mature and balanced understanding of her context, which is properly displayed in part, based on how she articulates her views of both races. Yet, her central interest is African-Americans and I would argue the integrity, intelligence, morality, and spirituality of Black women. Stewart remarks,

> How long shall the fair daughters of Africa be compelled to bury their minds and talents beneath a load of iron pots and kettles? Until union, knowledge and love begin to flow among us. How long shall a mean set of men flatter us with their smiles, and enrich themselves with our hard earnings; their wives' fingers sparkling with rings, and they themselves laughing at our folly?[36]

Stewart appears to desperately try to awaken the slumbered consciences of African-American women. She asserts they have God-given talents which are being suppressed by the duties of a slave, assigned according to the self-interest of Eurocentric-minded and White Supremacist people. Yet, African-American solidarity, especially within a Christian context, is achieved through the avenues of knowledge and love. White society is not the only oppressor of African-American women. Black womanizers are introduced into the discussion, or anyone who seeks to manipulate and take advantage of women. However, to a large extent, Anglo-American men can be placed within this category. The greater issue is a woman's self-worth. For Stewart, African-American women are gifted people who naturally deserve more than what slavery has forced upon them, but also those things that come because of compromise.

Stewart does not embody a spirit of division but that of reconciliation and edification. She never seeks to attack White society but demonstrates a realist interpretation of what she has seen and experienced. The inner transformation of Anglo-Americans is not the consequence of African-American social mobility. Rather, it can be seen as partially stemming from the synergistic relationship between God and non-European Christians, along with the humanity of African-Americans, in that they collectively work towards redeeming White humanity in various ways:

> The Americans do, and why should not you? Possess the spirit of men, bold and enterprising, fearless and undaunted. Sue for your rights and privileges. Know the reason that you cannot

---

36. Richardson, *Maria W. Stewart*, 37.

attain them. Weary them with your importunities. You can but die if you make the attempt; and we shall certainly die if you do not. The Americans have practiced nothing but head-work these 200 years, and we have done their drudgery. And is it not high time for us to imitate their examples, and practice head work too, and keep what we have got, and get what we can? We need never to think that anybody is going to feel interested for us, if we do not feel interested for ourselves.[37]

There is an element of success within failure that reveals itself in Stewart's words. She is aware that every human has natural rights and privileges. Yet, enslavement creates a distorted context whereby what is natural is reinterpreted as unnatural or nonexistent. For Stewart, there are only benefits from seeking one's freedom; even if they do not acquire it, these individuals will inevitably gain invaluable knowledge from the attempt itself.

Stewart returns to the hypocrisy and contradiction of Anglo-America. She scrutinizes the natural reaction an individual and community express when coming into the reality of their possible enslavement. In this particular discussion, we witness how Stewart is locating the lack of empathy, common sense, and humanity from proslavery Anglo-America. Mutual consideration, respect, and principles of equality and equity are not difficult concepts to understand. However, the human conscience that rejects the reality of human interrelatedness and interdependence inevitably lapses into a state of delusion and spiritual darkness. To a certain extent, Stewart is attempting to resuscitate the dying elements of the collective Anglo-American conscience and spirit, in that no culture, nation, or race exist in isolation but are solely dependent upon God who has created universal principles of equality:

> Did every gentleman in America realize, as one, that they had got to become bondmen, and their wives, their sons, and their daughters, servants forever, to Great Britain, their very joints would become loosened, and tremblingly would smite one against another; their countenance would be forced into action, their souls would recoil at the very thought, their hearts would die within them, and death would be far more preferable. Then why have not Africa's sons the right to feel the same? Are not

---

37. Richardson, *Maria W. Stewart*, 38.

their wives, their sons, and their daughters, as dear to them as those of the white man's?[38]

Stewart employs the American Revolutionary War (1775–1783) as the historical context from which Anglo-America could fully understand her perspective. She seeks to elicit the emotions and thoughts that have possibly been traumatic within the culture. Not to punish but to foster the healthy critical thinking and empathetic resonance required to establish a foundation for sincere repentance and reconciliation with the human-Other.

Within the greater context, Stewart is continually associating Christianity with American politics. For her, God's judgment and the complexities of sin are related to the contradiction and hypocrisy of Anglo-America's participation in slavery. Freedom within the perceived secular world is not detached from spiritual freedom. Anglo-Americans feared enslavement to the Anglo-British, and viewed their sociopolitical and religious freedom as being withheld and dictated by the oppositional-Other. Thus, Anglo-Americans feared dehumanization, enslavement, and oppression from the British and did everything in their power to avoid it. Stewart asks Anglo-America why they have chosen to withhold from non-Anglo-Americans the very things they have killed to maintain. She tentatively spoke on issues of which I interpret as exposing the difficulty Anglo-Americans had in discerning that they represented the Anglo-British to African-Americas. The tragic irony is that inequality and enslavement are never justified, and once imposed upon the human-Other, the human-Self is forced to deal with the reality of its fabricated inner world, and how they irrationally seek to impose it upon reality.

Anglo American society existed in a quasi-religious escapist world whereby they were justified and vindicated from false accusations. In this White Supremacist world, there is no divine judgment for creating and maintaining American slavery, in large part, through the assistance of the Christian church. Yet, for Stewart, this is a deceptive illusion as divine judgment will be experienced, and understood in complete self-awareness of our sins. She states,

> The blood of her murdered ones cries to heaven for vengeance against thee. Thou art almost become drunken with the blood of her slain; thou has enriched thyself through her toils and labors; and now refuseth to make even a small return. And thou

38. Richardson, *Maria W. Stewart*, 38–39.

has caused the daughters of Africa to commit whoredoms and fornications, but upon thee be their curse.[39]

It is a rather surreal experience when forced to prove your humanity to another person. The fact of being put in this position speaks volumes to the level of depravity of the person, or group for that matter, that demands such evidence. Yet, it takes humanity to acknowledge humanity, and when we have dehumanized ourselves, we will lose proper grounding in reality. This grounding alerts us to what may be common sense and easily verifiable information that does not rationally need justification. However, this is the general context many African and African-American slaves were forced into. Stewart is aware of the irrational view of Blacks that circulated within White Society. Her rebuttal and encouragement is expressed as,

> Trust in the Lord, and do good; so shalt thou dwell in the land, and verily thou shalt be fed. Encourage the noble-hearted Garrison. Prove to the world that you are neither ourang-outangs, or a species of mere animals, but that you possess the same powers of intellect as the proud-boasting American.
>
> I am sensible, my brethren and friends, that many of you have been deprived of advantages, kept in utter ignorance, and that your minds are now darkened; and if any one of you have attempted to aspire after high and noble enterprises, you have met with so much opposition that your souls have become discouraged.[40]

Stewart expresses her awareness of how African-Americans have been oppressed and she arguably demonstrates, from a sociological perspective, how the institution of slavery influenced the trajectory towards Black nihilism for many whose will was beaten to submission, and consequentially had no value in a world that they believed didn't apply to them, the free world. Stewart views herself and others as Ambassadors of Christ, and her ministry is to educate and support African-Americans, bringing them close to the full illumination of Christ Jesus.

---

39. Richardson, *Maria W. Stewart*, 39.
40. Richardson, *Maria W. Stewart*, 40–41.

CONCLUSION

Maria W. Stewart was a Christian influenced, in part, by the teaching of the Psalms and Proverbs. She demonstrated this through the biblical eloquence of her evangelical writing and ministry. She has written various articles, of which I have chosen one to engage. My aim was to provide an introduction to Stewart's faith and theology; only then could I attempt to do justice to presenting her to more readers. Authentic freedom does not exist apart from intellectual, moral, and spiritual improvement. This is what Stewart was seeking to convey to her audience. Although times have changed, the substance of these principles, at least for me, is universal and remains applicable to humanity. Stewart employed her freedom to help others achieve the same, and this is a journey we walk together on with Christ Jesus. Stewart's sociopolitical discourse was rooted within and upon an evangelical reading of scripture. This is not to minimize her denominational affiliation and influences, but is stated to direct the reader to the center of her life, of which she sought to expose everyone to Christ Jesus.

6

Julia A. J. Foote (1803–?)
"The Sanctified Preacher"

"Now may the God of peace Himself sanctify you entirely; and may your spirit and soul and body be kept complete, without blame at the coming of our Lord Jesus Christ."

(1 Thess 5:23)

INTRODUCTION

JULIA A. J. FOOTE, as I interpret her, was an influential evangelist and preacher. She was someone who clearly believed God called her to a ministry that extended beyond the concrete Christian church. Her character, speech, and relationships with people represented an individual who affirmed they not only had a relationship with God but that God had sanctified them for a life of self-sacrifice for the human-Other, in the glorification of Yahweh. This chapter will explore aspects of Foote's life and theology as articulated in her narrative. My aim is to extract certain events that helped shape her Christian identity, sense of belonging, and conceptions of shared-space with those considered the unsanctified and partially sanctified human-Other.

Foote was a controversial figure as a Black Christian woman who openly practiced evangelism and preaching without the permission of male authorities within her denomination. She was a Methodist but specifically within the African Methodist Episcopal church. An obvious aspect of her character and ministry was the rejection of opinions and man-made laws that opposed the Word of God.[1] Another dominant theme is Foote's emphasis on the reality of entire sanctification within our current earthly lives. Entire sanctification, as I interpret her articulation of it, bears similarity to what some Christians refer to as the Baptism of the Holy Spirit. Yet, it is difficult for me to discern whether she believed this or merely viewed the theological and realistic overlapping of the realities we define as entire sanctification, full salvation, and Baptism of the Holy Spirit. Regardless of how we view her beliefs and interpret her theology, Foote was adamant that she was not "teaching absolute perfection, for that belongs to God alone. Nor do I mean a state of angelic or Adamic perfection, but Christian perfection—an extinction of every temper contrary to love."[2] We will return to this important issue. Yet, beyond this interesting theological issue, Foote was clearly a faithful and even stubborn Christian woman, who was not ashamed of the Gospel and her calling to preach the Gospel to everyone, regardless of gender, race, and social status. Her life and ministry embodied the belief that God has truly saved her for communion with Him, and a sacrificial life of service to the wounded of the earth.

> A Brand Plucked from the Fire:
> An Autobiographical Sketch
> by
> Mrs. Julia A. J. Foote

FRONTISPIECE

Zechariah 3:2 is the initial scripture upon Foote's frontispiece. The third chapter consists of only ten verses but demonstrates a divine vision of Joshua, the High Priest, to Zechariah. These verses are reminiscent of Job 1:6–8, whereby Satan demeans Job's sincere faith in God. Yet, in this context, Zechariah, a human, is present and openly engages the angelic beings. Satan is the great deceiver and accuser of innocent and faithful children of Yahweh. Zechariah provides a portrait of Satan attempting to rob God of the very thing He desires, which is generally viewed as

1. Hanch, *Storied Witness*, 70.
2. Andrews, *Sisters of the Spirit*, 232.

genuine faith and obedience in love to Him. As in Job, in the context of Zechariah, Satan attempts to ridicule, discredit, and demean Joshua who is in visible need of forgiveness and reconciliation.

Joshua was dressed in filthy garments as he stood in the presence of the Angel of the Lord. The scene also alludes to Joshua experiencing the judgment of God. The reader is presented with the symbolism of Joshua's attire, and the implications of needing and about to receive salvation, sanctification, and cleansing from Yahweh. Joshua is dressed in homeless attire, which is representative of Israel and symbolic of her sins. The angel of the Lord rebukes Satan, stating, "Is this not a brand plucked from the fire?" Here is an articulation of a dominant theme within Foote's narrative that she applies to herself, and every person who embraces Christ as their Savior. God desires to forgive, redeem, and cleanse us of sin when we genuinely turn to Him, and we subsequently receive a special purpose to enact, embody, and live on earth that glorifies God. Foot exposes the listener and reader to her calling as a messenger of God. She willingly accepts that she and her ministry will be ridiculed, diminished, and rejected, but it does not matter because she is genuinely serving Yahweh. Thus, we witness early within the narrative the subtle alluding to the Baptism of the Holy Spirit, via entire sanctification, and the Baptism of Suffering, vis-à-vis earthly persecution.

The early message of the frontispiece directs the reader to a central theme of Foote's narrative. Her narrative is an account of the Gospel of Christ. Foote's life demonstrated how God rescued her. In this brief context, divine election and divine purpose are connected to the transformative power of Christ Jesus. Her story is deeply evangelical and Christological. She states "my object has been to testify more extensively to the sufficiency of the blood of Jesus Christ to save from all sin."[3] Foote had undertaken extensive periods of time dedicated to prayer to arrive at the point of writing her narrative. She displayed a deep concern that other evangelical colonial African-Americans displayed towards their race the reception of the Gospel message, embracing Christ as their Lord and Savior. Foote directly states, "My earnest desire is that many—especially of my own race—may be led to believe and enter into rest; 'For we which have believed do enter into rest' [Heb 4:3]—sweet soul rest."[4]

---

3. Andrews, *Sister Spirit*, 163.
4. Andrews, *Sister Spirit*, 163.

Spiritual rest is the consequential blessing from an authentic faith and love in Christ Jesus.

Jupiter Hammon (1711–1806) and Maria Stewart (1803–1879) expressed similar concerns regarding the immorality and blatant sins of some African-Americans. For Hammon and Stewart, the immoral lifestyles of enslaved people ironically made them the antithesis of genuine emancipation, as their lives were counterintuitive and counterproductive to authentic freedom. Nevertheless, Foote begins her narrative, like many others, from her place of birth, providing insight into her childhood and life before converting to Christianity.

The early part of her narrative is dedicated to articulating aspects of her childhood. It is complemented by exposing bad parentage and its consequences along with the importance of parents loving their children and properly raising them. Naturally, the ideal standard she employs is of Christianity as it relates to the Gospel message. Foote includes herself in this discussion. The reader is provided with a vision of God's presence in her early life. I argue, along with others, that one aspect of her ministry and theology was the restoration of Black parentage and traditional family structure that was essentially eviscerated throughout slavery.

CHILDHOOD IMPRESSIONS

"Honor your father and your mother, so that your days may be prolonged on the land which the LORD your God gives you"

(Exod 20:12)

"Train up a child in the way he should go, even when he grows older he will not abandon it"

(Prov 22:6)

Foote was born in Schenectady, New York, in 1823 as the youngest of four children to her mother. Her father had children from another woman. Foote, like those before her, finds it important to disclose information about her parents. Her mother was born a slave, but her father was initially free, only to suffer from the dehumanizing act of being stolen and forced into enslavement.

Although there were many, one of the most disheartening and barbaric aspects of colonial slavery was the total disregard for the Black family. Attached to this was the Anglo-American rejection of certain feelings and expressions of love from Black people. The assumption of many Anglo-Americans was that Black people, in being created for enslavement, did not have the normal human capacity to express and receive genuine love as epitomized by Anglo-Americans. An irrational level of ignorance, delusion, and dissonance is required to deny a human the natural right to be human. They are subjected to abuse and dehumanization when they successfully live as God intended them. Therefore, with this in mind, it becomes clear why there is an absence of positive stories of parents within the African-American slave narratives. Many African-American children were orphans or simply sold apart from their parents. These children became adults who were robbed of a safe home within the protection of their biological parents. Foote's childhood was different, but she was clearly conscious of the biblical view of parenthood and the firsthand experiences of being raised by Christians.

Foot introduces her parents at the initiation of her narrative in contrast to an abusive slave master. This particular context is employed to reveal aspects of her mother's character, one worth sharing with the world. It also demonstrated the depravity of some White masters who openly practiced sin within the institution of slavery. Foote's initial mention of her mother was not associated with prayer, singing together, or cooking her favorite meal. No, it was associated with experiencing a potential sexual assault from her master, and the further abuse she endured from rejecting his advances. We witness the inversion of morality within the institution of slavery according to the sinful pleasures of Anglo-American society. Foote's mother experienced further embarrassment and dehumanization from her mistress after disclosing the truth of her potential sexual assault.

People can react in different ways when forced to accept their weakness or confront an issue that causes them great pain. Generally, White mistresses reacted similarly when confronted with the knowledge of their husband's adultery, particularly with slave women. Typically, these pristine and cultured White Christian women behaved in barbaric ways, not towards their husbands, the men who had sworn an oath to love them before God, and those who wielded the most sociopolitical power within the nation, but towards some of the most vulnerable to society. Various Anglo-American women weaponized their racial allegiance above and beyond any universal empathy vis-à-vis their gender. The universal commonality to which we can naturally relate with one another was violated. Subsequently, those who were violated in this context had received a double portion of trauma and shame. Foote describes the dark complicity of her White mistress regarding her husband's sinful act by explaining,

> After the whipping, he himself washed her quivering back with strong salt water. At the expiration of a week, she was sent to change her clothing, which stuck fast to her back. Her mistress, seeing that she could not remove it, took hold of the rough tow-linen undergarment, and pulled it off over her head with a jerk, which took the skin with it, leaving her back all raw and sore.[5]

Sadism is a strong word that struggles to describe the reality of desiring and obtaining satisfaction at dehumanizing someone. Yet, it is an appropriate word to use when trying to understand some of the senseless acts of torture many African-American slaves endured under the guise of *discipline*. It becomes more difficult to understand when these desires and acts are practiced under the name of Christ Jesus. It takes a debased person with extreme narcissistic traits to torture someone for taking a moral stance against unrighteousness. These acts, at least for, represent what the Apostle Paul meant in Romans 1:28, "And just as they did not see fit to acknowledge God, God gave them up to a depraved mind, to do those things that are not proper."

Nevertheless, Foote's mother took a moral stance and accepted the consequences. Her righteousness was rewarded with a whipping, and inhumane treatment of her wounds, only to eventually be sold away from her family. These were common experiences for many African-American women. This event can also be interpreted as the grounding for Foote's discourse on the importance of loving parents and their moral and spiritual obligation to raise morally grounded children. The reader can safely assume that aspects of her mother's morality were placed within Foote at an early age.

Another intriguing event that depicted her parent's morality came within a particular crisis moment that was associated with the then-current Christian cultural perception of sin. Foote describes an event whereby her parents were leaving a dance with one of her siblings, who was a young baby. Her mother almost fell into a stream of water and drowned with her baby. For whatever reason, Foote's parents viewed this

---

5. Andrews, *Sister Spirit*, 166.

event as an example of divine intervention. The reader is not provided any specifics about why they assumed this, but only that they did, and desired to commit themselves to Christ. From this context, Foote introduces the subject of Christianity and connects this positive crisis moment to one of racial dehumanization. Foote demonstrates that moral and ethical lessons did not manifest solely in the secular world. They also developed within the Christian church, and whether inside or outside of a physical church, the integrity of her parents would continue to shine:

> Soon after, they made a public profession of religion and united with the M[ethodist] E[piscopal] Church. They were not treated as Christian believers, but as poor lepers. They were obliged to occupy certain seats in one corner of the gallery, and dared not come down to partake of the Holy Communion until the last white communicant had left the table.[6]

Foote's parents experienced racial discrimination similar to Richard Allen (1760–1831), Absolom Jones (1746–1818), and their congregation. Colonial Anglo-American Christianity divided the physical Church by race and social status. American slavery, through a Eurocentric lens, sought to usurp God's creative order in that White society sought to define the identity and sense of belonging of African-Americans, which was deeply connected to how they shared space with one another. African-Americans Christians, for the most part, almost always occupied the religious space within the church that was a replication of the social space outside of the church. Foote carefully chose two difficult contexts to examine regarding her parent's moral and spiritual self-awareness.

Foote did not shy away from discussing the irrationality of White Supremacy within the Christian church. I suspect Foote was providing examples of what was wrong about the American church, but she also sought to establish the things her ministry would confront, expose, and expunge from God's house. She recounts another event whereby her mother was offended in the church after making a reasonable mistake:

> One day my mother and another colored sister waited until all the white people had, as they thought, been served, when they started for the communion table. Just as they reached the lower door, two of the poorer class of white folks arose to go to the table. At this, a mother in Israel caught hold of my mother's dress and said to her, 'Don't you know better than to go to the table

---

6. Andrews, *Sister Spirit*, 167.

when white folks are there?' Ah! She did know better than to do such a thing purposely. This was one of the fruits of slavery. Although professing to love the same God, members of the same church, and expecting to find the same heaven at last, they could not partake of the Lord's Supper until the lowest of the whites had been served. Were they led by the Holy Spirit? Who shall say? The Spirit of Truth can never be mistaken, nor can he inspire anything unholy. How many at the present day profess great spirituality, and even holiness, and yet are deluded by a spirit of error, which leads them to say to the poor and the colored ones among them, 'Stand back a little—I am holier than thou.'[7]

The early experience of Christianity for Foote and her parents, as demonstrated by Anglo-American Christians, was the antithesis of the Gospel of Christ Jesus. The dehumanizing sectarian spirit of White Supremacy opposed the ecumenical spirit of Christianity. Those who claimed to be enlightened were deceptively blinded and lacked the self-awareness to see how they represented the spirit of the anti-Christ, not the Spirit of Christ. The destructiveness of White Supremacy affected the sacred ceremony of communion between God and His people. Foote articulates the level of self-righteousness that racism created when it was practiced and embodied within Christianity.

Foote's retelling of her early experience allows the reader to reflect on the possible initial construction of her identities, sense of belonging, and conceptions of shared-space with the human-Other, regardless of race, gender, and social status. She is establishing a grounding of Christian ethics and spirituality that influences the human-Self before its genuine conversion. Yet, Foote does not articulate her moral self-awareness solely relating to Anglo-American Christians. Foote is not preoccupied with issues of race and Whiteness. She has the moral self-awareness to properly assess her parent's moral judgment and contextualized Christianity relating to the testimony of Scripture. Foote is not ashamed to discuss the previous sinful lives of her parents, whom she believed dedicated unnecessary time to satisfying their flesh, as other Christians did before accepting Christ into their lives. One of the vices she discusses is drunkenness.

Consuming alcohol was acceptable to her parents before and after converting to Christianity. Their level of comfort with alcohol appears to cause discomfort within Foote, who reveals herself as a Christian who would advocate completely abstaining from it. Foote's crisis moment

---

7. Andrews, *Sister Spirit*, 167.

came as a child when she consumed alcohol without the direction of an adult. She explains,

> She [Aunt Giney] came in great haste, and at once pronounced me DRUNK. And so I was—stupidly drunk. They walked with me, and blew tobacco smoke into my face, to bring me to. Sickness almost unto death followed, but my life was spared. I was like a 'brand plucked from the burning' [Zech 3:2].
>
> Dear reader, have you innocent children, given you from the hand of God? Children, whose purity rouses all that is holy and good in your nature? Do not, I pray, give to these little ones of God the accursed cup which will send them down to misery and death. Listen to the voice of conscience, the woes of the drunkard, the wailing of poverty-stricken women and children, and touch not the accursed cup. From Sinai come the awful words of Jehovah, 'No drunkard shall inherit the kingdom of heaven' [1 Cor 6:10].[8]

It is difficult to assess the severity of Foote's crisis moment as a child. Perhaps she is embellishing the event, or it is possible this is how she perceived it as a child. Regardless of our stance, it is interesting that she acknowledged the presence of God's grace and protection of her life before accepting salvation. If this is the line of reasoning, the drunken event is a possible foreshadowing of divine intervention, mercy, and calling upon her life for a greater purpose. The reader can safely assume it was service to God vis-à-vis preaching the Word of God. We are presented with the first reference to Zachariah 3:2 within the main text apart from the narrative's frontispiece. Foote uses this event to provide a warning, a biblical lesson to her readers, especially those who are parents.[9] To a certain extent, the deeper issue may not be our theological stance on the permissibility of consuming alcohol. Instead, it is the focus on the parent's responsibility from God to raise morally grounded children in the hopes that they mature into strong Christian adults. Christian ethics and morality extended beyond the issue of drunkenness. It also touched on the important reality of reconciliation and redemption. We witness this in part through Foote's early experiences with various Anglo-Americans.

---

8. Andrews, *Sister Spirit*, 168.
9. Hanch, *Storied Witness*, 75.

THE LORD'S PRAYER

Memories Between Father and Daughter

> "Our Father in heaven, hallowed be your name, you kingdom come, your will be done, on earth as it is in heaven. Give us today our daily bread. And forgive us our debts, as we also have forgiven our debtors. And lead us not into temptation, but deliver us from the evil one" (Matt 6:9–13)

We are provided a selective image of Foote's upbringing. She does not express whether her grandparents on her mother's and father's side of the family were Christian. Nor do we know if Foote's parents grew up in Christian households. We are only told they genuinely converted after a significant event and devoted themselves to Christ. Perhaps this is a primary reason why they never forced or coerced Foote to convert at a young age. Foote's parents appeared to model Christian character and faithfulness, allowing their lives to be a testimony to Foote, along with their love as parents. Foote's parents may have also represented Christian forgiveness and reconciliation. They still opened their hearts and home to certain Anglo-Americans rather than allow their abuse and torment to scar their spirit, making them bitter, and ultimately distorting their relationship with God.

Foote discusses two significant events that shaped her childhood development. One event appears to have been in the context of a local Church revival, and the other stems from a possible close friendship between her parents and an Anglo-American woman. The two events centered on the biblical testimony of the Lord's prayer (Matt 6:9–13; Luke 11:1–4). Even at eight years old Foote was exposed to the uniqueness of church revivals. Upon attending one, she was met by an adult man, possibly a preacher, who made a brief but impactful impression on her perception of God and His Word.[10] Referencing this encounter, Foote explains,

> He prayed for me long and loud. I trembled with fear, and cried as though my heart would break, for I thought he was the Lord, and I must die. After they had gone, my mother talked with me and my soul more than she ever had before, and told me that this preacher was a good man, but not the Lord; and that, if I were a good girl, and said my prayers, I would go to heaven.

---

10. Hanch, *Storied Witness*, 80.

This gave me a great comfort. I stopped crying, but continued to say, "Now I lay me." A White woman, who came to our house to sew, taught me the Lord's prayer. No tongue can tell the joy that filled my poor heart when I could repeat, "Our Father, which art in heaven." It has always seemed to me that I was converted at this time.[11]

It is interesting that Foote had a somewhat ominous or overwhelming dread of the Lord. This was not instilled by her parents, who appeared to be lax in their practice of Christianity compared to her as an adult. Nevertheless, a sense of reverence is expressed, and we can reflect on the possible sense of dread she may have felt from experiencing everyone's words and actions during the revival. We can also logically reflect on the possible self-awareness she experienced regarding feeling the Spirit's presence at the event. The revival marked a moment whereby young Foote was establishing a new identity, sense of belonging, and conception of shared-space with the human-Other. This event was the synthesis of God making His presence more felt and visible even within Foote's natural ignorance as a young child, in conjunction with her making mature decisions on how she will respond to God.

During the revival, she chose to love and be guided by love. Foote chose communication with God through genuine prayer. She did not employ selective obedience with a façade of holiness. Foote gestures at the sometimes ambiguity of our salvation. For her, it was attached to the encouragement of the Black preacher and her mother's correction. Another significant event was being taught the Lord's prayer by an Anglo-American woman. We are provided a positive example of Whiteness within the confines of Black space. Whiteness was not viewed as an intrusion but was warmly invited within sanctified space through the Spirit for the glory of Christ. The revival and Foote's childhood home connect two people from different races who are siblings within the Body of Christ, both instilling invaluable lessons within Foote that shape her identity, sense of belonging, and share-space with the human-Other. Foote's father is included, and he provides a very touching moment for her that she may have valued more than she articulated within her narrative.

Foote spends a lengthy amount of time discussing her childhood at the beginning of her narrative. It complements her direct and indirect emphasis on the value of having Christian parents, and their divine

---

11. Andrews, *Sister Spirit*, 169.

responsibility to raise God-loving children. This makes a particular event with her father special, as it represents the deep intimacy a father and daughter can experience in Christ. The nature of Christian influence is seen within this event. We are challenged to reflect on how God engages everyone as they come together to learn about His Word. Foot did not have to be a Christian to experience the presence of the Spirit around her. She received a powerful awareness of Him through her parents as they embodied a Christlike life as enslaved children of God.

Literacy and Christianity have a unique relationship within African-American culture. Countless slaves attempted, and some succeeded, in learning how to read and write with the Bible as their primary text. Foote's father conducted family worship through the ability to partially discern English alphabets. For whatever reason, this had a great impact on Foote, as it probably was the grounding for her intellectual stimulation. It was rare for a slave to read, albeit sparingly, and for that person to use their ability to worship God in community with other people. Foote possibly desired these experiences and responsibilities, all of which stemmed from her genuine interest in Yahweh. She recounts a particular special occasion with her father by explaining,

> One day, when he was reading, I asked him to teach me the letters. He replied, "Child, I hardly know them myself." Nevertheless, he commenced with "A," and taught me the alphabet. Imagine, if you can, my childish glee over this, my first lesson. The children of the present time, taught at five years of age, can not realize my joy at being able to say the entire alphabet when I was nine years old.[12]

The excitement a young girl has with spending quality time with her father, in this context, developed through Christianity and literacy. The alphabet wasn't the uniqueness of the event. Rather, it was the person, her father, who carved out time to teach Foote everything he knew and that few adults had obtained. Foote's father, in many ways, helped establish another conduit of communication for God to empower Foote's character, relationship with Him, and her future ministry. All of this influenced how she articulated her identity, sense of belonging, and conception of shared space with the human other.

The importance of a parent's influence upon their children is noticeably emphasized at the beginning of Foote's narrative. She displayed a

---

12. Andrews, *Sister Spirit*, 170; Hanch, *Storied Witness*, 80.

patient and meticulous description of her parents' character before and after their conversion. Foote takes the opportunity to connect this to the importance of inviting Christ into those memorable moments. No child is too young to be exposed to the Word of God, regardless of their inability to fully comprehend their situation and the content being spoken to them. The most important element is exposing them to the presence of God and the relationships between Him and adults until their cognitive abilities mature. The emphasis on Christian parenthood is interesting and mysterious as Foote never explains what inspires this deep inner interest within her. The reader can imagine it was possibly a major theme within her evangelism, preaching, and everyday discourse with people. Foote's words of encouragement can be gleaned from statements like this,

> Dear children, with enlightened Christian parents to teach you, how thankful you should be that "From a child you are able to say that you have known the Holy Scriptures, which are able to make you wise unto salvation, through faith which is in Christ Jesus" [2 Tim 3:15]. I hope all my young readers will heed the admonition, "Remember now thy Creator in the days of thy youth" [Eccl 12:1], etc.[13]

Foote is not ashamed of the Gospel, and she is not insecure about presenting it to her readers. There is something special about the relationship between God, child, and parent, and this includes surrogates. Enslavement had reduced and relatively eliminated healthy conceptions of respect, love, guidance, and sacrificial love of a parent to their child for African-Americans. Foot was conscious of this and, as I interpret her, sought to recreate what was partially lost.

Foote also emphasizes the relationship between parent and child through the creation account. She employs the monumental act of Adam and Eve's disobedience to YHWH ushering in the Fall of humanity. Foote particularly discusses ignoring God's voice. Most interpretations emphasize Adam's shame as the primary cause of him avoiding God when beckoned. However, Foote places an emphasis on the consequence of sin relating to some new innate natural fear. She states,

> It was not a strange voice; it was a voice he had always loved. Why did he flee away, and hide himself among the trees? It was because he had disobeyed God. Sin makes us afraid of God, who is holy; nothing but sin makes us fear One so good and so kind.

---

13. Andrews, *Sister Spirit*, 170.

> It is a sin for children to disobey their parents. The Bible says: "Honor thy father and thy mother" [Exod 20:12].[14]

Foote frames Adam's relationship with God as that between a son and father. Adam ignoring God's voice was an additional act of disobedience, as the first brought about sin, and the second was a paradox from the first, as it stemmed from the original sin and subsequently supported the initial sin. The power of our ethical and moral inner conviction of sin is not overwhelming to the extent that we cannot repent and seek forgiveness. Foote connects this to the early relationship between parents and children, which echoes the testimony of the Prodigal Son (Luke 15:11–32).

Lessons of parenthood blended with the relationship of children to adults. For Foote, the responsibility of obedience was not isolated solely to kinship, and race for that matter. She articulates a story that developed between her and adult Anglo-Americans that insinuates the consequences of adults violating their divine responsibility.

VIOLATED TRUST AND THE WANING OF LOVE

Some colonial African-Americans were forced into contexts whereby they were naturally exposed to the ideology of White supremacy and the Anglo-Americans who embodied it. However, others were also exposed to those who did not exhibit the dehumanizing ideology. These African-Americans were exposed to the true humanity of White society that desperately sought to establish themselves within the veil of quasi-deification. Black and White humanity nurtured one another in healthy contexts to the point of establishing genuine love and reconciliation, inside and outside of the Church. Foote provides an interesting aspect of her young life that expressed the positive reality of this engagement. At ten years old, Foote was sent to care for a prominent Anglo-American family that was disabled and suffered from various illnesses. She expresses a deep connection with two members of the family that are rarely expressed in colonial African-American discourses:

> They had no children, and soon became quite fond of me. I really think Mrs. Prime loved me. She had a brother who was dying with consumption, and she herself was a cripple. For some time after I went there, Mr. John, the brother, was able to walk from

14. Andrews, *Sister Spirit*, 170.

his father's house, which was quite near to ours, and I used to stand, with tears in my eyes, and watch him as he slowly moved across the fields, leaning against the fence to rest himself by the way.[15]

Foote doesn't elaborate on the specific contours of their relationship. She only briefly discusses it, and the assumption holds that the greater purpose of this information is to demonstrate the presence of racial reconciliation between Black and White society. These relationships were the light that glimmered within the darkness of colonial America and demonstrated the reality of mutual, reciprocal, and self-sacrificial love. This connection was applicable to Mrs. Prime and her brother. Foote articulates the compassion and possible empathy she had for him.

Mr. Prime suffered from a terminal illness, and for whatever reason, it ignited not only curiosity but genuine concern for his salvation. The touching aspect of their relationship is felt in Foote questioning Mr. Prime's prayer life: "One day, as he started for home, I stepped up to him and said, 'Mr. John, do you say your prayers?' and then I began to cry. He looked at me for a moment, then took my hand in his and said: 'Sometimes I pray; do you?' I answered, 'Yes sir.' Then said he, 'You must pray for me'—and turned and left me. I ran to the barn, fell down on my knees, and said: 'Our Father, who art in heaven, send that good man to put his hand on Mr. John's head.' I repeated this many times a day as long as he lived."[16] Naturally, Mr. Prime was considerate enough not to overwhelm a 10-year-old with the details of his illness. A sign of his character can be gleaned from asking a young Black girl for prayer. A rare but transformative event that demonstrated their hearts. Foote is carefully demonstrating the redemptive qualities of Whiteness, not as a racialized-philosophical concept, but as the representative of a collective body of humanity, that is made in the Imago Dei, and if sincerely Christian, conformed to the Imago Christi.

Young Foote's relationship with the Primes was close to the extent they financially supported her education. Even within a school, she had pleasant experiences with Anglo-American children and teachers. This did not distort Foote's perception of White Supremacy and Anglo-American culture; it likely grounded it within the testimony of the Bible and a form of Christian realism. She was not a racial assimilationist but a

---

15. Andrews, *Sister Spirit*, 171.
16. Andrews, *Sister Spirit*, 171.

racial realist. Nevertheless, part of the significance of mentioning her relationship with the Primes is related to the nature of parenting and moral character instilled in children. Yet, in this context, it is child and adult that transcend racial discrimination. Foote is consistent in her narrative in that she always finds room to connect a secular or universal principle to the Gospel message:

> Parents, are you training your children in the way they should go? Are you teaching them obedience and respect? Are you bringing your little ones to Jesus? Are they found at your side in the house of God, on Sunday, or are they roving the streets or fields? Or, what is worse, are they at home reading books or newspapers that corrupt the heart, bewilder the mind, and lead down to the bottomless pit?[17]

The focus is Christ, not the pleasures of the world, as she and others had naturally been tempted to enjoy. Foote's worldview encompasses the familial relationships that transcend race, gender, and class. She emphasizes the universal call of God via the Gospel and Jesus' sacrifice on the cross as the means to reconcile former enemies into the family of God. There is a duality of the form of reconciliation Foote is emphasizing in these contexts: reconciliation between God and humanity that creates genuine reconciliation between the races. The interesting element of Foote's narrative bears similarity to Jarena Lee. Both women, as children and young adults, demonstrated the character and moral understanding of Christ but had not yet confessed Christ as their Lord and Savior. They exhibited knowledge of scripture and the immorality and sin that accompany the perception of failing or offending God.

THE EXPERIENCE OF SUICIDAL IDEATION

Children who are morally grounded can experience the darker aspects of acknowledging their immorality and sins. Some do not have the cognitive and emotional maturity to search for a balance of knowing they are a sinner and understanding they are saved, redeemed, and reconciled with God and humanity in Christ Jesus. Jarena Lee was another woman who experienced suicidal ideation. Foote is similar, and the experience of suicidal ideation is deeply connected to a temporary falling out with the Primes.

17. Andrews, *Sister Spirit*, 171.

Some of the most compassionate colonial Anglo-Americans displayed moments of paternalistic aggression or superiority. These areas serve as the ambiguous space between White Supremacy and White delusion regarding the permissibility of irrational but self-justified violence as a discipline. Foote was whipped with rawhide by Mrs. Prime because she believed Foote had stolen some little pound cakes, although she sternly denied it. We are never told why Mrs. Prime did not believe Foote. The reader of the narrative is not given any indication of Foote acting in a way that entertained thievery or an immoral character. Up to this point in Foote's narrative, we are given a definitive positive view of Foote's integrity, even to the point of her being borderline self-righteous.

Nevertheless, Foote argued for her innocence, and she experienced the rage of Mrs. Prime through strict whipping. Unfortunately, this event was interpreted as a betrayal for Foote, and it changed her views and relationship with the Primes. The reader is forced to interpret this event also as a biblical violation of the divine responsibility older adults have over children. Foote expresses anger and disbelief at how she was treated by Mrs. Prime. Mrs. Prime is depicted as someone who did not think or act from any rational moral grounding, but instead, reacted from irrational emotionalism. Mrs. Prime was established in contrast to young Foote, who was a morally grounded girl, dedicated to living the right way, who was also shown that a person can still be punished when innocent of a violation. Everyone must face their weakness with an individual or group who has authority over them and has chosen to "discipline" them according to their moral standard, even if their decision is immoral or a sin. Evidently, the whipping had a traumatic effect upon Foote. She associated her feelings from the betrayal with those of a former teacher of hers who committed suicide after committing murder. Foote explains,

> That night I wished over and over again that I could be hung as John Van Paten had been. In the darkness and silence, Satan came to me and told me to go to the barn and hang myself. In the morning I was fully determined to do so. I went to the barn for that purpose, but that boy, whom I disliked very much, was there, and he laughed at me as hard as he could.[18]

The tight bond between Foote and Mrs. Prime was waning from this event of betrayal. The strong and irrational emotions of a child are fully displayed through Foote's account. The interesting element of this event

---

18. Andrews, *Sister Spirit*, 175.

is upon entering the potential context of suicide, she is met with the likely culprit, the individual who stole the little pound cakes.

Satan is articulated by Foote as the great deceiver. He is portrayed as seeking to capitalize on this event to destroy God's potential plans for Foote regarding her ministry. The interesting aspect of Foote's moral self-awareness is the inability of her at that age to see how suicide was defined as a sin, but she had the awareness to discern that her anger and attempt to physically hurt the young boy was immoral. She viewed her anger towards the young boy as a second violation of God's Word, of which she needed to repent, seeking God's forgiveness and restoration. Foote's conception of ethics and morality continued to develop as she grew and experienced the contours of an enslaved African-American woman. At this point, it is likely that Foote has already accepted Christ as her Lord and Savior. The difficulty with her narrative, as with others, is that they have difficulty expressing the context and moment of conversion primarily because of their theological maturity and convictions. Naturally, many Christians do not know the exact hour, minute, and second of conversion. However, some do reflect on the presence of moral conviction and the desire to change as a general indication of their salvific journey. Nevertheless, Foote continues to emphasis the importance of moral self-awareness in her narrative, and the reader is presented with an event that bore eerie similarity to her parents when they were young.

FOOTE'S BACKSLIDING

"The Little Methodist Fool"

Often the lines can become blurred between the Holy Spirit convicting us of our sins and us inappropriately assuming the responsibility to reprimand ourselves. This becomes problematic for some, as their desire to be obedient and please the Lord can lapse into extremism. False conceptions of holiness and an accompanying imposition of judgmentalism can develop. This was an important lesson for Foote. She was possibly becoming a zealous teenager who focused entirely on being distinct from the world. At this point in her life, Foote's parents had relocated the family to Albany, New York, and then attached themselves to a Methodist church. She was like any other human regardless of religious and areligious dispositions. Foote struggled with embracing a particular perspective of Christianity that tended to emphasize God's grace and mercy. She describes a particular as,

> The last time I made a public effort at dancing I seemed to feel a heavy hand upon my arm pulling me from the floor. I was so frightened that I fell; the people all crowded around me, asking what was the matter, thinking I was ill. I told them I was not sick, but that it was wrong for me to dance. Such loud, mocking laughter as greeted my answer, methinks is not often heard this side the gates of torment, and only then when they are opened to admit a false-hearted professor of Christianity.[19]

Foote demonstrates another example of the ambiguity of moral convictions we sometimes experience. Logically, she was possibly struggling with the secular cultural acceptance of dancing against a certain religious disavowal prior to this particular dance. She still attended and this brought about an interesting psychological and spiritual experience. Foote discerned the cause and source of the "pulling," and for whatever reason was transparent enough to disclose it among people who could not appreciate it. Yet, to be fair, under normal conditions the crowd's reaction seems plausible.

Nevertheless, Foote was mocked and called "a little Methodist fool," because this mysterious event seemed out of context.[20] The reader is struck wondering whether this is a coincidence Foote shared with her parents or simply an embellished retelling of an anticlimactic secular event. If we remember, as a child her mother and sibling almost died upon leaving a dance. That crisis moment was interpreted as a central expression of divine intervention in relation to calling them to salvation. The reader is forced to reflect on the possibility of the same message being presented to Foote. Skepticism aside, she likely experienced a legitimate confrontation with God, a heightened moral self-awareness from Him, progressively sanctifying Foote for a greater ministerial purpose. This initial embarrassing event has progressed into an influential communal testimony. Foote explains, "an invisible presence seemed to fill the place," and this likely was the Holy Spirit, who saturated the dance, disturbing the participants and causing them to leave.

It is here that Foote repeats a phrase that she feels characterizes her life: she was "plucked as a brand from the burning." The perception and

---

19. Andrews, *Sister Spirit*, 178.
20. Hanch, *Storied Witness*, 86.

possibility of Foote's religious extremism is felt in her belief that God's judgment would fall upon her if she continued to dance. Now we must view dancing as representative of something more powerful, a sin, or the potentiality of sin, that could cause a rupturing of the relationship between her and God. It is not the simple act itself since there are biblical references to dancing within positive contexts of worship. The central importance of this event was primarily Foote's obedience to God's action and how she could possibly become a living testimony to Him according to His will. There is a mystery as to why and how the crowd was left speechless by the presence of God within the room and eventually left without saying a word. We can either assume God was likely preparing the participants for His presence before the event, lacerating the callousness of their hearts and consciences. Or Foote is employing some religious embellishment to dramatize this unique event that she only experienced.

The confusing aspect of the story is the ambiguity of the event once juxtaposed with other events within her narrative. For example, Foote later mentions her mother encouraging her to attend a family event after the crisis moment at the dance where she was pulled to the floor. Apparently, according to Foote's narrative, her mother believed she was possibly exhibiting an extremist religious reaction during that moment. Despite this, Foote was convinced that she did not misinterpret God during that moment. She also proceeds to chastise her mother for encouraging the sinful practice of dancing. This is in conjunction with admitting to the reader her knowledge of the positive biblical testimony of dancing. Foote honestly believes she was spared God's judgment by not continuing to dance and levies a stern rebuke of mothers who lack the moral self-awareness to discern what is and is not sinful cultural practices. Foote remarks that, "Mothers, you know not what you do when you urge your daughter to go to parties to make her more cheerful. You may even be causing the eternal destruction of that daughter. God help you, mothers, to do right."[21] There is the conflict between two conceptions of Christian ethics and spirituality between Foote and her mother. It is amazing she exhibited this level of moral and spiritual self-awareness before she accepted Christ as her Lord and Savior.

---

21. Andrews, *Sister Spirit*, 179.

FULL CONFIRMATION OF SALVATION

Many colonial African-Americans experienced dramatic conversion experiences. Colonial Black evangelicals struggled with the heightened self-awareness of their sin and those that permeated society. This was a sign of their genuineness, experience of divine revelation, relationships with God, and calling into ministry. Foote also experienced a dramatic conversion, one that culminated from God progressively reaching out to her, showing more of Himself, and how much she needed to sacrifice to be with Him.

Foote experienced the salvific presence and confirmation of Christ at the age of fifteen at a Sunday church meeting.[22] The voice of God was unavoidable that night. During that meeting, the minister read Revelation 14:3 regarding the signs of a new song. The verse emphasizes the uniqueness of the Elect, the 144,000 who were the only people able to sing a divine song. For whatever reason, Foote was inclined to focus on how sinful she was relating to the holiness of God, as she listened to this verse preached. She experienced a deep sense of unworthiness that appeared to border upon self-degradation. I state this in relation to the entirety of her narrative. Foote appeared to constantly strive to achieve a sense of self-worth or a separate, heightened divine confirmation of her sanctification. Foote could not ignore a voice that perpetually spoke to her: "Such a sinner as you are can never sing that new song." This voice was not an imaginary projection of Foote's conscience. It wasn't an illusory manifestation of trauma in Foote's life. The voice was of God, and He desired that she, as Foote believed, would arrive at a basic understanding of the effects of sin, the damage and delusion it inflicts upon the human mind.

The theological lesson the reader is forced to grapple with is that God does remind us of our sins and this remembrance is not a punishment. God does not receive any pleasure from convicting us of sins. The person, if genuine, must be purified from the debilitating effects of self-worship vis-à-vis the acquiring of their self-interest, in part through fleshly pleasure. Everyone must come to a mature understanding of who they are apart from Christ and how we become who God intended for us to be, not as isolated individuals but in a community with one another. Foote finally reached her moment of self-negation and submitted to Christ: "In great terror I cried: 'Lord have mercy on me, a poor sinner!'"[23] From her own testimony, Foote describes herself as previously swaying back and

---

22. Hanch, *Storied Witness*, 89.
23. Andrews, *Sister Spirit*, 180.

forth about genuinely committing to a Christian lifestyle. This explains the perception of the dramatic dancing event relating to her conversion experience. God was chipping away at the callousness of Foote's heart and conscience. He was freeing her from the allure of sinful deception whereby one is deadened to the concrete existence of God, human sin, and how much humanity needs its Creator.

Often, it is difficult for us to accept the simplicity of life. I imagine that our fallen humanity is captivated by some internal insecurity, and that aspect of us is perpetually fed by a complex network of deception, misunderstanding, and disbelief that makes us think truth and fact exist and can only be achieved through extreme difficulty and struggle. Foote shares another experience with Jarena Lee. They both had difficulty accepting the legitimacy of their conversion. Doubt crept into their heart, and as they both understood it, Satan attempted to deceive them.

Foote describes her struggle, stating, "One week from the time of my conversion, Satan tempted me dreadfully, telling me I was deceived: people didn't get religion in that way, but went to the altar, and were prayed for by the minister. This seemed so very reasonable that I began to doubt if I had religion."[24] Upon communicating with a trusted minister, he confirmed that rituals did not save people. Rather, it is their faith and love in Christ as their Lord and Savior. Ultimately, God sent an earthly messenger to confirm to Foote what He was continually speaking to her. Here is another powerful event in Foote's life that she grafted into her ministry. Foote's experience, as I understand it, bears similarity to the heightened sense of self-awareness Martin Luther (1483–1546) experienced regarding the Apostle Paul's words regarding the just shall live by faith alone.

Nevertheless, for Foote, genuine salvation is not works-based or ritualistic. It does not provide a psychological aesthetic. True faith and love of God are creations of God and lovingly given to us through His grace. We are only gifted with these realities and everything they entail when we seek to understand God as God is, and choose to submit to Him, growing in love for him and the human-Other.

THE DOCTRINE OF SANCTIFICATION

Theologically, Foote developed a dogmatic belief and adherence to the doctrine of entire sanctification in our earthly lives. She referred to it also

---

24. Andrews, *Sister Spirit*, 181.

as *full salvation*. Her narrative displays the positive and negative aspects of adhering to this belief. Foote routinely references opposition to the doctrine of entire sanctification and her claim to have achieved it. Opposition in different ways comes from her parents, the main minister of their church, Foote's husband, and various other Christians. The belief of entire sanctification was a controversial topic among colonial American Christians, and still is currently within select Christian communities. Yet, the dynamics of this belief and how it was possibly practiced takes a rather interesting turn within the context of colonial slavery and its inversion of Christian principles according to race.

Nevertheless, the doctrine itself tends to create certain unavoidable realities for its adherents, as they are typically characterized in two ways. From one perspective, the adherent may perpetually struggle with the awareness of their sins, in the sense of constantly wrestling with inner embarrassment and shame. Their awareness of sin stimulates an almost inner compulsion to not only reject/repent of their sin, but quickly acquire some sense of righteousness. There is the negative and persistent need to seek some final confirmation of their salvation, as awareness of their sinfulness is equated to an ambiguous doubt of sorts regarding their salvation. Therefore, the adherent may seek the final conquering of sin in their earthly lives whereby they do not struggle with sin in any stretch of the imagination. On the other hand, adherents may assume a level of entire sanctification or full salvation where they present themselves as no longer struggling with sin. They have obtained a heightened communion with God through the empowerment of the Holy Spirit. Additionally, these adherents may always seek to invite other Christians to this heightened spiritual reality, interpreting the rejection of entire sanctification as sinful doubt. An example of this is seen in Foote's inability to handle her anger when she is hit by her younger brother.

> One day, as I was sitting at work, my younger brother, who was playing with the other small children, accidentally hit me in the eye, causing the most intense suffering. The eye was so impaired that I lost the sight of it. I was very angry; and soon pride, impatience, and other signs of carnality, gave me a great deal of trouble. Satan said; 'There! You see you never were converted.' But he could not make me believe that, though I did not know the cause of these repining within.[25]

---

25. Andrews, *Sister Spirit*, 182.

Anger may have been a persistent sin in Foote's early life. She struggled with it relating to the betrayal of Mrs. Prime regarding the stolen cake. Foote believed a local boy she disliked was the true culprit, and upon seeing him laugh at her, she states "All at once my weak feelings left me, and I sprang at him in a great rage, such as I had never known before; but he eluded my grasp, and ran away, away, laughing."[26] Nevertheless, beyond these examples, the dogmatism of Foote is further witnessed when she rejects the advice of the main preacher of her church, a possible class leader of the church, and her parents who rejected earthly entire sanctification, telling her that it was normal for Christians to struggle with sin. Her internal response to them was, "What delusion!"[27] The reader is forced to reflect on why she assumed spiritual maturity above her elders, at least in this situation. We can respect her desire, and any Christian for that matter, to achieve a life of sinlessness for the glory of Christ. Foote's conception of entire sanctification or full salvation, for her at least, can only be achieved through the power of the Holy Spirit.

Yet, to be fair, Foote was possibly surrounded by people who did not clearly comprehend the doctrine of sanctification. We can only rely upon her account. Foote discusses her preacher, class leader, and parent's interpretation of sanctification by stating,

> I told my parents, my minister, and my leader that I wanted to be sanctified. They told me sanctification was for the aged and persons about to die, and not for the one like me. All they said did me no good. I had wandered in the wilderness a long time, and now that I could see a ray of the light for which I had so long sought, I could not rest day nor night until I was free.[28]

For whatever reason, both parties clearly did not view themselves as being sanctified but had still achieved salvation. Theologically this is unbiblical as sanctification, at least for most Christians, begins after salvation and the Christian undergoes this process throughout their life. Sanctification appears to mirror some works-based models to achieve it, as the elderly and those facing death have obtained it. The knowledgeable reader is forced to reflect on the contours of their definition of sanctification and how it is biblically justified. Perhaps their definitions are associated to both longevity of life and the suffering one experiences. Nevertheless, the

---

26. Andrews, *Sister Spirit*, 175.
27. Andrews, *Sister Spirit*, 183.
28. Andrews, *Sister Spirit*, 185.

desire for entire sanctification or full salvation became somewhat of a relative compulsion for Foote. The absence of achieving it had thrust Foote into bondage from which she sought emancipation. It can be argued that self-inflicted trauma can be manifested by desiring something that doesn't exist or can never be obtained. Does this apply to Foote?

Foote never clarifies who those "old people" were that achieved sanctification. Perhaps they are Christian elders of her community. There is a striking irony expressed by Foote regarding her self-awareness and critical thinking related to her central message of children obeying their parents. She has consistently preached this principle throughout her narrative; however, she chose to disobey her parent regarding the acquisition of sanctification. Foote found the sanctified old people of almost mythological lore and received their wise counsel: "Sanctification was for the young believer, as well as the old."[29] Despite this confirmation, Foote is still unsettled, as she still is without it, according to her perspective. Eventually, Foote believes and acquires entire sanctification. She never articulates the exact moment or context of this relatively evasive event. We are only provided with her experiences, whereby it is confirmed and implied through her engagement with disbelieving Christians.

Opposition to this doctrine and the perception of her acquisition is seen within her family and her new congregation: "Others disbelieved and ridiculed this 'foolish doctrine,' as they called it, saying it was just as impossible to live without committing sin as it was to live without eating, and brought disjointed passages of Scripture to bear them out."[30] The reader is forced to reflect upon their position regarding entire sanctification, and the positioning of the empathy regarding both parties. The Christians who opposed Foote, at least from her own description, had possibly viewed or sensed some self-righteousness within her. An example of this is seen in a response of Foote's husband regarding her acquisition of entire sanctification and his inability to obtain it:

> My husband had always treated the subject of heart purity with favor, but now he began to speak against it. He said I was getting more crazy every day, and getting others in the same way, and that if I did not stop he would send me back home or to the crazy-house. I questioned him closely respecting the state of his mind, feeling that he had been prejudiced. I did not attempt to contend with him on the danger and fallacy of his notions, but

---

29. Andrews, *Sister Spirit*, 186.
30. Andrews, *Sister Spirit*, 193.

simply asked what his state of grace was, if God should require his soul of him then. He gave me no answer until I insisted upon one. Then he said: "Julia, I don't think I can ever believe myself as holy as you think you are."[31]

We must understand Foote's reasoning from the position that salvation is only truly confirmed as the reception of entire sanctification. There is almost a space of ambiguity between her understanding of salvation and sanctification. She affirmed her husband's salvation prior to this event, but her theology appears to require a finality, the culmination of union between God and humanity, vis-à-vis, entire sanctification. Her husband appears empathetic but stands firm in his theology, acknowledging their conflicting views of holiness. For him, holiness as Foote articulates it, is a state that he rejects because of its irrationality, not some false belief of his struggle with sin.

CONCLUSION

Despite this issue, Foote was a genuine Christian with an influential ministry that glorified Christ. She was someone who did not accept the presence and dehumanizing consequences of sin in our lives. We may assume this is largely influenced by the presence and struggle of sin in her life, not by any measure of self-awareness from her moral understanding and intelligence. Rather, it likely stemmed from divine revelation according to God's will and His purpose for her life.

Foote was more than an African-American woman fighting for gender equality through the advancement of conservative feminism. These were aspects of her identity as she advocated for the biblical legitimacy of her calling to preach, and every woman God has called into ministry. Yet, we must realize her love for Christ and the strong desire to live a life of self-sacrifice were the reasons we are blessed to learn as little as we have within her narrative. The controversial theological issue of entire sanctification is intriguing. Whether we agree or disagree with the doctrine, it had undoubtedly shaped Foote's Christian identity, sense of belonging, and how she conceptualized her share-space with the human-Other—not through force or coercion, but willfully from the sincerity of her heart and spirit.

---

31. Andrews, *Sister Spirit*, 196.

7

Homage to Harriet E. Wilson
An Evangelical Reading of "Our Nig"

"He predestined us to adoption as sons and daughters through Jesus Christ to Himself, according to the good pleasure of His will."

(ROM 8:15)

"OUR NIG," PROVIDES AN intuitive testimony of colonial African-American feminism and a critical evaluation of superficial American Christianity.[1] Harriet E. Wilson articulated some universal struggles, hopes, pains, and joys many African-American women experienced during slavery.[2] However, the most touching, through my interpretive lens, is the subtle presentation of Wilson's desire to be loved by her biological mother, and the absence of her mother, within a context of servitude under the extreme abuse from a pseudo-mother figure, embodied by a Christian

---

1. My intent within this interpretation of Wilson's work is not to provide a complex historical account of her authentic life and those she portrays within her narrative. This lies beyond the scope of the chapters, and my attempts would do injustice to the scholars I have gleaned from who have articulated impressive influential work. See Boggis et al., *Harriet Wilson's New England*; Foreman et al., *Harriet E. Wilson*; Gates and Wilson, *Harriet E. Wilson*; Gates et al., *Our Nig*.

2. Historians have discovered her real name to be Harriet E. "Hattie" Adams. She was born to Joshua Green, an African-American man whose job was viewed as a "hooper of barrels." Wilson's mother was Margaret Adams, and Anglo-American woman whose occupation was a "washerwoman." See Foreman et al., *Harriet E. Wilson*, vii, xiv, xxvi.

proslavery Anglo-American woman.³ Theologically, the significance of Wilson's narrative, at least in part, achieves further clarity through the biblical testimony of *spiritual adoption*. The slave child, orphaned and in search of parental and familial love, undergoes a seemingly endless search for love, only to be partially withheld by the emotionally, psychologically, and spiritually stunted people around her. However, she is fully embraced by those who truly embody the Gospel narrative.⁴

Wilson does not focus on presenting an overt theological message to the reader. In many regards, she expressed a subtle but influential Christian faith within the narrative. Wilson relies on her Christian lifestyle rather than a bombardment of doctrinal statements to engage the human-Other. The theological significance of her narrative is clever in its delivery, establishing the ability to incite self-reflection and empathy within the reader. Wilson's life represents the various ways we can be influenced beyond our self-awareness, subsequently influencing the human-Other in edifying ways that are representative of the Fruit of the Spirit.⁵

In presenting my Evangelical interpretation of "Our Nig," I want you to consider a few perspectives. First, human disagreement and division are natural. They are not inherently immoral and wicked. However, they can become skewed tools for immorality if those individuals outside of a particular community are demoralized and dehumanized simply because they are outsiders. By their very existence, outsiders presuppose a certain level of human difference, establishing that they do not represent anyone within the community or the community itself. Immorality, oppression, and dehumanization begin with the skewed belief that the outsider could never be grafted into the community, which supports additional irrational beliefs and societal structures of injustice. This belief manifests destructive consequences when the outsider is forced to stay outside the community, with no possible way of being grafted within it. Alternatively,

---

3. I interpret Wilson's work as what some scholars refer to as *creative nonfiction*. Her narrative has elements of embellishment fused with various factual events and people. In my opinion, the narrative is also noticeably infused with Christian principles, although in real life, Mrs. Wilson was a spiritualist within a non-Christian tradition. Foreman et al., *Harriet E. Wilson*, xxiii, xxiv.

4. My interpretation of Our Nig, in part, is influenced by the colonial reality of African and African-American families being routinely torn asunder through a total disregard for Black humanity. The slave auction block is the profane space, believed to be sanctified by White self-interest in the dismemberment of colonial Black familial connections.

5. I am framing my interpretation in relation to Galatians's reference to the Fruit of the Spirit (5:22–23). The ethical/moral grounding and character of everyone called into question within Wilson's narrative, are assessed by their embodiment of said Fruit.

when outsiders become part of the community, they are likely subjected to systemic immorality, oppression, and dehumanization, which imposes a hierarchy of human value upon them.

Secondly, the biblical narrative clearly understands this, especially concerning the principles of alienation, adoption, and kinship. These three principles are implied within the Apostle Paul's discussion of the Fruit of the Spirit. Paul's discourse clarifies the interconnectedness of salvific faith, righteousness, and justification, which subsequently creates the Christian's *identity*, *sense of belonging*, and conceptions of *shared space* with the human-Other. For me, Mrs. Wilson's narrative expresses a persistent conflict between the Fruit of the Spirit and the *Deeds of the Flesh*. The narrative also demonstrates the complexity of human influence between the human-Self and the Human-Other. Mrs. Wilson expresses the anti-Gospel essence of proslavery Anglo-American Christianity, as it demonstrates defiant opposition to proper Christianity. Within these types of relationships, I argue, were situated forms of the colonial Black conscience, and the trials it endured through the emotional and psychological realities classified as dehumanization and humanization.[6]

In considering these perspectives, we begin an evangelical interpretation of the narrative of Mrs. Harriet Wilson, once an alienated child who sought inclusion and adoption into a loving family. As an adult, she matured and blossomed into the woman she yearned for. Wilson's narrative begins with a perceptive introduction to her mother, Mrs. Mag Smith.[7]

MRS. MAG SMITH

The Muse of Despair and Self-Pity

"For among them are those who slip into households and captivate weak women weighed down with sins, led on by various impulses."

2 Timothy 3:6

---

6. I am emphasizing the principles of the Great Commission (Matt 28:16–20), the Kingdom (family) of God consisting of both Jews and Gentiles (Rom 11:11–31), and the two New Testament commandments to love God with the entirety of our existence, and humanity as we love ourselves (Matt 22:36–40). Collectively, they provide glimpses of the complex mutual identity of sacrificial love shared between Yahweh and humanity. Earthly classifications of division and dehumanization are transcended.

7. Wilson's mother's real name was "Margaret Ann Smith." Foreman et al., *Harriet E. Wilson*, xxvii.

Mag was Wilson's biological mother. She was an Anglo-American woman, apparently ostracized from Anglo-American society. Ambiguity is a central term for her, as Wilson does not clarify what her mother endured. Perhaps she was unaware of the events that led to her mother's unfortunate condition. Yet, Wilson subtly alludes to possible reasons for the reader to speculate reasonably. I interpret Mag as a representative of a peculiar embodiment of the Deeds of the Flesh. This perspective complements my interpretation of Anglo-American society in Wilson's narrative as representing a pseudo-chosen people under a fabricated set of quasi-divine commands that aims to mirror the Old Testament Law. Generally speaking, *proslavery* Anglo-American society perceived itself as obtaining authority that endowed its adherents with secular socio-racial salvation, sanctification, and righteousness.

As Wilson portrays her, Mag represents those whom the Apostle Paul spoke of in 2 Timothy 3:6. Mag was a woman weighed down with sin and bore the burden of trauma experienced through abuse, abandonment, neglect, and isolation. Wilson describes, albeit vaguely, her mother's inability and lack of desire to redeem herself. Mag appears as someone who somehow cannot find healing from those events and people who influenced the trajectory of her life. Mag represents an aspect of the Deeds of the Flesh because she situates herself within despair and self-pity. In describing her mother, Wilson states,

> Lonely Mag Smith! See her as she walks with downcast eyes and heavy heart. It was not always thus. She *had* a loving, trusting heart. Early deprived of parental guardianship, far removed from relatives, she was left to guide her tiny boat over life's surges alone and inexperienced. As she merged into womanhood, unprotected, uncherished, uncared for, there fell on her ear the music of love, awakening an intensity of emotion long dormant.[8]

Wilson never clarifies who created the pain in her mother's life. She only states that her mother was once happy. Wilson also alludes to an eerie similarity between her and Mag. Both women were deprived of a loving connection with their parents and forced to mature alone. Isolation and a disconnection from the individuals around them created a sense of vulnerability and unwantedness within mother and daughter. The introduction to the narrative, which centers on Wilson's mother,

---

8. Andrews, *Classic African American Women's Narratives*, 144.

provides an underlying connection between them as Wilson emphasizes their mutual experiences as adults, transcending geography and time. Both women embodied similar identities, a sense of belonging, and shared space. I interpret this as an expression of generational spiritual and secular "sins." The behavioral and psychological influence of parents upon their children.

Mag's humanity is rejuvenated through a deep love for, and apparently from, a particular gentleman. This love becomes a blessing and a curse as it brings life to her for a moment but eventually subjects her to feelings of despair and rejection. For Wilson, her mother was ultimately left heartbroken and abandoned with a child, forced to assume the sole responsibility of caring for their needs. Historically, this was a social nightmare for many colonial women. Here is another *prophetic* reference connecting mother and daughter revealed towards the end of the narrative. Unfortunately, Mag's first child, for uncertain reasons, died. Wilson provides a grim account of her mother's reaction to what most women would experience as a devastating event. Wilson complements her mother's perspective by stating,

> "God be thanked," ejaculate Mag, as she saw its breathing cease; "no one can taunt *her* with my ruin." Blessed release! May we all respond. How many pure, innocent children not only inherit a wicked heart of their own, claiming life-long scrutiny and restraint, but are heirs also of parental disgrace and calumny, from which only long years of patient endurance in paths of rectitude can disencumber them.[9]

Mag's reaction to her daughter's death bears an eerie similarity to some colonial African-American women, who believed their children's death was the best opportunity for freedom. For Mag, death was a blessing for her firstborn. The reader's imagination is left to wander, pondering the possible events and people who assisted in creating her trauma. The accumulation of events and people, whether deliberate or not, caused Mag to fear for her firstborn's safety and the possibility of her experiencing a miserable life. The potential cause stems from Mag's guilt, shame, and alienation. Again, we see an expression of fear regarding the transference of parental sin upon their children.

Wilson, at least on the surface, appears to agree with her mother. However, we must reflect upon the broader significance of her ability to

---

9. Andrews, *Classic African American Women's Narratives*, 145.

empathize with her mother. Generally speaking, an individual's immoral lifestyle creates denigrating consequences, initially for the individual and inevitably, to some extent, for those within their network of friends and family. It applies to everyone, regardless of race, gender, or social class. Wilson appears to empathize with her mother, speaking from her adult experiences, which coincide with this principle. Wilson was an orphan, like countless other slave children during colonialism, who experienced the duality of yearning for their biological parents and subsequently faced with the task of overcoming trauma created by them. The reader of her narrative should consider Wilson is possibly reasoning from the perspective that her mother, like herself, was perhaps influenced by the decisions of her biological parents too. Nevertheless, according to Wilson, her mother seemed to wallow in despair, refusing to return to her former life, distancing herself from once intimate friends who sought to help her:

> Occasionally old acquaintances called to be favored with help of some kind, which she was glad to bestow for the sake of the money it would bring her; but the association with them was such a painful reminder of by-gones, she returned to her hut morose and revengeful, refusing all offers of a better home than she possessed. Thus she lived for years, hugging her wrongs, but making no effort to escape. She had never known plenty, scarcely competency; but the present was beyond comparison with those innocent years when the coronet of virtue was hers.[10]

Wilson articulates the self-contradictory nature that her mother displayed. Mag refused salvation, sanctification, and redemption from outside and within. Yet, she had the self-awareness to recognize her miserable condition and claimed to want a life of love and acceptance, but refused to do the basic things to achieve it. The reader can logically speculate on what Mag's innocent years and the *coronet of virtue* entailed. Perhaps Wilson is alluding to her sexuality and the violation of it, whether forcibly or through deception.

Wilson describes her mother experiencing trauma from three events: those that left her alone in the world without a family, the abandonment by a man she believed loved her, and losing her first child. In this context, the reader is situated within ambiguity, trying to determine if Wilson is legitimately unaware of the particularities her mother endured, or if she

---

10. Andrews, *Classic African American Women's Narratives*, 145.

is withholding them from respect and love. We do not know anything concretely beyond Mag's social alienation influencing her to seek refuge among *strangers*.

WILSON'S CREATION NARRATIVE BEFORE THE FALL

"You shall not oppress a stranger, since you yourselves know the feelings of a stranger, for you also were strangers in the land of Egypt"

(EXOD 23:9)

The Old Testament provides numerous verses articulating Yahweh's love and acceptance of humanity. He demonstrates this, particularly within the context of ancient Israel's relationship with the human-Other who walks with them in peace. Accepting the human-Other for who they are is a righteous attribute among many oppressed people throughout history. It is also a common occurrence historically within African-American culture. In this area, we witness the Bible's influence upon African-American culture, and from a secular perspective, the lesson comes through employing basic empathy for the human-Other, through one's personal experience of oppression.

At some point, Mag was isolated, alone, and struggling to support herself. She resided within an African-American community, finding relative peace and sanctuary among the outcasts of society. Mag eventually became associated with a Black man named Mr. Jim. Jim often spoke with Mag, engaging in general conversations about her well-being:

> "How much you earn dis week, Mag?" Asked he one Sunday evening. "Little enough, Jim. Two or three days without any dinner. I washed for the Reeds, and did a small job for Mrs. Bellmont; that's all. I shall starve soon, unless I can get more to do. Folks seem as afraid to come here as if they expected to get some awful disease. I don't believe there is a person in the world but would be glad to have me dead and out of the way." "No, no, Mag! Don't talk so. You shan't starve so long as I have barrels to hoop. Peter Greene boards me cheap. I'll help you, if nobody else will."[11]

---

11. Andrews, *Classic African American Women's Narratives*, 146.

According to Wilson's account, Jim, a gentle and caring man, initially suppressed his deep yearning for Mag. Jim was aware of Mag's loneliness and, for unknown reasons, perceived her as having a *pure* heart devoid of hate, discrimination, and White supremacist ideology. Jim uttered to himself, "She'd be as much of a prize to me as she'd fall short of coming up to the mark with white folks. I don't care for past things. I've done things 'fore now I's 'shamed of. She's good enough for me, any how."[12] Wilson depicts Jim as a Christ-like figure. He is an archetype of love who provides a lost soul with acceptance, forgiveness, and redemption. Jim honored his decision to provide for Mag. He made certain she had food to eat and other necessities.

Finally, the day presented itself when Jim could no longer conceal his love for Mag. After careful reflection, he gathered the courage to approach Mag, hoping she was receptive and reciprocal to his true feelings for her. Mag's living conditions, alienation from Anglo-American society, and loneliness became the quasi-justification for Jim's proposal, "You's had trial with white folks, any how. They run off and left ye, and now none of 'em come near ye to see if you's dead or alive. I's black outside, I know, but I's got a white heart inside. Which you rather have, a black heart in a white skin, or a white heart in a black one?"[13] Jim posed an ethical question to Mag. This question elicited self-awareness and challenged an individual's loyalty to race or love. It provided a glimpse into the actual state of the individual's heart.

Jim intentionally employed conceptions of race through a paradigm of yearning, belonging, and acceptance. White apathy and rejection were in opposition to Black empathy and acceptance. To a certain extent, Jim posed a rhetorical question to Mag, as her present condition provided what he believed to be the obvious answer. Jim loved Mag, and this was a love that transcended race and social standing. However, the central issue stemmed from Mag's heart and feelings for Jim. Could she reciprocate genuine love for him? Did Mag have a deep loyalty to her race, which shaped her conceptions of love and empathy?

Wilson, keenly aware of Anglo-American society's views on race and intermarriage, speaks of Mag and Jim's marriage as an *amalgamation*. However, as I read Wilson's words, she subtly critiques Anglo-American society. The supposed union of two loving people, regardless of race,

---

12. Andrews, *Classic African American Women's Narratives*, 146–47.
13. Andrews, *Classic African American Women's Narratives*, 147.

was an affront to Anglo-American society. It violated an individual's allegiance to their race and defilement of Whiteness. We partially witness this in Wilson's words regarding her mother: "She has sundered another bond which held her to her fellows. She has descended another step down the ladder of infamy."[14] Sexual intercourse and marriage between races represented the ceasing of White purity and sanctification. Blackness infringed upon Whiteness and skewed White existence. However, what becomes of those individuals and communities birthed from the union of two races?

Wilson eventually reveals Jim as her biological father. The nature of whether her mother genuinely loved him or merely tolerated him from convenience remains unclear. Perhaps her love is concealed through self-pity. We receive a subtle indication of how Wilson may have perceived their union as she recounts her father's illness:

> A few years and a severe cough and pain in his side compelled him to be an idler for weeks together, and Mag had thus a reminder of by-gones. She cared for him only as a means to subserve her own comfort; yet she nursed him faithfully and true to marriage vows till death released her. He became the victim of consumption. He loved Mag to the last. So long as life continued, he stifled his sensibility to pain, and toiled for her sustenance long after he was able to do so.[15]

The reader is compelled to acknowledge Wilson's continuous focus on her father's love as she contrasts it with her mother's self-pity. There is a Gospel correlation in this context. An intrinsic alluding exists in terms of a pitiful sinner who, in dismissing the importance of repentance, is enclosed in a self-imposed prison, weighed down by guilt, shame, embarrassment, and sin. Transformation and a better life are well within their grasp, but for various reasons, the individual chooses to stay within self-pity, reframing it in terms of being a victim of circumstances, events, and people who have inflicted trauma upon them beyond their control. Wilson stresses the importance of her mother's decline into racial, and sociopolitical anathema concerning her association and intimacy with Blackness. Mag's preoccupation with her former life makes it difficult to completely accept the genuine Black love and peace presently awarded to

---

14. Andrews, *Classic African American Women's Narratives*, 147.
15. Andrews, *Classic African American Women's Narratives*, 148.

her. The inability to forgive herself and embrace a new life only exacerbates the trauma from past events and people before she met Jim.

Mag succumbs to more tragedy through the death of Jim, a dedicated provider and faithful lover. Yet, Wilson does not focus on the death of her father and the significance of it in her life. Her mother remains the focus and the state of self-pity that shaped her identity and existence. Her father's death serves as another context to question her mother's sincerity and the presence of selfishness within her self-pity. Here, we see a possible third correlation between mother and daughter: the inability to focus upon genuine love and allow it to transform your life.

Wilson displays a peculiar approach to minimizing or arguably dismissing the relevance of her father's love. The reader may find themselves seeking to discern whether, intentionally or not, she minimizes the only positive Black male presence in her narrative. Her father is undoubtedly a loving figure. However, the reader could argue she portrays his love in an almost irrational way, as her mother, the primary recipient of his love, does not appear to value it and consequently does not deserve it. Nor does Mag seem to have the self-awareness and desire to reciprocate this level of love, which she only received in the alternative reality to the ideal life she desired. I refer to this as a tragic irony within the relationship between the human will and desire. The things and people we desire may not be a blessing but a curse to us, but since we want them, our will and minds cannot recognize and seek those things and people who bless us.

Nevertheless, Mag finds another companion, a man named Mr. Seth Shipley.[16] Shipley was a business partner of Jim. The reader could assume Mr. Shipley received a wealth of information from Jim about his wife, her past, and her then-current inability to provide for her family after his death. It is interesting to see Wilson describe her mother's sources of empowerment, free will, and decisive action articulated within her femininity, sexuality, and ability to attract suitable companionship from African-American males. In this context, the underlining theme was the continuous questioning of Mag's inability to recognize and reciprocate sincere love,

> How Mag toiled and suffered, yielding to fits of desperation, bursts of anger, and uttering curses too fearful to repeat. When both were supplied with work, they prospered; if idle, they were hungry together. In this way their interests became united; they planned for the future together. Mag had lived an outcast for years. She had ceased to feel the gushings of penitence; she had

---

16. Foreman et al., *Harriet E. Wilson*, xxvii–xxviii.

crushed the sharp agonies of an awakened conscience. She had no longings for a purer heart, a better life. Far easier to descend lower. She entered the darkness of perpetual infamy. She asked not the rite of civilization or Christianity. Her will made her the wife of Seth. Soon followed scenes familiar and trying.[17]

The *Muse of Despair and Self-Pity* descends to quasi-apostasy, rejecting her human destiny and her ideal-Self as revealed through sincere love. How has this affected Wilson's childhood? How has her mother's influence and character, as interpreted through the deeds of the flesh, shaped Wilson's sense of belonging, identity, and shared space with the human-Other?

Wilson describes four characteristics of her mother. They reinforce her questionable respect for Mag, as the perception of love is relatively non-existent. First, the ceasing of penitence is a strong proclamation. For what or who should Mag seek forgiveness? Is it forgiveness from an individual, community, or God?

The reader's thoughts focus on questions within a space of ambiguity between assumptions and speculations. The disregard for penitence is associated with the trauma Mag endured. The trauma likely influenced the state of her fragmented conscience. The reader is left to reflect upon the bombardment of possible abuse and dehumanization, which caused the deconstruction of her identity and self-awareness. Thirdly, we can interpret the absence of a desire for a pure heart and a better life as a central moral issue. How does Mag perceive a pure heart, and what is required of a person to obtain and sustain it?

Answers to this remain unclear. We only know that Mag believes the answers are deeply associated with the acceptance and love, at least partly, from the White community that ostracised her. A pure heart is necessary for a better life. The disavowal of said heart is the repudiation of a better life. A striking consequence of this progression is Mag's reluctance or inability to create a family and small community which provided the acceptance, healing, and love she desired. Fourthly, civilization and Christianity become examples of humanization, normality, stability, and general conceptions of healthiness. Society creates these types of standards and subjects them to everyone within itself. Yet, my main point is that Mag disavowed them. What are the opposite realities of civilization and Christianity? Moreover, what forms would an individual's sense of

---

17. Andrews, *Classic African American Women's Narratives*, 148.

belonging develop into, and how would this shape their identities, along with occupying shared spaces with the human-Other?

Possible answers to these questions would be, to some extent, barbarism and atheism: the repudiation of her humanity, which is intrinsically associated with the rejection of God. A dark progression into despair and self-pity related to the alienation from an individual's race, gender, and the absence of God as the final source for reclaiming one's humanity. For some, the reality and perception of their value are required to *live* genuinely. *Existence* is the consequence of that alienation, not life, but an existence within an alternative and inferior community. Mag must construct relationships that would not have existed if her estrangement from the ideal White community had not occurred. Nor would she experience the love and acceptance the secondary community provided if she was not worthy of it, or could not recognize and reciprocate what was given to her. The climax of this procession is in the declaration that, according to Wilson, Mag's will "made her the wife of Mr. Seth Shipley."[18] Who is Seth? A superficial replacement? Is he a suitable provider, conditioned by the deplorable state of Mag?

Seth becomes the subtle antithesis of Wilson's father, Jim. Seth is the charlatan who influenced Mag to commit the ultimate sin. To some extent, Seth represents the snake in the Garden of Eden. As the snake spoke to Eve, Seth conversed with Mag, employing her to sacrifice her children for the sake of *their* comfort, as it provided less resistance to living in a way more appropriate to them. However, Mag, like Eve, is not innocent and appears to be self-aware of the devastating consequences she will create by abandoning her children:

> "It's no use," said Seth one day; "we must give the children away, and try to get work in some other place." "Who'll take the black devils?" snarled Mag. "They're none of mine," said Seth; "what you growling about?" "Nobody will want any thing of mine, or yours either," she replied.[19]

We could present the argument that Mag was merely placating Seth and suppressing the desire to keep her daughters. Nevertheless, Mag would eventually decide whether to choose her husband, Jim, or her daughter, young Frado, who would mature to become Mrs. Wilson. Wilson provides another glimpse into her mother's heart and moral aptitude.

18. Andrews, *Classic African American Women's Narratives*, 148.
19. Andrews, *Classic African American Women's Narratives*, 148.

The reader views this in that Mag was keenly aware of Mrs. Bellmont, the *Muse of Bitterness and Vindictiveness*. Mrs. Bellmont developed a repulsive but deserved reputation within their community. She was a woman with an aggressive, malicious, and violent temperament. Mrs. Bellmont played an influential role in Wilson's life as her antagonist and the embodiment of the *Deeds of the Flesh*.

Mag's self-awareness is displayed in Wilson's articulation of her mother's description of Mrs. Bellmont as "a right she-devil.[20]" Mag was aware of Mrs. Bellmont's destructive personality, to the point that her abusive nature made it difficult for her kind husband, Mr. Bellmont, to hire long-term assistance for their home. Yet, the cruel nature of Mrs. Bellmont did not deter Mag from concocting a scheme to abandon her daughter into the care of Mrs. and Mr. Bellmont. Whether Mrs. Wilson knew her mother loved her is not the question, but to what extent. There appears to be a subtle indication of this, which underlines her critique of Mag and her ability to reciprocate love. The reader is placed in a position by Wilson whereby we are to reflect on Mag's inability to strengthen her will and find the resolve to break free from the bondage, at least in part, of which she has encased herself.

Mrs. Wilson shares an incident whereby she and a young childhood friend were playing together but somehow wandered away, becoming lost. Mag and Jim desperately sought her whereabouts. However, they could not locate her, and Mag's anxiety and fears began to overcome her. Guilt, too, was an overwhelming emotion. Wilson describes her mother reflecting on the thought that she, as young Frado, must have discovered the plan to abandon her. Yet, Wilson assures the reader that she was utterly oblivious to this plan during this period. Young Frado was still a child of innocence and naivety: "Mag was relieved to know her child was not driven to desperation by their intentions to relieve themselves of her, and she was inclined to think severe restraint would be healthful."[21] The reader can reflect upon how Wilson felt about this. What emotions may have overwhelmed her, and soothed the resentment or anger she may have had for Mag before this revelation?

This event within the narrative seems somewhat insignificant, extracted from a different context, and forcefully placed before the climax of Wilson's abandonment, her mother's greatest sin. However, the

---

20. Andrews, *Classic African American Women's Narratives*, 149.
21. Andrews, *Classic African American Women's Narratives*, 150.

significance of this event, real or imaginary, is the intentional attempt to describe the possible suppressed emotions, feelings, and love within Mag for her young daughter, Frado. Wilson may want the reader to be aware of her mother's love amidst her fragmented heart and skewed conscience. Unfortunately, deception, the lack of fear, avoidance of responsibility, and disconnectedness from the future consequences of her actions led Mag to the Bellmont's residence, with the unacknowledged *gem* of her life, young Frado:

> A knock at the door brought Mrs. Bellmont, and Mag asked if she would be willing to let that child stop there while she went to the Reed's house to wash, and when she came back she would call and get her. It seemed a novel request, but she consented. Why the impetuous child entered the house, we cannot tell; the door closed, and Mag hastily departed. Frado waited for the close of day, which was to bring back her mother. Alas! It never came. It was the last time she ever saw or heard of her mother.[22]

Wilson positions the reader to reflect upon the possible emotions and thoughts that may have overwhelmed her mother. An individual can imagine that although this was the last time she heard from Mag, it was not possibly the last time for Mag. Mag knew where her daughter was and could learn of her well-being.

The significance of Mag to her daughter is complex yet quite familiar to a small demographic of colonial Anglo-American women. In her then-current state, Mag's identity as an Anglo-American woman represented the receiving element of the dehumanizing consequences of Whiteness turning against itself. Many Anglo-American women experienced socio-racial abandonment, oppression, and rejection if they chose to empathize and love Blackness as the human-Other. Mag represented defiled-Whiteness, which was perceived to have committed socio-racial apostasy through unfaithfulness to the illusion of White superiority. Socio-racial unrighteousness, as defilement, must be expunged from Anglo-American society; otherwise, it will spread its tainted nature within the community. Colonial White Supremacy and White Nationalism are reinterpreted as a variant of The Law, which creates the perception of these ideologies embodying and endowing its adherents with forms of socio-racial salvation, sanctification, and righteousness. Whiteness as a social construct, not the intrinsic humanity of those classified as such,

---

22. Andrews, *Classic African American Women's Narratives*, 151.

bears the illusion of religious and secular authority. The perception of authority and obedience to the laws and people that represent it govern the moral principles of White supremacy. Whiteness, as White supremacy, represents the fragmentation of the human conscience, which struggles to discern fantasy from reality as it seeks to make imaginative irrational constructs influential aspects of reality.

Mag represents the passive embodiment of the Deeds of the Flesh: The Muse of Despair and Self-Pity. She signifies the sinner's non-malicious and unintentionally rebellious nature, who nevertheless disavows God's Word and their human destiny. Mag is also representative of a contradiction. She is a victim of apparent abuse, neglect, and rejection, which developed her weakened human will. However, there appears to be a glimmer of goodness within Mag's heart, but she is lost in the world, struggling to grasp the self-awareness and determination necessary to obtain healing. The consequence is a distorted relationship between her and Frado.[23] From an evangelical perspective, Mag characterizes the words of the Apostle Paul in Romans 7:15–20,

> I do not understand what I am doing; for I am not practicing what I want to do, but I do the very thing I hate. However, if I do the very thing I do not want to do, I agree with the law, that the law is good. But now, no longer am I the one doing it, but sin that dwells in me. For I know that good does not dwell in me, that is, in my flesh; for the willing is present in me, but the doing of the good is not. For the good that I want, I do not do, but I practice the very evil that I do not want. But if I do the very thing I do not want, I am no longer the one doing it, but sin that dwells in me.

Wilson constructs a narrative whereby she articulates a yearning for her mother's love, which begins by subtly demonstrating her mother's inability to love herself and those who deserve it in her life. The reader may ask a series of questions. How has Mag's inability to reciprocate love affected young Frado's yearning for her mother's love? Which aspects of Wilson's father, Jim, positively influenced her character and conception

---

23. Scholars have discovered that Wilson's mother died sometime after leaving Wilson with the Bellmont family. Margaret was in a domestic violence relationship with her lover and died of alcohol consumption at some point. Margaret's obituary was stated by the "Coroner's jury" in the local newspaper, *Farmer's Cabinet*, on March 27, 1830. See Foreman et al., *Harriet E. Wilson*, xxviii–xxix.

of love? Does this have any bearing on Wilson's view of race and gender as a *bi-racial* woman identifying primarily as Black during colonialism?

FRADO: THE MUSE OF STRENGTH AND RESILIENCE MEETS

Mrs. Bellmont—The Muse of Bitterness and Vindictiveness

There will always exist conflicts of the human will between individuals whenever there is essential interaction. In part, understanding how and why these conflicts occur can be derived by determining the intent of the individuals, the purpose of the conflict, who initiated it, and whether someone's self-interest was fulfilled from the outcome. Wilson and Mrs. Bellmont engaged in a lifelong contest of the human will, initiated by Mrs. Bellmont but impressively withstood by Wilson. Their relationship is a central issue within the narrative that shapes Wilson's character and influences the development of her Christian theology.

The Apostle Paul stated in Ephesians 6:12, "For our struggle is not against flesh and blood, but against the rulers, against the powers, against the world forces of this darkness, against the spiritual *forces* of wickedness in the heavenly *places.*" This biblical truth has a psychological element that complements the spiritual aspect that Paul mentions. To some extent, the spiritual forces of wickedness can be interpreted as the dark psyche of the human mind and the corrupt nature of the heart. In this context, we will examine the dehumanizing relationship between Wilson and Mrs. Bellmont. I am concerned about pushing beyond the superficial layer of racism and White Supremacy that exploits the differences in pigmentation. They are important; however, I also seek to examine who and what Wilson represented to Mrs. Bellmont. In part, their relationship demonstrates the conflict between Whiteness and Blackness vis-à-vis, Mulatto, but theologically, the Deeds of the Flesh against the fruit of the Spirit. They displayed two unique characters representing two ethical paradigms that influenced how they understood and embodied their sense of identity, sense of belonging, and shared-spaced with the human-Other.

The Bellmont family was somewhat divided by their beliefs regarding European dominance and the ambiguous acknowledgment of racial equality.[24] Their division represents a form of collective *fragmented-Whiteness*. Whether an intentional writing ploy or the natural results of her life, Wilson continually contended with narcissistic White femininity: Mrs. Bellmont and her daughter Mary. The relationship between Wilson and these women can be contrasted with her relationship with Mr. Bellmont and his two sons, John and Jack. Thus, to some extent, we witness the warring within Whiteness, the battle between Flesh and Spirit. Yet, Mr. Bellmont represented a passive and timid example of righteousness for Wilson:

> Mr. Bellmont was a kind, humane man, who would not grudge hospitality to the poorest wanderer, nor fail to sympathize with any sufferer, however humble. The child's desertion by her mother appealed to his sympathy, and he felt inclined to succor her. To do this in opposition to Mrs. Bellmont's wishes, would be like encountering a whirlwind charged with fire, daggers and spikes. She was not as susceptable of fine emotions as her spouse. Mag's opinion of her was not without foundation. She was self-willed, haughty, undisciplined, arbitrary and severe.[25]

Yet, the reader is justified in questioning Wilson's view of Mr. Bellmont concerning his marriage to Mrs. Bellmont, and his seemingly *impotent* attempts to stop her abusive ways. The very nature of how many slaves defined *good* and *righteousness* concerning their masters was always subject to critique. Those who believed a master and mistress could logically be deemed good were considered to have a distorted conscience and sense of Self. For some, a good enslaver could not logically exist. Nevertheless, as young Frado, Wilson would find a new home where she would be viewed as an outcast, a nuisance, and an inconvenience by some members of the Bellmont family, and a blessing to others.

---

24. Some of the actual names of the Bellmont family consisted of Sally Hayward (Aunt Abby), Nehemiah Hayward Jr. (Father: Mr. John Bellmont, father), Rebecca S. Hutchinson (Mother: Mrs. Bellmont, Mrs. B, and the She-Devil), George Milton Hayward (Oldest brother: James Bellmont), Charles S. Hayward (Brother: Jack Bellmont), and Rebecca Smith Hayward (Sister: Mary Bellmont). For a complete description of the family and their names, see Foreman et al., *Harriet E. Wilson*, xix–xxii.

25. Andrews, *Classic African American Women's Narratives*, 151.

REPUDIATED-BLACKNESS

What to do with Frado?

The value of Frado's existence was a perpetual issue during her childhood and teenage years. The initial questioning shaped the deceptive plan of Wilson's mother, Mag, but was also problematic for the conscience of Mrs. Bellmont and her insidious daughter Mary.

> "I don't want a nigger 'round *me*, do you, mother?" asked Mary. "I don't mind the nigger in the child. I should like a dozen better than one," replied her mother. "If I could make her do my work in a few years, I would keep her. I have so much trouble with girls I hire, I am almost persuaded if I have one to train up in my way from a child, I shall be able to keep them awhile. I am tired of changing every few months."[26]

Frado was renamed "Nig," by the Bellmont family. In this context, she represented a form of Blackness that *intruded* upon Whiteness and White space. For Mrs. Bellmont and Mary, Frado embodied an identity of reluctant acceptance and compromising belonging, as if it were a burden that they, representative of Whiteness, had to bear because of their superiority in the world. Mrs. Bellmont and Mary intentionally established themselves as the antithesis of Frado. Thus, the stage was set for the conflict between the Muses and Mary. How is young Frado to negotiate and define her identity as a Black-Mulatto? In what ways can she establish a sense of belonging among fragmented-Whiteness? Furthermore, can she withstand and navigate through the insecurities, willful ignorance, and perpetual abuse from Mrs. Bellmont and Mary as *they* seek to define her existence perpetually?

The first year of young Frado's life with the Bellmont family was full of abuse, loneliness, and isolation. Frado was six years old and maintained the responsibilities of an adult female servant. She routinely cared for the Bellmont's farm animals and served the family within the capacity of a house servant. Nevertheless, Mrs. Bellmont and Mary constantly tested young Frado's will, as she gradually realized there was no other option but to stay with the Bellmonts. The whereabouts of her mother, Mag, were unknown.

Young Frado was six years old and routinely endured acts of violence from Mrs. Bellmont and Mary. Often, this came through the

---

26. Andrews, *Classic African American Women's Narratives*, 151–52.

habitual strikes to her head as the primary means of discipline. According to Wilson's account,

> These was great annoyances to Frado, and had she known where her mother was, she would have gone at once to her. She was often greatly wearied, and silently wept over her sad fate. At first she wept aloud, which Mrs. Bellmont noticed by applying a rawhide, always at hand in the kitchen. It was a symptom of discontent and complaining which must be "nipped in the bud," she said.[27]

Mrs. Bellmont, the Muse of Bitterness and Vindictiveness, employed dehumanization through the façade of discipline to correct the perceived discontent of an *ungrateful* slave girl. Young Frado was denied the natural and reasonable expressions of her humanity, through emotions and feelings incited from specific traumatizing experiences. Mrs. Bellmont sought to reinterpret Frado's humanity, by punishing her for reacting as any human would.

Nevertheless, the rationale and behavior of Mrs. Bellmont reflected *her* inhumanity, apathy, and indifference. They also represent a form of escapism, which rejects and seeks to suppress anything and anyone who represents reality. In this context, for Mrs. Bellmont to reside within reality is to become aware of her skewed conscience and heart and young Frado's true humanity. Young Frado yearned for her mother amid abandonment and abuse from Mrs. Bellmont. Frado, the young Muse of Strength and Resilience, withstood the dehumanization from Mrs. Bellmont for an entire year. Frado, a young child, endured what many adults could not bear.

We must wonder if Frado's strength only intensified Mrs. Bellmont's wrath. If so, this alludes to, albeit slightly, Proverbs 25:21–22, "If your enemy is hungry, give him food to eat; And if he is thirsty, give him water to drink; For you will heap burning coals on his head, And the Lord will reward you." What can psychologically develop within immoral individuals and communities who oppose you? Can they become further enraged by their inability to break you, and your ability to sustain your humanity amid the constant onslaught of inhuman treatment?

Through the skewed conscience of the immoral human-Self, even the obedience it demands from the human-Other can incite internal rage, as well as irrational and compulsive acts of violence. I present

---

27. Andrews, *Classic African American Women's Narratives*, 153.

this as another example of the Deeds of the Flesh. For Mrs. Bellmont, Frado did not deserve to function as a human, displaying emotions that were symptomatic of her trauma. Mrs. Bellmont prioritized her skewed desires above Frado's humanity. Adherents of White Supremacy exist in a state of self-dehumanization whereby they are often compulsive, unaware of their psychological fragmentation, and impulsive in their attempts to dehumanize Black humanity. For these individuals, avoidance and denial form a destructive relationship to create escapism within an illusory White supremacist world. Ironically, the rejection of Black humanity is employed to develop and sustain the mechanisms of their self-dehumanization.

Education is often viewed as a means of empowering and developing our humanity. The withholding of education is a form of oppression. It can function to suffocate the human development of the oppressed individual and community. Frado, like many other slaves and indentured servants, experienced the vitality education provided, even amid attempts to withhold or distort it.

FORMAL & INFORMAL EDUCATION

Young Frado's Early Lessons of Equality & Love

One of the best examples of cognitive dissonance and confirmatory bias within Eurocentric and White supremacist reasoning stemmed from the different views of whether African slaves should be educated. African slaves were deemed innately inferior and lacking the capacity for literacy. They were also deemed unable to construct a legitimate civilization. These beliefs, and others, were maintained despite the presence of intelligence among the slaves.

The presence of literacy among the slaves revealed the fragmented nature of the Eurocentric conscience. Black intelligence relating to a strong desire to learn had exposed the irrationality of White Supremacist reasoning. The internal fragmentation intensified as slave laws were created to keep African slaves ignorant and dependent upon Anglo-Americans. From this context, we gain insight into the fragmented conscience of Mrs. Bellmont and Mary, regarding their views of young Frado's worthiness in being educated:

> Mrs. Bellmont was in doubt about the utility of attempting to educate people of color, who were incapable of elevation. This subject occasioned a lengthy discussion in the family. Mr. Bellmont, Jane and Jack arguing for Frado's education; Mary and her mother objecting. At last Mr. Bellmont declared decisively that she *should* go to school. He was a man who seldom decided controversies at home. The word once spoken admitted of no appeal; so, notwithstanding Mary's objection that she would have to attend the same school she did, the word became law.[28]

Within the fragmented White-conscience, the perception and realization of equality evoked some of the most erratic outbursts of wrath towards the Black slave. Mary, a young version of her mother, undoubtedly felt Frado was not worthy of proper education. Mary never articulated a rational explanation for this view other than Frado was a *nigger*, and thus, being educated was unobtainable. Mary employs cognitive dissonance and confirmatory bias as the possibility of Frado proving her Eurocentric views as irrational was dismissed entirely. Rather than observe Frado's progress, Mary insisted on invoking violence upon her as a means of punishment, and possible alleviation from the frustration of experiencing the perception of equality with a slave.

Fragmented-Whiteness is seen within the collective conscience of the Bellmont family. Wilson never elaborates on why the family appeared divided regarding racial beliefs. Mrs. Bellmont and Mary clearly embodied the skewed notions of Eurocentric ideologies. However, Mr. Bellmont, Jack, James, and Grandma Bellmont disavowed White supremacy and expressed timid ideas of racial equality. It is uncertain whether they had notions of racialized paternalistic ideologies. The binary-oppositional views that began to split American society were expressed within many Anglo-American families, such as the Bellmonts. The self-dehumanizing and violent White supremacist views of Mrs. Bellmont and her daughter Mary clashed with the humanizing and timid views of Mr. Bellmont, Jack, James, and Grandma Belmont. Within fragmented-Whiteness, young Frado exhibited a mysterious sense of stability and strength within contexts that would have broken adults. This elicits the question: Who and what were the sources of Frado's strength and refinement of her will?

Young Frado was conscious of race and her identity as a Black-Mulatto, but these identities are not used to employ racialized escapism or skewed racialized politics. Ethics and morality are central to young

---

28. Andrews, *Classic African American Women's Narratives*, 154.

Frado, and they are cemented within the perception of her humanity. Love and acceptance from and for her mother appeared to sustain her through the abuse and turmoil of her childhood. However, from her account, her father, Mr. Jim, may have influenced the development of her character more than she initially realized.

Principles of love and empathy are observed within Anglo-Americans who have and continue to oppose White supremacist reasoning. A glimmer of these attributes is observed in some of the darkest contexts and people within colonialism. Redemption and reconciliation are desired goals and can be obtained in ways that rejuvenate the human spirit. Redemption and reconciliation are achieved in various degrees and often unexpectedly. Young Frado endured racism, not only from adults but also from her peers, but amid these debilitating experiences arose lessons of love, and the rejuvenation of her humanity:

> All followed, and, after the bustle of securing seats was over, Miss Marsh inquired if the children knew "any cause for the sorrow of that little girl?" pointing to Frado. It was soon all told. She then reminded them of their duties to the poor and friendliness; their cowardice in attacking a young innocent child; referred them to one who looks not on outward appearances, but on the heart. "She looks like a good girl; I think *I* shall love her, so lay aside all prejudice, and vie with each other in shewing kindness and good will to one who seems different from you," were the closing remarks of the kind lady. Those kind words! The most agreeable sound which ever meets the ear of sorrowing, grieving childhood.[29]

Miss Marsh embodied the relationship of love, ethics, and responsibility, which led by example. White femininity, through Miss Marsh, stands in contrast to Mrs. Bellmont and Mary. The decisive statement from Miss Marsh, "I shall love her," is the catalyst for recognizing Frado's sorrow and the urge to help heal her from it. Healing occurred, in part, through aligning empathetic-Whiteness with the ailing Black-Mulatto, and initiating self-awareness within ignorant-Whiteness, that was unaware of its self-dehumanization in its attack upon the Black-Other. For Miss Marsh, racial allegiance and solidarity were an irrational illusion in the presence of organic deliberate love for the human-Other. Where do our responsibility and accountability reside? Evidently, Miss Marsh believed it rested within justice and equality for everyone, regardless of racial and social class.

29. Andrews, *Classic African American Women's Narratives*, 154.

8

Homage to Harriet Wilson
The Concluding Evangelical Reading of "Our Nig"

"For God has not given us a spirit of timidity, but of power and love, and discipline [sound mind]."

(2 TIM 1:7)

"So for one who knows the right thing to do and does not do it, for him it is sin."

(JAS 4:17)

SELF-AWARENESS THROUGH THE HUMAN-OTHER

THE BIBLICAL TESTIMONY CREATES a unique relationship between power, love, and discipline. Intricately connected, each element cannot exist isolated from one another, as each component contributes to the existence of the other. The Apostle Paul, encouraging young Timothy to be confident in his ministry, assures him that God is always present. The presence of God extends from outside the human body to the indwelling of the Holy Spirit, who provides the Fruit of the Spirit. In this context, I emphasize the Spirit equipping the believer with power, love, and discipline. There are many purposes for this, one of which is to assist the believer in embodying sacrificial love for the human-Other, within our service to

Christ. Additionally, the essence of God and how He lives in communion with His Children can also positively influence those who do not identify with them.

Timothy, for Paul, had demonstrated a genuine faith in Christ, initially observed within his mother and grandmother, Eunice and Lois. From this perspective, the principles of power, love, and discipline were taught to him at a young age, modeled by the women who raised him. The nature and complexity of human and divine influence are observed within this testimony and those alike. The overall conscience and disposition of timidity, shame, and disbelief are confronted and overcome wherever the genuine Christian conceptions of power, love, and discipline reside. Within this perspective, we must question the conscience and contextualized Christianity of the Bellmont family concerning colonial slavery, and attempts, whether accomplished or failed, to embrace the racialized-Other.

Within a different context, James, the brother of Jesus, confronted what appeared to be Christians practicing and embracing their desire to sin. James's attempts to awaken their moral conscience were by articulating Christian ethics via oppositional principles and the destructive consequence of sinful decisions. For James, people sin through a level of self-awareness that will *always* hold them accountable and responsible within the conscience of God. Thus, Christians are commanded to do what is morally/ethically upright according to their intelligence and moral aptitude. To do otherwise reaps natural and divine judgment upon the individual and community. Interestingly, as I interpret Wilson's narrative, this becomes a central principle in critiquing the collective conscience and contextualized Christianity of the Bellmont family.

Beneath the surface, the Bellmont family was entrenched in Eurocentric colonial reasoning like many other Anglo-American families. They were deeply divided about their beliefs about the legitimacy of slavery. Yet, those within the family who viewed the institution as questionable or immoral, were inevitably revealed to be inept in abolishing the institution. Generally speaking, I suggest certain inept anti-slavery Anglo-Americans, like their proslavery counterparts, could not obtain the self-awareness necessary to acknowledge their inhumanity that developed from participating, and benefiting from the institution. The presence of young Frado, like other slaves, was a catalyst for the divisions within some Anglo-American families and parts of American society. Frado established an intimate bond with Mr. Bellmont, Jack, James, Aunt

Abby, and other family members. Their bonds ruptured the White conscience of these individuals, forcing them to question Eurocentric reasoning, the institution of slavery, and the nature of the slave's humanity. Frado's relationships exacerbated the Bellmont family's division, not in the sense of creating a noticeable distancing between members or severance of communication. The Eurocentric reasoning of Mrs. Bellmont and Mary was the sole reason for this. Instead, the Bellmont's disagreement on the legitimacy of slavery, and the constant moral awareness of whether they were doing what was right, became relatively unavoidable concerning Frado's influence in their lives. Frado represents a troubling anomaly, one that alerts the fragmented White conscience of its true nature, and the fragile Eurocentric world it has created, and desperately seeks to sustain.

Mrs. Wilson shifts the narrative to display this division within the Bellmont family. An exploration of the internal fragmentation of Whiteness ensues. The narrative eventually moves from a surreal example of empathetic-Whiteness vis-à-vis Miss Marsh and the *transformed* school children. It proceeds to a dehumanizing event that situates itself as a binary-opposite to the compassion and love displayed by Miss Marsh and the children. The narrative of Miss Marsh portrayed the redemption, at least to a certain extent, of dehumanized-Whiteness (children), as it is transformed through love to become a rudimentary existence of a potential empathetic-Whiteness. For Wilson, if White children could utilize their freewill to commit to loving a Black child, it is possible to assist White adults to achieve the same results. Wilson expresses the duality of Anglo-American adults and children embodying the spirit of power, love, and discipline in acquiring empathy and *reconciliation*. These are necessary to humanize themselves and the racialized-Other.

QUESTIONING WHITE SELF-AWARENESS

Nevertheless, one of the most frustrating elements of colonialism is the examples of Anglo-Americans who demonstrated self-awareness in knowing the institution of slavery and the dehumanization of slaves was reprehensible. Yet, they still appeared socio-politically inept and avoided the necessary sacrifices to abolish the institution. These individuals, unaware theologically of how they have sinned and fallen into the judgment of God, inevitably created a web of self-deception that pushed them further from acknowledging this biblical truth. For me, these individuals represent the ambiguous nature of *timid-Whiteness* and the representation of *biblical lukewarmness*. Living in a state of hypocrisy and confusion, they attempted to appease the Eurocentric mind and simultaneously sought to create and maintain a healthy bond with African slaves. History records how some Anglo-Americans had not obtained true empathetic resonance and self-sacrifice for the racialized-Other, but appeared to have deceived themselves into thinking they had. Wilson crafts an intricate interplay between the three aspects of Whiteness: Empathetic, Timid, and Depraved.

As Anglo-American Christians, in embracing and rejecting slavery, what *spirit* did the Bellmont family embody? Moreover, how are we to perceive the nature of a sinner, when Anglo-Americans who claimed to be self-aware of the dehumanizing institution of slavery, continued to participate and benefit from it? Here, the narrative shifts to Mary, the representation of depraved-Whiteness, and its attempts to assert itself upon the African-Other.

MARY'S MALICIOUSNESS

At a young age, Mary was greatly influenced by her mother and cultivated a deviant nature. Inevitably, like her mother, Mary chose to remain within the unacknowledged state of self-dehumanization through her abuse and apparent hatred for young Frado. Mary, as a representative of depraved-Whiteness, stood in opposition to Frado, but also against their academic peers and Miss Marsh. Miss Marsh chose to love Frado, and the example of Miss Marsh influenced the children. The critical aspect of this testimony was the ability of the children, at that current moment, to reflect and decide what course they believed was rational and morally correct. They displayed the spirit of power, love, and discipline. Miss Marsh and the children's decision to love Frado further revealed Mary's resentment and disdain toward Frado. Mary recommitted herself to abusing Frado and, consequently, plunged deeper into self-dehumanization. In doing so, Mary became a potential Muse to the Deeds of the Flesh.

Mary was infuriated by her inability to influence her academic peers. In response, she attempted to remind Frado of her role within society. After school, upon coming to a stream, Mary sought to push Frado in, but "in the struggle to force her over, she lost her footing and plunged into the stream."¹ Their academic peers witnessed this incident. Mary, seeking to conceal her embarrassment and devious intentions, created a narrative to sanctify her reputation to her mother, exclaiming, "Nig pushed me into the stream."² Frado did not sit idle as she corrected Mary by accurately recounting what occurred to Mrs. Bellmont. However, within the Eurocentric mind, truth conveyed through the intellect, integrity, and mouth of the racialized-Other is readily rebuked and rejected. Infuriated by Frado, Mrs. Bellmont remarked to Mr. Bellmont, "Will you sit still, there, and hear that back nigger call Mary a liar?"³ Unhinged and wrathful, the Muse of Bitterness and Vindictiveness sought assistance punishing Frado.

However, timidity and impotence represented Mr. Bellmont's actions as he rejected the irrationality of Mrs. Bellmont and Mary's accusations: "How do we know but she has told the truth? I shall not punish her."⁴ Mr. Bellmont leaves the scene without attempting to secure Frado's safety from his wife and daughter. He was fully aware of their abusive nature towards her. Yet, they were more preoccupied with de-escalating their disagreement. Young Frado endured more abuse from Mrs. Bellmont and Mary. It stemmed from Mary's inability and lack of desire to acknowledge the truth, rejecting any notion of loving Frado. Situations like this were common within colonial slavery: the unprovoked, undeserved, and irrational acts of violence upon the slave's existence. For some, Anglo-Americans justified this treatment simply from their will.

Jack, aware of Mary abusing Frado, questioned his sister on the irrationality of her actions and was immediately stopped by their mother: "You shall never talk so before me. You would have that little nigger trample Mary, would you? She came home with a lie; it made Mary's story false."⁵ Mrs. Bellmont defended Mary, as Mary was a replication of herself. Mrs. Bellmont would succumb to similar judgment if Mary were found deceitful and malicious. Jack, too, represented timid-Whiteness. He displayed the impotence to do what was necessary, beyond a rational verbal confrontation against the self-dehumanizing conscience of his mother and sister: "The school-children happened to see it all, and they tell the same story Nig does. Which is most likely to be true, what a dozen

1. Andrews, *Classic African American Women's Narratives*, 155.
2. Andrews, *Classic African American Women's Narratives*, 155.
3. Andrews, *Classic African American Women's Narratives*, 155.
4. Andrews, *Classic African American Women's Narratives*, 155.
5. Andrews, *Classic African American Women's Narratives*, 155.

agree they saw, or the contrary?"[6] Jack's words were ineffective against his mother: "It is very strange you will believe what others say against your sister." "I think it is time your father subdued you."[7] Mrs. Bellmont provided her reinterpretation of events according to her self-interest. She presented her interpretation of events as if only Whiteness could represent and speak truth into existence. In her world, and that of other White supremacists, Whiteness embodied and defined what was true. Thus, for Mrs. Bellmont, Blackness represented a binary-opposite to Whiteness, as it represented lies and could not possibly speak truth against Whiteness.

Mr. Bellmont did nothing to rebuke or negate the possibility of Frado being abused again. Infuriated by his mother and sister's actions, Jack sought to comfort Frado. Yet, a telling statement from Wilson's account reveals the skewed conscience of Jack. Upon crossing paths with his mother, Jack retorts: "If that was the way Frado was to be treated, he hoped she would never wake again."[8] According to Wilson, Mr. Bellmont appeared indifferent to the situation until he noticed Jack's emotional involvement. This context displays the interplay between two forms of the colonial White conscience, which sought to establish a healthy bond with the Black conscience but could not do so because of their skewed state, which could not allow them to make the necessary sacrifices against a more depraved White conscience.

The troubling and frustrating aspect of contexts like these is discerning why some Anglo-Americans were useless against abolishing institutional slavery. Jack would rather young Frado succumb to death than for him to procure the means to stop the abusive acts from his mother and sister. Jack represents a form of White conscience, White fragmentation of timidity that has the presence of genuine sympathy for the racialized-Other but cannot establish the physical and practical means to truly empathize with the racialized-Other vis-à-vis attempting to abolish the institution of slavery. Jack's impotence remains within the context of figurative language. Wilson connects this form of White conscience to Mr. Bellmont. He displays aloofness and emotional numbness. Mr. Bellmont's emotions were not ignited, nor was his humanity touched until he viewed Jack's emotional reaction to Frado's abuse.

6. Andrews, *Classic African American Women's Narratives*, 155.
7. Andrews, *Classic African American Women's Narratives*, 156.
8. Andrews, *Classic African American Women's Narratives*, 156.

Aunt Abby displayed the same sentiments and ineptness as Mr. Bellmont and Jack. Aunt Abby and Mr. Bellmont discussed the incident whereby Mrs. Bellmont repeatedly kicked Frado, and this discussion provides further clarity to the conscience of timid-Whiteness. Mrs. Wilson recounts their discussion:

> Aunt Abby returned to her apartment, followed by John, who was muttering to himself. "What were you saying?" asked Aunt Abby. "I said I hoped the child never would come into the house again." "What would become of her?" "You cannot mean *that*," continued his sister. "I do mean it. The child does as much work as a woman ought to; and just see how she is kicked about!" "Why do you have it so, John?" asked his sister. "How am I to help it? Woman rule the earth, and all in it?" "I think I should rule my own house, John," "And live in hell meantime," added Mr. Bellmont.[9]

Aunt Abby and Mr. Bellmont were morally conscious of Mrs. Bellmont's deviancy towards Frado, and her overall hostile personality. Wilson repeatedly layers her narrative with her childhood confrontations with Mrs. Bellmont, all connected with the presence and acknowledgment of the abuse by those deemed righteous. Yet, Wilson may have articulated an intentional mystery regarding why everyone appeared unable to stop Mrs. Bellmont. In this context, James 4:17 reiterates that moral self-awareness creates the command to choose, practice, and seek to embody righteousness. To do otherwise elicits divine judgment, stemming from rebelling against what is right and being unfaithful to Yahweh. Nestled between these actions and reactions, is the unknowing relinquishing of the individual/community's humanity, at the expense of dehumanizing the human-Other. We must also question Frado's self-awareness for not scrutinizing Aunt Abby, Mr. Bellmont, Jack, and James's inability to protect her from abuse.

The power of human influence is remarkable and often expresses itself beyond our self-awareness. Likewise, we must acknowledge how human influence is naturally connected to morality and our spiritual nature. Frado's existence and unique conscience could not rupture the callous hearts and seared consciences of Mary and Mrs. Bellmont. However, Frado's presence and rebelliousness were conduits of the responsibility and accountability unto God that Mary and Mrs. Bellmont rejected. Frado

---

9. Andrews, *Classic African American Women's Narratives*, 159.

was a positive influence on Mr. Bellmont and Jack. They experienced the deep conviction of their sin while obtaining the self-awareness to discern what was right. Still, in seeking to negotiate with depraved-Whiteness, they made themselves complicit and inept in fighting against slavery and recognizing their inhumanity. Young Frado sustained her humanity, strong will, and pleasant personality, not in isolation but within the presence of empathetic-Whiteness, as humanized-Whiteness. I interpret this as the mysterious fortitude of the Muse of Strength and Resilience. Yet, another important aspect of Frado is how she expressed portions of her developing theological reflection amid the growing self-awareness of her Blackness within a Eurocentric world.

FRADO'S DEVELOPING THEOLOGY

Does My Blackness Influence How I Perceive God?

James and Frado have established an interesting bond at this point in the narrative. The context in question occurred after a violent outburst by Mrs. Bellmont, whereby she repeatedly kicked Frado, because of an act she deemed disrespectful. The conversation between James and Frado is intriguing because it demonstrates the clash between two moral standards. One standard is controlled by race vis-à-vis Eurocentric reasoning, and the other is emancipated from racialized logic governed solely by common sense. Each individual's moral standard positions the burden of responsibility upon the other. Connected to this is an example of how some colonial African Americans reflected theologically on race, viewed through a White Supremacist lens and how they reacted against it. James, like his father, Mr. Bellmont, and brother Jack, represented timid-Whiteness as the moral responsibility to be righteous is levied upon young Frado, not his mother, Mrs. Bellmont:

> "Are you glad I've come home?" asked James.
> "Yes; if you won't let me be whipped tomorrow."
> "You won't be whipped. You must try to be a good girl," counselled James."
> "If I do, I get whipped," sobbed the child. "They won't believe what I say, Oh, I wish I had my mother back; then I should not be kicked and whipped so. Who made me so?"
> "God," answered James.
> "Did God make you?"

"Yes."
"Who made Aunt Abby?"
"God."
"Who made your mother?"
"God."
"Did the same God that made her make me?"
"Yes."
"Well, then, I don't like him."
"Why not?"
"Because he made her white, and me black. Why didn't he make us *both* white?"
"I don't know; try to go to sleep, and you will feel better in the morning," was all the reply he could make to her knotty queries.[10]

James represented refuge, safety, and a potential quasi-messianic hope for liberation and love. In many ways, he appeared to be aware of how Frado viewed him. James initiated the conversation not in an attempt to legitimize Frado's beliefs and feelings, which subsequently condemned his mother for her immoral actions. Instead, he centers himself within the discussion, playing on Frado's feelings for him as an anesthesia within her psyche and heart. As an object of distraction, James could have attempted to manipulate Frado by reinforcing his mother's ethical standard that depicts Frado as being the cause of her suffering. "You must be a good girl" is met with Frado's reinforcement of despair and relativism, as she believes the moral responsibility rests on James's mother, Mrs. Bellmont. Being a good child did not determine Mrs. Bellmont's abusive nature. She has and will continue to self-justify what she wants and desires.

Frado becomes emotionally transparent as she reveals the person her heart desires: her mother, Mrs. Mag Smith. Mag is the true finite savior in Frado's life, the Christlike figure she desperately awaits. Frado provides a sudden shift in the conversation with James whereby she questions her existence: "Who made me so?" We witness five interesting questions by Frado, of which James answered "God." God is discussed as the Creator of everything, including human differences, used to enslave and punish a particular demographic. James's theology is accurate, albeit simplistic, devoid of necessary explanation for someone seeking honest answers through her trauma. God created everything. He made Frado,

---

10. Andrews, *Classic African American Women's Narratives*, 162.

Aunt Abby, and James. These were positive creations. However, this God also created Mrs. Bellmont and the racial distinctions between Black and White people. Thus, initially, Frado assumes God is responsible for her pain and suffering stemming from her supposedly ordained inferior Blackness. The reader of the text could imagine the logical sequence of internal questioning and assumed answers that consumed Frado's mind. The implication is that Yahweh, if responsible for some people's suffering, is not worthy to be worshipped. I interpret this as a subtle play on questioning theodicy and expressing a natural human response to rejecting God. Frado, like everyone else, initially seeks to understand God from sociopolitical issues. She has not learned to rely primarily upon divine revelation, and to allow said revelation to influence her sociopolitical views. For now, race functions as a hermeneutic for her theology, not God, as God presents Himself through divine revelation intruding upon the human experience.

In this context, Frado functions as a typology of certain African Americans. She demonstrates a universal response to accepting or rejecting God amid experiencing intense pain and suffering. Frado is a form of Blackness that rejects God, not from the plausibility of His nonexistence, but from the influence of White Supremacist ideology upon their reasoning. Frado represents many Black people who viewed reality entirely or mainly through a racialized lens, thus categorizing religion according to ethnicities/races within a separatist/segregationist ideology. Nevertheless, the narrative eventually provides glimpses into the Bellmont family's contextualized Christianity, and through it, the reader witnesses the effects of White fragmentation.

THE BELLMONT'S CHRISTIANITY

The Introduction to White Christian Fragmentation

Wilson introduces the presence and influence of Christianity in her life at the age of fourteen. By then, eight years had passed within the Bellmont home, and Wilson has not provided any detailed reference to religion, nor the Bellmont's contextualized Christianity. Perhaps this is intentional, attempting to create speculation and anticipation within the reader. Wilson has expressed a vivid account of her inhumane treatment within the Bellmont home, and the potential revelation of their contradictory and hypocritical nature would have more clarity juxtaposed with any confession of religious obedience by the Bellmont family.

Mrs. Bellmont claimed Christianity as her own and articulated a contextualism that typified colonial Eurocentric proslavery Christianity. Her actions toward people she viewed as inferior were antithetical to basic Christian principles. Mrs. Bellmont's practice of Christianity was so far removed from the *essence* of Christianity, that I argue she embraced a Eurocentric Civil Religion laced with nuances of Christian principles. "Religion was not meant for niggers," stated Mrs. Bellmont. Young Frado never attended service with Mrs. Bellmont and Mary, and it is difficult to surmise the details of how *they* perceived Christianity supported slavery as well as justified their abusive nature. Mrs. Bellmont's statement represents the colonial Eurocentric belief, at least in part, that Black slaves had no spiritually redemptive qualities. For them, the Gospel narrative was not created for slaves, much like principles of human equality and freedom. Black humanity was a creation of God, designed to serve White humanity as White humanity represented God or a chosen race, and Black humanity represented God's devotees.

Regarding church attendance, Frado's immaturity and insecurity are revealed by her overwhelming focus on her supposed poor outward appearance. Whether she has prioritized an impressive outward appearance above and beyond exhibiting mature spiritual character is questionable. She repeatedly references her inappropriate, indecent attire, deemed insufficient for the "organized church." Frado's beliefs were likely influenced by Mrs. Bellmont and her contextualized Eurocentric Christianity. Yet, Frado and Mrs. Bellmont's views contradict those of Aunt Abby, who was not concerned with appearances but with the heart.

> Aunt Abby would take her to evening meetings, held in the neighborhood, which Mrs. B. never attended; and impart on her lessons of truth and grace as they walked to the place of prayer. Many of less piety would scorn to present so doleful a figure; Mrs. B. had shaved her glossy ringlets; and, in her course cloth gown and ancient bonnet, she was anything but an enticing object. But Aunt Abby looked within. She saw a soul to save, an immortality of happiness to secure.[11]

Thus, we witness the conflict between Eurocentric American proslavery Christianity and *sympathetic* Euro-American Christianity. Aunt

---

11. Andrews, *Classic African American Women's Narratives*, 169.

Abby was not an abolitionist. However, Wilson portrays her as a genuine Christian who is morally aware of the wickedness of slavery. Yet, this aspect of Aunt Abby was attached to a noticeable sense of sociopolitical helplessness against the institution. Sociopolitical ineptness in aiding the emancipation of the oppressed is typically associated with an irrational overemphasis on their spiritual salvation. Aunt Abby represents a form of Whiteness that struggles to understand itself against depraved-Whiteness.

Mrs. Bellmont was a religious *actress* who played the role of a dignified Christian woman. The elegance of her religious behavior and church attire, at least within her mind, represented her spiritual maturity. Yet, the illusion of piety was a distraction, an embellishment that typified the spirituality of many proslavery Anglo-American Christians. In many ways, the superficial religiosity of proslavery Christianity mimics that of the ancient Pharisees during Jesus' era, as expressed in Matthew 6:5 and Luke 18:11.

> "And when you pray, you are not to be like the hypocrites; for they love to stand and pray in the synagogues and on the street corners so that they will be seen by people. Truly I say to you, they have their reward in full" (Matt 6:5).

> "The Pharisee stood and began praying this in regard to himself: 'God, I thank You that I am not like other people: swindlers, crooked, adulterers, or even like this tax collector'" (Luke 18:11).

We can imagine a Eurocentric proslavery Christian thanking Yahweh for not making them Black and ignorant. Furthermore, we can reflect on how African Americans were deeply affected by this form of Christianity. Many African Americans rejected this form of proslavery Christianity, and others rejected Christianity. Yet, it is questionable how extreme contextualisms of African-American Christianity could have developed if they accepted a Eurocentric worldview. I am suggesting the consequential self-dehumanizing contextualism of African-American Christianity would progress beyond merely believing Jesus was White and the Black church being socio-politically inept against White Supremacy.

Nevertheless, Frado represents Black people without healthy exposure and opportunity to experience Christianity contextualized by African-American Christians. Examples of healthy contextual expressions of Black Christianity resided within the "Invisible Institution" and the independent African-American Churches. I must also include *interracial* Black churches led by Black pastors that consisted of Black people as the congregational majority, free from Eurocentric influences.

We must remember that Frado was someone who, according to the narrative, was detached from the African-American community. The detachment would have naturally affected her worldview. Frado's conception and self-awareness of her Blackness appear rooted or wholly dependent upon interpretations by fragmented Whiteness. Connected to this derived the contextualized theologies of Eurocentric proslavery, and the timid socio-politically ineptness of sympathetic Euro-American Christianity. Nevertheless, Aunt Abby and James were genuine Christians who deeply cared for Frado. Their character flaws and sociopolitical timidity should never negate or displace their heart for and obedience to Yahweh, as they understood Him. Their comprehension and obedience influenced both in aiding Frado into the Body of Christ. James shared the same sentiments as Aunt Abby:

> James encouraged his aunt in her efforts. He had found the *Saviour*, he wished to have Frado's desolate heart gladdened, quieted, sustained, by *His* presence. He felt sure there were elements in her heart which, transformed and purified by the gospel, would make her worthy the esteem and friendship of the world. A kind, affectionate heart, native wit, and common sense, and the pertness she sometimes exhibited, he felt if restrained properly, might become useful in originating a self-reliance which would be of service to her in after years.

Wilson articulates a subtle emphasis on Christology, alerting the reader to James's belief that Jesus as the Christ would be the One to provide her will with the peace and security she needed. For James, Christianity could enhance Frado's potential, empowering her by refining her moral and ethical self-awareness. Here is another point where it is safe to scrutinize James's intent and overall understanding of reality concerning responsibility. To an extent, he appears to avoid acknowledging his mother and White society's responsibility in caring for the human-Other, deconstructing systemic oppression and creating a world representing the Kingdom of God.

Additionally, Wilson articulates James as demonstrating a growing concern for Frado's future, apart from the Bellmont family, hopefully emancipated. Christianity, not a sociopolitical ideology, will serve as the source that grounds Frado as a mature and intelligent Black person contributing to society. Yet, James, Aunt Abby, and Frado knew this was difficult in the presence of Mrs. Bellmont and Mary. In this context, both women were depicted as standing in opposition to Frado and Jesus, who aligned himself with the poor and weak of the world. Within the broader context, concerning the embodiment of Christianity by Aunt Abby and James, lies an indirect critique of Mrs. Bellmont and Mary's contextualized Christianity.

Nevertheless, James continued to be a positive influence on Frado. He was a source of hope regarding freedom from Mrs. Bellmont and Mary's tyranny, as well as continual knowledge of the social beliefs of Anglo-Americans about race, politics, and Christianity. The influence of James upon Frado intensified as he became terminally ill. James intentionally reinforced his Christian beliefs to Frado, hoping she would come to affirm Jesus as the Christ and grow in her faith. At this point, we can assume Frado, at fourteen years old, had not received a genuine conversion experience. Theologically, she was still wrestling with the skewed contextualism of proslavery Anglo-American Christianity. Frado was committed to comprehending the purpose of her Black existence, as articulated through the Gospel narrative. She believed God existed and created humanity in all its complexities. Yet, what was the intrinsic purpose of Black existence in the world, and whether "there is a heaven for the blacks?"[12] Although she attended a racially and socially inclusive church, Frado still struggled with fully liberating herself from the influence of proslavery Christianity and White Supremacist beliefs.

Repentance ignites the genuine procession to our salvific and theological clarity regarding equality and freedom within God. The Anglo-American preacher of the church she attended explained, "Come to Christ," "All, young or old, white and black, bond or free, come all to Christ for pardon; repent, believe."[13] The Anglo-American pastor of Aunt Abby contextualized a biblical interpretation of the Kingdom of God and the Body of Christ, devoid of White Supremacist ideologies. Spiritually, everyone within humanity was equal in the mind of Yahweh. However, many colonial African-American Christians advocated the deep moral conviction of their sins via moral reprehensibility. Wilson captures this within her younger self by expressing Frado's desire to obtain needed theological answers to perplexing questions. Frado's conversion experience was natural and anticlimactic. It was a gradual spiritual experience that did not reveal itself as one moment and context.

Wilson contrasts her progression toward salvation with the irrational opposition of Mrs. Bellmont. Mrs. Bellmont represents the internal

---

12. Andrews, *Classic African American Women's Narratives*, 175.
13. Andrews, *Classic African American Women's Narratives*, 175.

confusion and contradiction of attempting to hold oppositional statements as equally valid and complementary. She was a Eurocentric White Supremacist who identified as a Christian. Mrs. Bellmont, according to Wilson, never felt responsible for her spiritual well-being, which supported her lack of empathy for and abusive nature towards young Frado. Wilson articulates the self-entitled and narcissistic personality of Mrs. Bellmont, as she prioritized her self-interest beyond a potential relationship between Frado and Christ. The Bible and salvation, in the hands of young Frado, represented emancipation. Yet, to others, it also represented irrational attempts at equality, and a laughable expression of piety by inferior Black people.

Wilson never articulated any complex theological reasoning from which Mrs. Bellmont expressed her views. Instead, Mrs. Bellmont employed basic Eurocentric and White Supremacist ideologies that functioned as hermeneutics within her contextualized Christianity. For her, Black people were inferior, and to be Christianized created a convoluted Black consciousness that desired and believed it could obtain illusory spiritual equality with White people. Mrs. Bellmont could not fathom any Black person reasoning from and practicing a reality that she deemed only White people could embody. She presents this supposed self-evident atrocity as the forewarning prophetic message she delivered previously, in seeking to deny Frado an opportunity to educate herself.

Nevertheless, returning to a previous point, the relationship between Mrs. Bellmont, and Frado also testifies to the skewed dependency or possessiveness Mrs. Bellmont exhibited over Frado. The tragic occurrence of James's death was overwhelming for Frado and the Bellmonts. As a committed Christian, James continued to preach Christ to Frado until he breathed his last breath. Yet, a more critical reality was Frado's continual search to understand herself concerning God and her oppressive life.

FRADO'S QUESTIONING

A Conflict of Theologies

Mrs. Bellmont desired to be a god-like figure to Frado, denying her the right to serve the God freely she claimed to worship. It was deemed irrational. We witness a subtle conflict within White religiosity through a conversation between Mrs. and Mr. Bellmont, relating to Frado attending church and whether her act was justified biblically: "I thought you

Christians held to going to church," remarked Mr. Bellmont. "Yes, but who ever thought of having a nigger go, except to drive others there?"[14] An escort was young Frado's original role on Sunday morning. She obediently drove Mrs. Bellmont and Mary to church but was never provided the luxury of participating in its services.[15]

Mrs. Bellmont, the Muse of Bitterness and Vindictiveness, displayed a deep wound and void within her humanity. She characterized elements of self-entitlement, narcissism, violence, and selective aggression that developed and expressed themselves toward young Frado. She embodied an emotional vacuum rejecting any empathy towards Frado, which influenced her to refuse young Frado the right to express her emotions. Mrs. Bellmont displayed outbursts of violence every time she could not avoid and control Frado's expressions of emotions, whether in happiness or misery. The inability to prevent Frado's emotions demonstrates a lack of control and power within Mrs. Bellmont. She is forced to acknowledge Frado's humanity through her failure to control Frado and the subsequent feeling of waning power in those contexts. Mrs. Bellmont had difficulty comprehending how self-awareness of Frado's humanity forced self-evaluation, in the sense of acknowledging her lack of humanity for the non-White human-Other.[16]

Naturally, young Frado, the Muse of Strength and Resilience, endured immense abuse and dehumanization among the Bellmont family. However, for whatever reason, the Bible became a source of genuine intrigue, and critical theological questions were the focus of intense emotional scrutiny. The interesting aspect of young Frado's search for the truth did not begin with punishing those who tormented her or developing a skewed racialized political theology of liberation. It was a general understanding of God as the Creator of her humanity, vis-à-vis Blackness, and why she and others suffered the way they did.

Wilson alerts the reader that through this journey, she uttered the prayer of the publican, "God be merciful to me the sinner."[17] For me, this is a central aspect of Colonial African-American Christianity. It is a foundational belief grounded in obedience to Christian doctrine, whereby the individual expresses a theological existential crisis of self-awareness

---

14. Andrews, *Classic African American Women's Narratives*, 177.

15. Andrews, *Classic African American Women's Narratives*, 168–69.

16. Andrews, *Classic African American Women's Narratives*, 157 (sun skin), 158 (irrational violence), 166 (dog), 168 (kitchen scum).

17. Andrews, *Classic African American Women's Narratives*, 177.

regarding their relationship to God and acknowledgment that they desire and need God. Young Frado is not preoccupied with a philosophy on the contours of Whiteness nor seeking to discern its redemption. Nor is race a *consuming*, governing hermeneutic in her discourse that shapes her theology. For Frado, in part, the source of understanding her Black existence was juxtaposed with the universal humanity shared with her White master and questioning why and how God could permit her current reality. Even in questioning God's will and creative power, God is sought to be comprehended as God is, not racialized or hyper-politicized. Frado eventually matures and desires to know God as demonstrated biblically, and from this understanding she can navigate through race and politics.

Mrs. Bellmont was a cruel and possessive mother who expressed disdain upon witnessing the affection James received from his wife, Aunt Abby, and Frado. Yet, James represented a central emotional, psychological, and theological object or space of conflict between Mrs. Bellmont and young Frado. From these two, we witness a clash between Eurocentric proslavery Christianity and a Black conscience experiencing a heightened spiritual self-awareness.

> Frado was becoming seriously ill. She had no relish for food, and was constantly over-worked, and then she had such solicitude about the future. She wished to pray for pardon. She did try to pray. Her mistress had told her it would "do no good for her to attempt prayer; prayer was for whites, not for blacks. If she minded her mistress, and did what she commanded, it was all that was required of her."
> This did not satisfy her, or appease her longings. She knew her instructions did not harmonize with those of the man of God or Aunt Abby's. She resolved to persevere.[18]

In this context, we witness the grace of God upon Frado and a prime example of what the Apostle Paul stated in 1 Corinthians 11:1, "Be imitators of me, just as I also am of Christ." Frado has not matured to rely first upon the testimony of scripture. We must acknowledge that she has not accepted Christ as her Lord and Savior. She is still searching for salvation by asking critical questions about God and her current situation. Yet, these are not essential observations at this point. What is central is her ability to scrutinize the irrational and unbiblical statements from Mrs.

---

18. Andrews, *Classic African American Women's Narratives*, 178–79.

Bellmont. Frado assesses Mrs. Bellmont's word against those she trusts and represents Christ: Aunt Abby and James.

For many Europeans and European descendants, colonialism marked a theological vacuum and rupture to their collective psyche, not only from our concrete reality but the *essence* of the Gospel. For many today, the ripple effect has created a generational legacy and theological tradition of Eurocentric Civil Religion. The contextualized Christianity and Eurocentric theology of Mrs. Bellmont represent the archaic rudiments of such religious expressions. As a Christian, Jesus, as the Christ, is not the center of Mrs. Bellmont's reality and theology. Instead, it is a fabrication of Jesus, representing the self-interest of the collective Eurocentric imagination. I argue that this Eurocentric Civil Religion, with its veneer of Christianity, convinced its practitioners that they could achieve specific goals: the usurpation of or the representation of God on earth. Prayer as deep spiritual communication is a central component of the Christian narrative, a product of and instrumentality of spiritual growth within the individual and group. Mrs. Bellmont represents the distortion of these beliefs and practices by seeking to usurp God as the center of affection and fulfillment in Frado's life.

Eurocentric Christianity repeatedly enforced the principle of God's inactivity in the lives of the slaves. Prayer is meaningless for the slave. Obedience to their White master becomes reinterpreted as a cloaked form of worship and reverence for Whiteness, representative of God's chosen people. For some, Whiteness represents a secondary mediator, attached to Christ Jesus, between God and humanity. However, even before an authentic salvific moment, young Frado acknowledges the irrationality of Eurocentric Christianity and Mrs. Bellmont's employment of it. Black rationality, *informed* but not spiritually transformed by religious principles, provides momentary segments of spiritual self-awareness, representative of obtaining the mind of Christ (1 Cor 2:16). The human mind, in this exposure to God's presence and activity, with assistance from God, can discern what is foundationally scripturally sound, and is harmonious with the Gospel narrative, against everything that is or may be intrinsically opposed to them. The Spirit reveals.

In many ways, James becomes a Christ figure to Frado. He was the source of deep intimacy and friendship for her. James also served as a source of sociopolitical hope and relative freedom, as he could have permanently freed Frado from Mrs. Bellmont and Mary. Unfortunately, James eventually died from a severe illness. He intentionally ministered to Frado and demonstrated to everyone his desire to enjoy eternal life with Christ. The last moments of James's life were not spent satisfying hedonistic desires or vain exploits.

Influenced by James, Wilson does not romanticize her journey toward spiritual self-awareness within the Christian tradition. She employs a practical form of realism in articulating the layers of reality that inform her developing contextual theology. We witness this, in part, at James's funeral and Frado reflecting upon her love for him in connection with her true thoughts about God: "As she saw his body lowered in the grave she wished to share it; but she was not fit to die. She could not go where he was if she did. She did not love God; she did not serve him or know how to."[19] Wilson demonstrates a level of honesty and transparency that few Christians have obtained. She acknowledges the source of her motivation in seeking God. We can also safely interpret her as revealing James as the stumbling block to genuinely *accepting* Christ as her Lord and Savior. It is also safe to assume that God revealed this truth to her, and she chose to receive it, not cloak it within false piety. "But just as it is written: 'Things which eye Has not seen and ear has not heard, and which have not entered the human heart, all that God has prepared for those who love him.' For to us God revealed them through the Spirit; for the Spirit searches all things, even the depths of God'" (1 Cor 2:9–10). Yet, it does not stop there. Wilson's honesty directs the informed reader to the two New Testament commandments: Luke 10:27, "And he answered, 'You shall love the Lord your God with all your heart, and with all your soul, and with all your strength, and with all your mind, and your neighbor as yourself.'"

Nevertheless, the Muse of Bitterness and Vindictiveness sought to correct Frado. Mrs. Bellmont's theology falsely projects selective relativism and a racialized hierarchy of human value into the Christian spiritual world. A Eurocentric theological creation account cannot fathom any relevance to notions of human equality, equity, and the affirmation of mutual humanization. Mrs. Bellmont sought to implant *learned helplessness* and *victimization* within Frado. She also desired to reinforce a Eurocentric worldview and theology into Frado's mind. Young Frado rejects Eurocentric proslavery Christianity, claiming that it doesn't represent the essence of the Gospel.

Aunt Abby and James were genuine spiritual beacons of light for young Frado. In many ways, timid Whiteness is ill-equipped and

---

19. Andrews, *Classic African American Women's Narratives*, 180.

sometimes unwilling to empower Blackness to achieve sociopolitical power. Yet, genuine Christians, regardless of race, do what is necessary for the spiritual empowerment of those deemed the oppressed. In this context, Christianity forced Europeans and European-Americans to turn against themselves when they needed to determine their supreme loyalty: Christ Jesus or their idolatrous social construction of Whiteness. For some, colonial European-American Christianity employed a form of cognitive dissonance that shielded the individual from acknowledging equality as a universal principle. Tragic irony expresses itself within the light of the Gospel that presents itself in the darkest moments of our lives, empowering people spiritually when they are socio-politically weak.

In returning to James, there is the subtle presence of possible romantic interest from young Frado. Wilson never states this nor carefully alludes to it. Yet, we must scrutinize why James was "the object of affection," not Jesus as the Christ. This was the central issue that Aunt Abby and a church minister had questioned. The conflict within Frado's heart was between an unhealthy desire for a person who became an idol within the context of salvation, occupying a position which only Jesus could fill. Frado needed to overcome this hurdle. Otherwise, she would merely commit the same sins as Mrs. Bellmont. Aunt Abby continued to minister to Frado after James's death. She did not do this in a paternalistic or condescending manner. Instead, Aunt Abby continued to represent Christ in Frado's life:

> She received her like a wanderer; seriously urged her to accept of Christ; explained the way; read to her from the Bible, and remarked upon such passages as applied to her state. She warned her against stifling that voice which was calling her to heaven; echoed the farewell words of James, and told her to come to her with her difficulties, and not to delay a duty to important as attention to the truths of religion, and her soul's interest.[20]

Aunt Abby demonstrates an interesting theology that shapes her witnessing to Frado. Abby articulates a form of *prevenient grace* in that she earnestly believed God was calling to Frado, and Frado, in return, was sincerely receptive despite her deep affection for James. There is no criticism or harsh judgment in this, as every believer must choose who or what is their life's central passion and love. We witness this particular decision summarized in Matthew 16:25, "For whoever wants to save his life will

20. Andrews, *Classic African American Women's Narratives*, 180–81.

lose it; but whoever loses his life for My sake will find it." Furthermore, Abby implies to Frado that her spiritual relationship with God is more important than her earthly struggles. Not in the sense that Frado should ignore or disregard the abuse she constantly endured. Instead, turning to Yahweh provides the transcendent means to overcome said oppression. But Christ must be first in her life, and she must wilfully dedicate her life to growing in union with the Godhead of Judean Christianity.

The struggle to place Christ as the central love of her life may not have been known by those around Frado. Aunt Abby and the minister of their congregation may have known. The persistent questioning of whether she was "serious" about converting to Christianity had created a moral and spiritual dilemma. The deeper theological issue rests on the reality that the Black slave had the intellect and ability to receive salvation and grow in their Christian identity. Naturally, these steps are only relevant because Christ died on the cross for Africans and Indians. The relationship between Aunt Abby, Frado, and God was a complete affront to the skewed theology of proslavery Christianity, exemplified by Mrs. Bellmont. Considering this, we may understand why Mrs. Bellmont expressed irrational interest and fear in Frado accepting Christ. Mrs. Bellmont was intent on routinely denouncing Frado and seeking to subdue the possibility of her becoming a Christian. Mrs. Bellmont articulates this irrationality within a previous conversation with Mr. Bellmont:

> I want your attention to what I am going to say. I have let Nig go out to evening meetings a few times, and, if you will believe it, I found her reading the Bible to-day, just as though she expected to turn pious nigger, and preach to white folks. So now you see what good comes of sending her to school. If she should get converted she would have to go to meeting: at least, as long as James lives.[21]

Mrs. Bellmont appears foolish and disconnected from her humanity and the God she claims to worship. Cognitive dissonance and confirmatory bias, the denial of White humanity intricately connected to the non-White human-Other, is expressed in Mrs. Bellmont's dismay at Frado's sincerity in accepting Jesus as her Christ, still after James's death. Frado expressed sincerity within her heart. She earnestly sought forgiveness and eternal life with God. Wilson portrays a scene whereby the White

---

21. Andrews, *Classic African American Women's Narratives*, 176.

preacher of her congregation invites her to his home, seeking the outward expression of what has occurred in her heart: accepting Jesus as Christ.

> The first opportunity they once more attended meeting together. The minister conversed faithfully with every person present. He was surprised to find the little colored girl so solicitous, and kindly directed her to the flowing fountain where she might wash and be clean. He inquired of the origins of her anxiety, of her progress up to this time, and endeavored to make Christ, instead of James, the attraction of heaven.[22]

For me, Frado's conversion experience occurred during that church service. James was no longer an idol in her heart but a loving Christian brother. Jesus was no longer a subtle inconvenience to her primary focus on James. Jesus was the center of Frado's life, and all other idols in her life had dissipated. Frado's new spiritual walk with God influenced her intellect and human-will. We witness this in part through a particular confrontation with Mrs. Bellmont.

FRADO'S REBELLION

Mr. Bellmont demonstrated his impotence and reluctance to stop Mrs. Bellmont's abuse of Frado. Again, we witness how timid-Whiteness exaggerates dehumanized-Blackness's moral and spiritual responsibility to maintain its escapism. Mr. Bellmont refused to acknowledge his inhumanity concerning his moral responsibility to hold Mrs. Bellmont accountable for her dehumanizing behavior:

> Mr. Bellmont found himself unable to do what James or Jack could accomplish for her. He talked with her seriously, told her he had seen her many times punished undeservedly; he did not wish to have her saucy or disrespectful, but when she was *sure* she did not deserve a whipping, to avoid it if she could. "You are looking sick," he added, "you cannot endure beating as you once could."[23]

Frado's young body, mind, and spirit had received senseless damage through years of service with the Bellmont family. It is astonishing to witness Mr. Bellmont admit his ineptness in alleviating Frado from mindless abuse. Mr. Bellmont displayed a presence of aloofness and cowardice that

---

22. Andrews, *Classic African American Women's Narratives*, 182.
23. Andrews, *Classic African American Women's Narratives*, 182.

his sons did not embody. Yet, a visual reminder of Frado's destitute condition did not deter Mrs. Bellmont from continuing to *discipline* her. A climax in the conflict between the two muses expressed itself when self-assertion, anger, and righteousness reached an emotional boiling point. On one occasion, Mrs. Bellmont sought an excuse to enact her physical torment, unprovoked upon Frado:

> She was sent for wood, and not returning as soon as Mrs. B. calculated, she followed her, and, snatching from the pile a stick, raised it over her.
>
> Stop!" shouted Frado, "strike me and I'll never work a mite more for you;" and throwing down what she had gathered, stood like one who feels the stirring of free and independent thoughts.
>
> By this unexpected demonstrations, her mistress, in amazement, dropped her weapon, desisting from her purpose of chastisement. Frado walked towards the house, her mistress following with the wood she herself was sent after. She did not know, before, that she had a power to ward off assaults. Her triumph in seeing her enter the door with *her* burden, repaid her for much of her former suffering.[24]

A depraved and fragmented mind will often reinterpret a subordinate's harmless, innocent, and ordinary act of obedience as defiance and an attempt at rebelling against and usurping their authority. Mrs. Bellmont assumed the role of judge and a quasi-god, at least in her mind, over young Frado. Mrs. Bellmont did not need any rational justification to enact her discipline; it was simply an exercise of her will that did not require approval, for approval was embedded within her desire to act as she did.

The assertion of Black humanity as a righteous force representing our concrete logical reality meets White inhumanity, an irrational compulsion representing a detached, self-aggrandized, imaginary world. In defending herself, Frado discovered an aspect of her humanity and freedom that Eurocentric Christianity and Mrs. Bellmont wanted to remain concealed. We also view a glimpse of Mrs. Bellmont's co-dependency with Frado. Frado's exertion of her humanity and morality had revealed Mrs. Bellmont's dormant fear of being alone, stripped of her illusions, and forced to confront her true Self. The overwhelming knowledge of

---

24. Andrews, *Classic African American Women's Narratives*, 182–83.

her reliance upon Frado created a debilitating dread within Mrs. Bellmont. Frado accomplished what Mr. Bellmont, Jack, James, and Aunt Abby could not: inflict unavoidable self-awareness within Mrs. Bellmont regarding her actions, recognizing her true humanity and weakness that she suppressed under the illusion of cultural sophistication, dominance, and religious piety. Yet, Frado's abuse was only reduced, not eliminated. Frado would experience another event that alleviated some of her abuse but through the death of an antagonist.

DEATH OF A DEMI-GOD & THE PATH TO EMANCIPATION

Frado, keenly aware of Mary's position in Mrs. Bellmont's world, referred to her as an *idol*. Mary was the image and extension of Mrs. Bellmont. Unfortunately, Mary became ill and died young after marrying and relocating to another state. Her death caused great distress to Mrs. Bellmont. Nevertheless, the fragmented world of Mrs. Bellmont continued to crumble. She was self-alienated, trapped within her self-inflated Eurocentric world, without her idol, the central person of her affection. Mary was a quasi-Christ figure in Mrs. Bellmont's life. Mary was a tyrant to Frado, to the extent that Frado did not express any sadness, depression, or dread from Mary's death. Thus, we are privy to another example of how Frado transcends Mrs. Bellmont. The relationship between Mrs. Bellmont and Mary contrasts with that of James and Frado. Yet, even within Frado's period of happiness and jubilee, Aunt Abby reminded her of the proper way to control her emotions. It was safe to enjoy freedom from abuse but not receive pleasure from an abuser's death.

Years passed, and young Frado reached her year of freedom. At 18, Frado was free. She was no longer an indentured servant to the Bellmonts. Frado, although forced, was able to endure what Mrs. Bellmont's children and other hired hands could not, not even Mary, which was to spend a reasonable amount of time in her presence. No one could tolerate Mrs. Bellmont. However, Mrs. Bellmont would try to manipulate Frado into staying with her, only to fail.

Nevertheless, Frado would experience physical illness and financial hardship that had her at the mercy of those within her community. She would even return a few times to the Bellmont's residence. However, she was not the young and healthy Frado she once was. In due time, Frado would meet, befriend, and eventually marry a suspicious character, supposedly a former house slave turned "lecturer." Young Frado experienced love; her relationship with this individual brought about heartache, disappointment, and a young son. Here, we witness another similarity between Frado and Mag. Frado's son provided her with someone, an extension of herself, who she could love and provide for in ways she did not experience as a child. The father neglected his son as much as he failed Frado. Willson articulates him as an individual who may have developed a general notion of superiority over the field slaves, even though he claimed to be an abolitionist. Physically, he did not carry the wounds or scars of a typical slave, as his body was devoid of any signs of abuse. He stands in contrast to Frado. Wilson admits she never questioned him about his former life as a slave, assuming it was just as traumatic as her experiences. Her husband would come and go from her life, eventually leaving, never to return. Yet, Wilson would experience something through someone who avoided her grasp for years: a loving and protective mother.

THE BLESSING OF AN EMPATHETIC MOTHER & FAMILY

Frado would grow to become a mature and discerning woman. Eventually, she met an Anglo-American Christian woman named Mrs. W. She rejected all Eurocentric reasoning as she remained committed to Christ Jesus and sought to care for Frado. Although briefly discussed, the relationship between Frado and Mrs. W. was humanizing, which provided Frado with someone she had desired since childhood: a mother and a family. Frado had a son and mother now, who both loved her. Moreover, even struggling to support herself and her child, she eventually met a couple who cared for her and her son as if they were their own. Wilson's *foster parents* loved them to the extent that they rejected and disavowed anyone who exhibited White supremacist beliefs, did not acknowledge Frado and her son or accept them as family.

As I interpret it, adoption, for Wilson, transcended the shallow notions of racialized politics, Eurocentric Christianity, and systemic oppression during colonialism because love and reconciliation were the driving forces in her life. The indisputable testimony of Wilson is, at least in part, her strength and resilience. Her life is a testimony of the pain and yearning some women experienced during colonialism. Wilson received the love and family she desired. Wilson did not obtain them from within the ideal people and situations. Yet, she accomplished something that her mother could not. Wilson established a genuine relationship with Christ and helped create and participate in a family that humanized her more than she ever experienced.

I interpret Wilson's narrative as a subtle theological narrative, a practical one that articulates aspects of African-American historical realism that elicits empathy within the reader's hearts. Her testimony, no matter how historically accurate it may be, is far-reaching and transcends the corrupt nature of White supremacy, Eurocentric Christianity, and racialized politics. Wilson was a woman who represented, at least to me, a muse of strength and resilience who eventually determined her identity, sense of belonging, and how she shared space with the human-Other.

Conclusion
The Authenticity of Our Christian Faith

MANY PEOPLE MAY DISAGREE, but I firmly believe the *authenticity* of our Christian faith cannot be mimicked. In this context, I must remind my readers that I am emphasizing the word authenticity. In a general sense, you are either authentic or inauthentic. Naturally, people can act and give a good to excellent theatrical performance. They can play a Christian through puppetry of Christian behavior and rhetoric. However, their ruse is still an existential façade. It lacks many things, especially a sincere relationship with the Holy Spirit.

The kernel of authenticity stems from our relationship with God, as the authenticity itself is an element of divine revelation intruding upon the human experience. Christian authenticity begins within and from Christ Jesus. It does not stem from the human imagination and the dark reality of self-deception. Christian authenticity exists because Christ Jesus exists and makes Himself a central figure in our lives. The kernel of Christian authenticity is also the consequence of humanity accepting the reality of God, and genuinely desiring to be reconciled with Him. Spiritual authenticity, at least from an evangelical perspective, can only derive from experiencing God as the "really real," the penultimate existence from which every other existence derives.

I am under the conviction that for some time, American Christianity, through its hyperpoliticization, has morphed into an inauthentic mimesis of genuine Christianity. Christianity, within its extremist forms, appears to be a hollow and superficial civil religion erected, in part, from racialized nationalism. Again, this is a universal judgment, as it applies to everyone, but for the sake of this conversation, I am speaking about Black people in America. In this, especially within the American academy, we view a litany of ambiguous secular humanist, religious, and spiritual beliefs that appear to be placed on common ground, as if qualitative and quantitative differences do not exist or are relevant. I find it deeply ironic that it isn't a divine force or being that unites everyone, but a social construction, and one created by those deemed the eternal-oppressor. Connected to this is the forced assumption that YHWH and one's religious faith in Him are necessary points of negotiation and compromise to achieve racial solidarity with the aim of complete sociopolitical emancipation from Whiteness. However, one's racial allegiance is not for dispute. You must sacrifice everything and everyone, including your God.

I often question the faith of Christians who seldom speak about their relationship with Christ, and/or speak more about their earthly identities above and beyond the nuances of their Christian faith. Again, I am making a general statement, one fueled by a universal judgment of humanity. Everyone, regardless of ethnicity, nationalism, race, or social standing, can fall prey to these assorted deceptions. Trust me, I am not suggesting our spiritual and earthly identities are mutually exclusive. Yet, I am implying the need for prioritization and the acceptance of one influencing the progression of the other. Our prioritization of our spiritual and earthly identities deeply influences our sense of belonging, and how we share space with the human-Other. One set is determined by YHWH and the other by humanity apart from YHWH.

In this context, I am increasingly disheartened by what passes as African-American Christianity, Black theology, the Black Church, and Black Christians. I am convinced that, at least for some, there is a dark correlation between sociopolitical freedom and authentic faith in Christ. In that, the more freedom some African-Americans have acquired, the more they relinquished a genuine faith in Christ Jesus. This lies at the heart of African-American culture and its struggle to assess and balance its views and embodiments of race relating to its relationship with religion. I am convinced that we once made genuine progress in this area during colonialism but have somehow regressed since the end of the Civil Rights Era. White people gave us more freedom, and some of us, in return, gave up our God.

The colonial evangelical African-Americans I discussed in this project displayed authentic Christian faith in Christ Jesus. The authenticity that they displayed and embodied is still present within our nation because, once again, it derives from Christ Jesus as the "really real." Yet, I am convinced that, because of our deep fascination, and obsession with constructs of race, and other identities, we have also forfeited influential aspects of our history that are attached to YHWH. Thus, as freedom comes, YHWH is ignored, and His historical presence in our ancestor's lives, and ours, is ignored as well.

Jarena Lee, Old Elizabeth, Maria W. Stewart, and Julia A. J. Foote are representatives of the authentic African-American Christian faith that we should never ignore, dismiss, or skew for our current racialized sociopolitical agendas. These women had colleagues and peers who were faithful to Christ and exhibited the Christian faith that shaped aspects of African-American culture and the United States. They understood the complexity of race but did not place it on par with YHWH as some concealed or openly justified idol. Rather, YHWH assisted them in refining their "Blackness" within Christ, not at the exclusion of the human-Other, but in redemption, regeneration, and reconciliation for everyone. My interpretation of these women does not end here, but it begins, and will attach itself to other African-Americans, both male and female, who have been dismissed, ignored, and rejected, not by White society, but by those African-Americans who claim to be enlightened and emancipated.

Bibliography

Allen, Clifton J. *Esther—Psalms*. Vol. 4 of *The Broadman Bible Commentary*. Nashville: Broadman, 1971.
Anderson, Victor. *Beyond Ontological Black: An Essay On African American Religious and Cultural Criticism*. New York: Continuum, 1995.
———. *Creative Exchange: A Constructive Theology of African American Religious Experience*. Minneapolis: Fortress, 2008.
Andrews, William. *Classic African American Women's Narratives*. New York: Oxford University Press, 2003.
———. *Sisters of the Spirit: Three Black Women's Autobiographies of the Nineteenth Century*. Bloomington: Indiana University Press, 1986.
Anthropological Society of London (ASL). *Memoirs Read Before the Anthropological Society of London*. 2 vols. London: Trübner, 1865.
Anyabwile, Thabiti M. *The Faithful Preacher: Recapturing the Vision of Three Pioneering African-American Pastors*. Wheaton: Crossway, 2007.
Anyabwile, Thabiti M., and Lemuel Haynes. *May We Meet in the Heavenly World: The Piety of Lemuel Haynes*. Grand Rapids: Reformation Heritage, 2009.
Baldwin, Lewis V. *There Is a Balm in Gilead: The Cultural Roots of Martin Luther King Jr.* Minneapolis: Fortress, 1991.
———. *To Make the Wounded Whole: The Cultural Legacy of Martin Luther King Jr.* Minneapolis: Fortress, 1992.
Ball, Charles. *Slavery in the United States. A Narrative of the Life and Adventures of Charles Ball, a Black Man, Who Lived Forty Years in Maryland, South Carolina and Georgia, as a Slave Under Various Masters, and Was One Year in the Navy with Commodore Barney, During the Late War*. New York: John S. Taylor, 1837. https://docsouth.unc.edu/neh/ballslavery/ball.html.
Banks, Jourden H. *A Narrative of Events of the Life of J. H. Banks, an Escaped Slave, from the Cotton State, Alabama, in America*. Liverpool: M. Rourke, 1861. https://docsouth.unc.edu/neh/penning/penning.html.
Baptist, Edward E. *The Half Has Never Been Told: Slavery & the Making of American Capitalism*. New York: Basic, 2014.
Barbour, Floyd B. *The Black Power Revolt*. Boston: P. Sargent, 1968.

Beach, William Waldo. "A Theological Analysis of Race Relation." In *Faith and Ethics: The Theology of H. Richard Niebuhr*, edited by Paul Ramsey, 205-24. New York: Harper Torchbooks, 1957.

Berger, Peter L., and Thomas Luckmann. *The Sacred Canopy: Elements of A Sociological Theory of Religion*. New York: Anchor, 1967.

———. *The Social Construction of Reality: A Treatise in The Sociology of Knowledge*. New York: Anchor, 1967.

Bernier, Francois. "A New Division of the Earth." *History Workshop Journal* 51 (2001) 247-50.

Blassingame, John W. *The Slave Community: Plantation Life in the Ante-Bellum South*. New York: Oxford University Press, 1972.

Blount, Brian K. *True to Our Native Land: An African American New Testament Commentary*. Minneapolis: Fortress, 2007.

Blumenbach, Johann Friedrich. *De Genesis Hamani Varietate Nativa*. N.p., 1781.

Boggis, Jerrianne, et al. *Harriet Wilson's New England: Race, Writing, and Religion*. Durham: University of New Hampshire Press, 2007.

Buffon, George Louis Leclerc de. *Natural History of Man*. N.p., 1778.

Carson, Clayborne, and Martin Luther King Jr. *The Autobiography of Martin Luther King Jr*. New York: Warner, 1998.

Carson, Clayborne, et al. "Martin Luther King Jr. as Scholar: A Reexamination of His Theological Writings." *Journal of American History* 78.1 (1991) 93-105.

Carter, J. Kameron. "Contemporary Black Theology: A Review Essay." *Modern Theology* 19.1 (2003) 117-38.

———. *Race: A Theological Account*. New York: Oxford University Press, 2008.

Cone, Cecil W. *The Identity Crisis in Black Theology*. Nashville: AMEC, 1975.

Cone, James H. "America: A Dream or A Nightmare." *Journal of the Interdenominational Theological Center* 13.2 (1986) 263-78.

———. "Demystifying Martin and Malcolm." *Theology Today* 51.1 (1994) 27-28.

———. *For My People: Black Theology and the Black Church. Where Have We Been and Where Are We Going?* Maryknoll, NY: Orbis, 1984.

———. *Martin & Malcom & America: A Dream or A Nightmare*. Maryknoll, NY: Orbis, 1991.

———. "Martin Luther King Jr. and the Third World." *Journal of American History* 74.2 (1987) 455-67.

———. "Martin Luther King Jr., Black Theology, Black Church." *Theology Today* 40.4 (1984) 409-20.

———. "The Theology of Martin Luther King Jr." *Union Seminary Quarterly Review* 40.4 (1986) 21-39.

Cooley, Timothy Mather. *Sketches of the Life and Character of the Rev. Lemuel Haynes*. New York: John S. Taylor, 1839.

Cooper, Valerie C. *Word, Like Fire: Maria Stewart, The Bible & The Rights of African Americans*. Charlottesville: University of Virginia Press, 2012.

Cundall, Arthur E. *Psalms—Malachi*. Daily Bible Commentary. Philadelphia: A. J. Holman, 1973.

Deburg, William L. Van, ed. *Modern Black Nationalism: From Marcus Garvey to Louis Farrakhan*. New York: New York University Press, 1996.

DeWolf, L. Howard. "Martin Luther King Jr. as Theologian." *Journal of the Interdenominational Theological Center* 4.2 (1977) 1-11.

Dickerson-Cousin, Christina. *Black Indians & Freedman: The African Methodist Episcopal Church & Indigenous Americans, 1816–1919*. Urbana: University of Illinois Press, 2021.
Douglas, Kelly Brown. *The Black Christ*. Maryknoll, NY: Orbis, 1994.
Downing, Frederick L. "Martin Luther King Jr. as Public Theologian." *Theology Today* 44.1 (1987) 15–31.
Drake, St. Clair. *The Redemption of Africa and Black Religion*. Chicago: Third World, 1970.
Elizabeth. *Memoir of Old Elizabeth: A Coloured Woman*. Philadelphia: Collins, 1863. https://docsouth.unc.edu/neh/eliza1/eliza1.html.
Evans, G. R. *The Roots of the Reformation: Tradition, Emergence and Rupture*. Downers Grove, IL: IVP Academic, 2012.
Evans, Tony. *The Tony Evans Bible Commentary: Advancing God's Kingdom Agenda*. Nashville: Holman Reference, 2019.
Fairclough, Adam. *Martin Luther King Jr*. Athens: University of Georgia Press, 1995.
Foreman, P. Gabrielle, et al. *Harriet E. Wilson: Our Nig or, Sketches from the Life of a Free Black*. New York: Penguin Group, 2005.
Fredrickson, George M. *Racism: A Short History*. Oxford: Princeton University Press, 2002.
Freire, Paulo. *Pedagogy of the Oppressed*. New York: Continuum, 2005.
Gaebelein, Frank E., et al. *Psalms, Proverbs, Ecclesiastes, Song of Songs*. Vol. 5 of *The Expositor's Bible Commentary: With the New International Version of the Holy Bible*. Grand Rapids: Zondervan 1991.
Garber, Paul R. "Black Theology: The Latter Day Legacy of Martin Luther King Jr." *Journal of Interdenominational Theological Center* 2 (1975) 100–113.
———. "King Was a Black Theologian." *Journal of Religious Thought* 31.2 (1975) 16–32.
Gates, Henry Louis, Jr., and Harriet E. Wilson. *Harriet E. Wilson: Our Nig or; Sketches from the Life of a Free Black: Harriet E. Wilson*. New York: Vintage, 2002.
Gates, Henry Louis, Jr., et al. *Our Nig or, Sketches from the Life of a Free Black*. New York: Vintage, 2011.
Goffman, Erving. *The Presentation of Self in Everyday Life*. New York: Anchor, 1959.
González, Justo L. *The Early Church to the Dawn of the Reformation*. Vol. 1 of *The Story of Christianity*. New York: Harper One, 2010.
Gruen, Arno. *The Betrayal of the Self: The Fear Of Autonomy In Men And Women*. Berkeley: Human Development, 1988.
Hanch, Kate. *Storied Witness: The Theology of Black Women Preachers in Nineteenth-Century America*. Minneapolis: Fortress, 2022.
Hannaford, Ivan. *Race: The History of an Idea in the West*. Baltimore: John Hopkins University Press, 1996.
Harris, Marvin. *The Rise Anthropological Theory: A History of Theories of Culture*. London: Routledge & Kegan Paul, 1969.
Hopkins, Dwight N. *Down, Up, and Over: Slave Religion and Black Theology*. Minneapolis: Fortress, 2000.
———. *Introducing Black Theology of Liberation*. Maryknoll, NY: Orbis, 1999.
———. *Shoes That Fit Our Feet: Sources for a Constructive Black Theology*. Maryknoll, NY: Orbis, 1993.
Hopkins, Dwight N., and George Cummings. *Cut Loose Your Stammering Tongue: Black Theology in the Slave Narratives*. Maryknoll, NY: Orbis, 1991.

Irons, Charles F. *White and Black Evangelicals in Colonial and Antebellum Virginia: The Origins of Proslavery Christianity.* Chapel Hill: University of North Carolina Press, 2008.

Issac, Benjamin. *The Invention of Racism in Classical Antiquity.* Princeton: Princeton University Press, 2004.

Ivory, Luther D. *Toward a Theology of Radical Involvement: The Theological Legacy of Martin Luther King Jr.* Nashville: Abingdon, 1997.

Jennings, Willie James. *The Christian Imagination: Theology and the Origin of Race.* New Haven: Yale University Press, 2010.

Johnson, Ruby F. *The Development of Negro Religion.* New York: Philosophical Library, 1954.

Jordan, Winthrop. *White over Black: American Attitudes Toward the Negro, 1550–1812.* Baltimore: Penguin, 1968.

Kaplan, Sidney. *The Black Presence in the Era of the American Revolution, 1770–1800.* Washington, DC: Smithsonian Institute, 1973.

King, Martin Luther, Jr. *A Call to Conscience: The Landmark Speeches of Dr. Martin Luther King Jr.* New York: Little, Brown, 2001.

———. *Strength to Love.* Minneapolis: Fortress, 2010.

———. *The Trumpet of Conscience.* Boston: Beacon, 2010.

———. *Where Do We Go From Here: Chaos or Community.* Boston: Beacon, 2010.

———. *Why We Can't Wait.* New York: Signet Classics, 2000.

King, Martin Luther, Jr., and James M. Washington. *A Testament of Hope: The Essential Writings And Speeches Of Martin Luther King Jr.* New York: Harper One, 1986.

Laing, R. D. *Self and Others.* London: Tavistock, 1961.

Latourette, Kenneth Scott. *Beginnings to 1500.* Vol. 1 of *A History of Christianity.* San Francisco: Harper & Row, 1975.

Levinas, Emmanuel. *Humanism of the Other.* Translated by Nidra Poller. Urbana: University of Illinois Press, 2006.

Lindley, Susan Hill. *"You Have Stept Out of Your Place": A History of Women & Religion in America.* Louisville: Westminster John Knox, 1996.

Linnaeus, Carolus. *Systema Naturae.* Leyden: n.p., 1735, 1753.

Linne, Carl von. "The God-Given Order of Nature." In *Race and the Enlightenment: A Reader,* edited by Emmanuel Chukwudi Eze, 10–14. Cambridge: Blackwell, 1997.

MacCulloch, Diarmaid. *Christianity: The First Three Thousand Years.* New York: Viking, 2009.

May, Cory J. "The Racialized-Politics within African-American Studies as Evidenced by the Dismissal of the Work of Jupiter Hammon, and the Conservative Tradition of African-American Slave Christianity." PhD diss., University of Aberdeen, 2018.

McCarthy, Thomas. *Race, Empire, and the Idea of Human Development.* Cambridge: Cambridge University Press, 2009.

McCoskey, Denise Eileen. *Race: Antiquity and Its Legacy.* London: IB Tauris, 2012.

McDonald, Soraya Nadia. "The Complicated Feminism of Amber Rose's SlutWalk." *Washington Post,* October 5, 2015. https://www.washingtonpost.com/news/arts-and-entertainment/wp/2015/10/05/the-complicated-feminism-of-amber-roses-slutwalk/?noredirect=on&utm_term=.7d82cafcfdd6.

Montagu, Ashley. *Man's Most Dangerous Myth: The Fallacy of Race.* New York: Oxford University Press, 1974.

Moody, Joycelyn. *Sentimental Confessions: Spiritual Narratives of Nineteenth-Century African American Women*. Athens: University of Georgia Press, 2003.

Morgan, Philip D. *Slave Counterpoint: Black Culture in the Eighteenth-Century Chesapeake & Lowcountry*. Chapel Hill: University of North Carolina Press, 1998.

Mellon, James. *Bullwhip Days: The Slaves Remember. An Oral History*. New York: Avon, 1990.

Moses, Wilson Jeremiah. *Classical Black Nationalism: From the American Revolution to Marcus Garvey*. New York: New York University Press, 1996.

———. *The Golden Age of Black Nationalism*. Oxford: Oxford University Press, 1988.

The New American Standard Bible. La Habra: Lockman Foundation, 2020.

Niebuhr, H. Richard. *The Meaning of Revelation*. Louisville: Westminster John Knox, 2006.

———. *Radical Monotheism and Western Civilization: With Supplementary Essays*. Lincoln: University of Nebraska Press, 1960.

Niebuhr, Reinhold. *Beyond Tragedy: Essays on the Christian Interpretation of History*. London: Nisbet, 1941.

———. *The Children of Light and the Children of Darkness: A Vindication of Democracy and a Critique of Its Traditional Defense*. Chicago: University of Chicago Press, 2011.

———. *Faith and History: A Comparison of Christian and Modern Views of History*. London: Nisbet, 1949.

———. *Human Destiny*. Vol. 2 of *The Nature and Destiny of Man*. New York: Scribner's Sons, 1943.

———. *Moral Man & Immoral Society: A Study In Ethics and Politics*. New York: Scribner's Sons, 1960.

———. *Pious and Secular America*. New York: Scribner's Sons, 1985.

———. *The Self and the Dramas of History*. New York: Scriber's Sons, 1955.

Niebuhr, Reinhold, and D. B. Robertson. *Love and Justice: Selections from the Shorter Writings of Reinhold Niebuhr*. Gloucester: Peter Smith, 1976.

Othow, Helen Chavis. *John Chavis: African American Patriot, Preacher, Teacher, and Mentor (1763–1838)*. Jefferson: McFarland & Company, 2001.

Otto, Rudolf. *The Idea of the Holy: An Inquiry into the Non-Rational Factor in the Idea of the Divine and Its Relation to the Rational*. Oxford University Press: London, 1958.

Peck, John, and Lemuel Haynes. *A Descent on the Universal Plan Consecrated: Or, Universal Salvation Explained*. Madison: Arion & Lodge, 1831.

Pennington, James W. C. *The Fugitive Blacksmith; or, Events in the History of James W. C. Pennington, Pastor of a Presbyterian Church, New York, Formerly a Slave in the State of Maryland, United States*. London: Charles Gilpin, 1849. https://docsouth.unc.edu/neh/penning49/penning49.html.

Peterson, Carla L. *"Doers of the Word": African-American Women Speakers & Writers in the North*. New Brunswick, NJ: Rutgers University Press, 1998.

Richardson, Marilyn. *Maria W. Stewart, America's First Black Woman Political Writer: Essays and Speeches*. Bloomington: Indiana University Press, 1987.

Sernett, Milton C. *Black Religion & American Evangelicalism: White Protestants, Plantation Missions, & the Flowering of Negro Christianity, 1787–1865*. Metuchen: Scarecrow, 1975.

Simmons, Martha, and Frank A. Thomas. *Preaching with Sacred Fire: An Anthology of African American Sermons, 1750 to the Present*. New York: Norton, 2010.

Smedley, Audrey. *Race in North America: Origin and Evolution of a Worldview*. Boulder: Westview, 1993.

Stampp, Kenneth M. *The Peculiar Institution: Slavery in the Ante-Bellum South*. New York: Knopf, 1956.

Sterling, Marion Wilson. *The Slave Narrative: Its Place in American History*. Washington, DC: Harvard University Press, 1988.

Stewart, Austin. *Twenty-Two Years A Slave, And Forty Years A Freeman; Embracing A Correspondence Of Several Years, While President Of Wilberforce Colony, London, Canada West*. Rochester: William Alling, 1857. https://docsouth.unc.edu/fpn/steward/steward.html.

Stewart, Maria W. *The Collected Meditations of Mrs. Maria W. Stewart*. Berkeley, CA: Mind Editions, 2021.

Valenti, Jessica. "SlutWalks and the Future of Feminism." *Washington Post*, June 3, 2011. https://www.washingtonpost.com/opinions/slutwalks-and-the-future-of-feminism/2011/06/01/AGjB9LIH_story.html?utm_term=.c24bfddbdafo.

Walter, Kristin. *Maria W. Stewart and the Roots of Black Political Thought*. Jackson: University Press of Mississippi, 2022.

Warner, Laceye C. *Saving Women: Retrieving Evangelistic Theology and Practice*. Waco: Baylor University Press, 2007.

Weber, Thomas. *Deep Like the Rivers: Education in the Slave Quarter Community, 1831–1865*. New York: Norton, 1978.

West, Cornel. *Prophecy Deliverance: An Afro-American Revolutionary Christianity*. Philadelphia: Westminster, 1982.

Wheatley, Phyllis. *The Collected Works of Phillis Wheatley*. Edited by John Shields. New York: Oxford University Press, 1988.

Williams, Don. *Psalms 1–72*. Communicator's Commentary. Waco, TX: Word, 1986.

Wills, Lawrence M. *Not God's People: Insiders and Outsiders in the Biblical World*. Lanham, MD: Rowman & Littlefield, 2008.

Woodson, Carter G. *The History of the Negro Church*. Washington DC: Associated, 1921.

Wright, Donald R. *African Americans in the Colonial Era: From African Origins through the American Revolution*. Wheeling: Harlan Davidson, 2000.

Yetman, Norman R., ed. *When I Was a Slave: Memoirs from the Slave Narrative Collection*. Mineola: Dover, 2002.

www.ingramcontent.com/pod-product-compliance
Lightning Source LLC
Chambersburg PA
CBHW050846230426
43667CB00012B/2165